## Succeeding and Adult Dyslexia

There is a need to demonstrate the potential that dyslexic adults have to achieve success despite the difficulties often associated with dyslexia. A focus on adults with dyslexia is pertinent given that individual life experiences have the potential to make dyslexia in adulthood more variable in manifestation than in childhood. This book offers a comprehensive discussion of the relationship between dyslexia and success based on current understanding derived from theory and practice, including the challenges of dyslexia in work-related contexts and a range of possible solutions. It presents a framework to conceptualise adult dyslexia and these individual difficulties and provides a basis for success. Personal stories of adult dyslexics who have faced work-related challenges are included alongside a set of strategy-based solutions for dealing with and responding to such challenges. This is an essential resource for dyslexic adults themselves, as well as coaches, human resources departments, and managers in organisations and training institutions.

**Carol Leather** is Director of Training at Independent Dyslexia Consultants, UK, where she provides coaching and training across a range of occupations. She is also a consultant to several UK government departments and public service organisations, advising on assessment and adjustments in the workplace.

**John Everatt** is Professor of Education at the University of Canterbury, New Zealand. He has worked and given talks and lectures on dyslexia in many parts of the world. His research focuses on dyslexia identification and intervention, but also on the individual and situational factors that influence the consequences of learning difficulties.

# Succeeding and Adult Dyslexia

Personal Perspectives, Practical Ideas, and Theoretical Directions

**Carol Leather**
*Independent Dyslexia Consultants*

**John Everatt**
*University of Canterbury*

Shaftesbury Road, Cambridge CB2 8EA, United Kingdom

One Liberty Plaza, 20th Floor, New York, NY 10006, USA

477 Williamstown Road, Port Melbourne, VIC 3207, Australia

314–321, 3rd Floor, Plot 3, Splendor Forum, Jasola District Centre,
New Delhi – 110025, India

103 Penang Road, #05–06/07, Visioncrest Commercial, Singapore 238467

Cambridge University Press is part of Cambridge University Press & Assessment,
a department of the University of Cambridge.

We share the University's mission to contribute to society through the pursuit of
education, learning and research at the highest international levels of excellence.

www.cambridge.org
Information on this title: www.cambridge.org/9781108844819

DOI: 10.1017/9781108953696

© Carol Leather and John Everatt 2024

This publication is in copyright. Subject to statutory exception and to the
provisions of relevant collective licensing agreements, no reproduction of any part
may take place without the written permission of Cambridge University Press &
Assessment.

First published 2024

*A catalogue record for this publication is available from the British Library*

Library of Congress Cataloging-in-Publication Data
Names: Leather, Carol, author. | Everatt, John, author.
Title: Succeeding and adult dyslexia : personal perspectives, practical
ideas, and theoretical directions / Carol Leather, Independent Dyslexia
Consultants, John Everatt, University of Canterbury.
Description: Cambridge, United Kingdom ; New York, NY : Cambridge
University Press, 2024. | Includes bibliographical references and index.
Identifiers: LCCN 2023027443 | ISBN 9781108844819 (hardback) |
ISBN 9781108948883 (paperback) | ISBN 9781108953696 (ebook)
Subjects: LCSH: Dyslexics – Life skills guides – Popular works. |
Dyslexics – Vocational guidance – Popular works. | Dyslexia – Popular
works.
Classification: LCC RC394.W6 L38 2024 | DDC 616.85/53023–dc23/eng/20230817
LC record available at https://lccn.loc.gov/2023027443

ISBN 978-1-108-84481-9 Hardback
ISBN 978-1-108-94888-3 Paperback

Cambridge University Press & Assessment has no responsibility for the persistence
or accuracy of URLs for external or third-party internet websites referred to in this
publication and does not guarantee that any content on such websites is, or will
remain, accurate or appropriate.

# Contents

| | |
|---|---|
| *List of Figures* | *page* vi |
| *List of Tables* | vii |
| *Acknowledgements* | viii |

### Part I

| | | |
|---|---|---|
| **1** | Introduction | 3 |
| **2** | Adult Dyslexia | 25 |
| **3** | Theoretical Perspectives on Success | 59 |

### Part II

| | | |
|---|---|---|
| **4** | Strategies Contributing to Success | 89 |
| **5** | Literacy and Language Issues and Strategies | 138 |
| **6** | Effective Communication | 168 |
| **7** | Dyslexia in the Workplace | 190 |
| **8** | Organisational Influences on Success | 223 |
| **9** | Personal Perspectives of Dyslexia and Career Success | 267 |
| **10** | Summary and Conclusions: A Revised Framework | 300 |

| | |
|---|---|
| *References* | 309 |
| *Index* | 321 |

# Figures

| | | |
|---|---|---|
| 2.1 | Framework for understanding adult dyslexia | *page* 28 |
| 2.2 | Profile of the average performance of 100+ dyslexic adults | 54 |
| 4.1 | Representation of an 'average' adult dyslexic profile | 98 |
| 4.2 | Representation of a simple model of information processing | 102 |
| 4.3 | Representation of information processing focusing on the key areas of processing discussed in the book | 108 |
| 4.4 | Illustration of word-finding differences | 114 |
| 4.5 | Mapping plans to complete tasks on time | 122 |

# Tables

| | | |
|---|---|---|
| 3.1 | Internal and external factors of success | page 83 |
| 3.2 | A model for working towards career success | 85 |
| 4.1 | Skills, with activity examples, related to metacognitive processing | 113 |
| 8.1 | Example of enablement document or a personal work passport | 236 |
| 8.2 | Training, coaching, mentoring, and counselling | 241 |
| 8.3a | Type of computer-based resources used by contributors (text) | 249 |
| 8.3b | Type of computer-based resources used by contributors (general) | 251 |
| 10.1 | Framework for representing key elements of adult dyslexia and success | 302 |

# Acknowledgements

We would like to thank everyone who has contributed to this book. There are too many people to mention by name but thank you for sharing your ideas, your knowledge, your insights and your experiences of dyslexia. Thank you, too, for the dyslexic people we have worked with over the years for your sharing your challenges and the solutions you have found.

The information you have all shared with us has inspired and enabled us to write this book, which we will hope will lead to successes – both big and small – for many more dyslexic people.

# Part I

# 1

# Introduction

In this book, we aim to discuss issues related to dyslexia in adults and provide a framework for understanding these issues. We also aim to consider the challenges faced by adults with dyslexia, particularly in the workplace, and the potential solutions for overcoming these challenges. The framework for understanding the challenges of adult dyslexia is that of the authors, but many of the ideas about how to deal with the challenges are provided by individuals who have experienced a lifetime of dyslexia and who may be seen as relatively successful in their chosen field of employment. The inspiration for writing this book came from working with dyslexic people in a wide range of occupations, so we have focused on the world of work rather than education. Although these ideas relate primarily to the workplace, many are also relevant to adult education contexts.

Although the occurrence of dyslexia in adults has long been recognised, the specific challenges faced in adulthood are often overlooked. The focus of this book is on how the challenges in adulthood can be very different from those in childhood, even if they stem from the same underlying causes. The book should be relevant to all those interested in dyslexia. This includes dyslexic adults themselves – indeed, many of the strategies we discuss are aimed at adults with dyslexia, and therefore we discuss many in the second person (i.e., 'you'). We also believe some of the ideas and strategies are of particular relevance for those dyslexic adults who are starting out on their career journeys. The transition from college or university into the world of work can be unexpectedly challenging. We also hope it is of value to those working alongside adult dyslexics – workmates, colleagues, managers, and human resources (HR) departments – by providing ideas about what dyslexia is and what impact it can have in the workplace. Likewise, those working with adult dyslexics – coaches, trainers, tutors, or assessors – or students or researchers studying dyslexia, may find it helpful. Furthermore, the family and friends of those with dyslexia, children and adults alike, may find it informative. Finally, although we have focused on dyslexia, the ideas around career success and also the strategies in Part II may be of interest to people with associated syndromes such as dyspraxia or deficits in attention (such as in Attention Deficit Hyperactivity Disorder), as although the causes of these are very different, the challenges can be similar.

It may be that some aspects of this book are more relevant for some readers than for others. Part I presents the theory, while Part II explores how the theories underpin the practical strategies. While we have presented our ideas in a particular order, one that makes sense to us, we would encourage you all to find your own way through the book; for example, you may prefer to read the last chapter first to get an overview of the book or you may find the personal stories of our dyslexic contributors the most helpful (see Chapter 9). Awareness and understanding are the initial points for dealing with

Introduction

the challenges and finding solutions. We hope that the ideas in this book provide these starting points.

Part I provides the background to what we see as adult dyslexia and how we see this relating to issues of success, particularly in employment (Chapters 1–3). Part II (Chapters 4–9) focuses on strategies to deal with various aspects of work, hopefully providing the reader with possible solutions that they can tailor to their own circumstances and needs. These strategies are contained in comments/stories told us by adults with dyslexia, though we present our own interpretations of these comments/stories so as to fit with the content of the book. The final chapter (Chapter 10) summarises these ideas and gives our final concluding thoughts. Before we discuss these ideas, though, we need to present what we see as the background to dyslexia in adults.

## 1.1   Dyslexia over the Lifespan

Dyslexia is often seen as a childhood disorder. The focus of practitioners, policy makers, and researchers on the problems faced by dyslexic children when learning the basic skills of reading and writing has led to this perception. However, dyslexia is not something that an individual grows out of. It typically influences aspects of an individual's experiences across their whole life. Dyslexia in adulthood may not be experienced in the same way as dyslexia in primary school; the two are very different contexts. While, quite rightly, literacy is the main concern in the school years, this may not be true in adulthood as people may have developed their literacy skills to a competent level. Hence it may be necessary to deal with adult dyslexia in somewhat different ways to that proposed for dyslexia in childhood. To understand this, we need to look at what we know (and do not know) about dyslexia from childhood to adulthood.

Part I

One starting point is to consider what dyslexia is in terms of its definition. The definition provided by the International Dyslexia Association is probably the most long-serving one around today; it seems to have stood the test of time. This definition states that dyslexia is

> a specific learning disability that is neurological in origin. It is characterized by difficulties with accurate and/or fluent word recognition and by poor spelling and decoding abilities. These difficulties typically result from a deficit in the phonological component in language that is often unexpected in relation to other cognitive abilities and the provision of effective classroom instruction. (International Dyslexia Association, 2002, https://dyslexiaida.org/definition-of-dyslexia/)

There is a fuller version of this definition of dyslexia available on the International Dyslexia Association's website. However, this is not the only definition that has been used to discuss dyslexia. There are many alternatives that have been proposed over the 100-plus years that dyslexia has been recognised and studied (see Kirby & Snowling, 2022). A consideration of the more common types of definition suggests that most focus on four key elements (see discussions in Everatt & Denston, 2020). These focus on the difficulties associated with dyslexia and can be summarised as follows:

1. Difficulties relate to accurate and/or fluent reading and writing/spelling developing incompletely or with great difficulty.
2. Difficulties are apparent at the word level and are persistent despite access to learning opportunities that are effective with most individuals.
3. Difficulties are unexpected in relation to typical development, or relative strengths, in non-literacy areas.
4. Difficulties are due to differences in the way language is processed, particularly the phonological component of language.

We discuss each of these elements in turn later.

Introduction

## 1.1.1 Elements 1 and 2: Reading and Writing Issues

The first element focuses on the most obvious feature of dyslexia: reading and writing difficulties. Many perspectives on dyslexia focus on the idea that reading and writing/spelling develop incompletely or with great difficulty. This suggests that individuals with dyslexia will have problems with reading and writing, but that it is not impossible for them to learn to read and write. For most, the development of good reading and writing skills takes time and may require appropriate support, although for some people there may be aspects of reading or writing that remain a problem even after long-term learning. For example, many adults with dyslexia who are in higher education continue to show difficulties with spelling accuracy even though word reading accuracy may be good compared to many people in the general population.

The second element relates to the first but focuses on when the difficulties with reading and writing occur and how they can be long-lasting. This suggests that difficulties are apparent at the word level and are persistent despite access to learning opportunities that are effective with most individuals. The focus on word-level reading (sometimes referred to as decoding) and word-level writing (i.e., spelling) means that difficulties will be experienced early in learning – from the very start of the child's experience with letters and words. Equally, the earlier difficulties are identified, the more effective the intervention. Therefore, much of the focus in terms of developing interventions has been on early identification and support. This is again why many focus on dyslexia in childhood – it is the way to avoid many of the difficulties experienced by dyslexics. However, if identification does not occur, then learning may be less than efficient. It is also the case that the severity of difficulties can determine the success of interventions and the length of time that an intervention needs to be implemented. Therefore, although a focus on young children beginning to learn to read/write is understandable, procedures to support older individuals should also be useful, and they may need to take account of additional problems. This is the reason why most definitions refer to the persistence of difficulties and why there is a need to consider the impact of dyslexia in adulthood as well as in children.

Persistence, though, can also mean that the experience of difficulties can change with age. For example, the problems experienced by the dyslexic individual at the word level can then impact on other elements of literacy learning, such as reading comprehension and text writing (we discuss such consequences further in the rest of this book). Thus, as the child grows up, the range of difficulties stemming from early word-level difficulties may increase: letter and single-word reading/spelling problems at the age of five or six and may lead to reading comprehension problems and text production weaknesses through school and into adulthood. This then needs to be taken into account in support procedures (specialist lessons/coaching). Similarly, single-word decoding interventions may not work effectively with many adults who perceive comprehension as the focus of literacy skills. Interventions may need to embed decoding strategies within procedures that benefit comprehension to ensure that the adult recognises their usefulness and practises them.

### 1.1.2 Element 3: Specificity, Comorbidity, and Neurodiversity

The third element suggests that difficulties with reading and writing are unexpected in relation to typical development in non-literacy areas. However, literacy skills can impact on most areas of education unless appropriate interventions or accommodations are used. This element is one of the reasons why assessments often look at factors outside of reading and writing development (we discuss this point later). Looking at other factors can help identify the impact of learning difficulties (i.e., the consequences that we discuss when covering the fourth element) but may also help explain literacy assessment findings if an individual is using compensatory strategies. For example, some adults slow reading down to allow strategy use, rather than being slow readers because they are slow at processing information. Assessments of areas outside of reading and writing may also identify co-occurring difficulties (referred to by some as comorbidities) that can impact on learning, and which may need additional attention/intervention.

Dyslexia can co-occur with dyspraxia (problems with co-ordinating movements) or deficits in attention (such as in Attention Deficit Hyperactivity Disorder), and effective support may also be needed here to avoid them interfering with learning during a dyslexia intervention. Issues of comorbid difficulties can make identifying support more complex. They may increase the range of difficulties that advice and support needs to take into account. In addition, such co-occurring conditions, along with the individual differences discussed in this book, can lead to a range of issues when trying to determine what is, and what is not, dyslexia (see discussions in Everatt & Denston, 2020). We do not have the space to discuss all the alternative perspectives that may have derived from this mix, but some of the perspectives set out here may be of interest to the reader; this may particularly be the case if the reader feels that what they have experienced throughout learning is very different from the framework used in this book. Note that the framework is based on our current understanding, which is derived from both research and practice. In many ways the phonological processing deficit is the dominant view of dyslexia, but there are alternatives. Some of these alternatives have reasonable levels of supporting evidence, though typically not as much as for the key feature (phonology) of the fourth element in this framework. However, other perspectives are very mixed in their evidence: they either contradict the experiences of most dyslexics or are inconsistent with the evidence in the literature. Indeed, some are contradictory with themselves or with related viewpoints.

As an example, the view that coloured overlays can be a way to support students with dyslexia often contradicts statements about the use of coloured lenses and the precise colour needed for such lenses to be effective (see Wilkins, 2005, and contrast with Suttle et al., 2018). If a precise colour is needed, as a colour prescription requires, then the overlays should not work as they are not precise. If overlays do work, then a precisely coloured lens is not necessary. Equally, taking out light through overlays and lenses relates to the background light in a room. If the background light changes (e.g., from sunlight to the light produced by an electric bulb), then a precise colour will need to change also. This is not to say that reducing the glare from a white piece of paper cannot help – reducing glare may help many by increasing the length of time that they can concentrate without feeling tired from having to look at mostly white paper for a long time. However, this is not dyslexia-specific enough in a framework for understanding dyslexia. Hence, although issues of visual stress and colour-based supports may be related to the experiences of some with dyslexia, they are not a fundamental feature of the majority's experience and may be better understood as an important comorbidity when considering support.

The same can be said of other areas that have been associated with dyslexia. If the reader wants to consider other dyslexia

## Introduction

perspectives that have been linked to visual processing issues, the following might be helpful:

1. Irlen (1991; https://irlen.com/) for a discussion of scotopic sensitivity (sometimes referred to as Meares/Irlen syndrome) as a potential cause of dyslexia-related difficulties – this perspective has a number of key differences from some views that argue for the use of coloured overlays or lenses (again contrast with Wilkins, 2005).

Other perspectives include:

2. Stordy and Nicholl (2000; and see www.fabresearch.org/viewItem.php) for a discussion of nutritional deficits that may be related to some aspects of dyslexia, particularly the fast processing of information within the brain that has been associated with some visual processing weaknesses – though again, the evidence is mixed and some of the features of nutrient deficiencies (such as skin problems) are not the type of characteristics we see experienced by most adult dyslexics;
3. Tallal et al. (1997; www.scilearn.com/) for initial discussions of auditory temporal processing deficits that may be found in individuals with language-related processing difficulties and which have then been linked with the visual temporal processing deficits that some have argued to be the reason for visual sensitivity (see Stein, 2019); and
4. Davis (1997; and consider www.dyslexia.com/) about the presence of artistic talent as a requirement for an identification of dyslexia (which we do not agree with as we find many dyslexic adults who are not great artists).

The recent views on visual and auditory temporal (or magnocellular) processing ideas can be found in Stein (2019), which brings together many of the ideas related to visual processing deficits outlined earlier. However, the need to explain more auditory processing differences between those with and without dyslexia (including the phonological effects discussed later) has led to the need to assume there are problems processing information at speed (the temporal part of the term) in both the visual and auditory domain. This is an example of a visual explanation that includes explanations of language-related deficits within its overarching theory.

We could include similar discussions about interpretation problems associated with motor deficit or automaticity deficit viewpoints (see Everatt & Denston, 2020 for such a discussion), but this is not the focus of the current book. If you want to look at some of the ideas related to motor deficit theories of dyslexia, then maybe consider the ideas of Goddard, Blythe and others at www.inpp.org.uk/, and contrast these with Levinson at www.dyslexiaonline.com/treatment/treatment.html. Also see the relatively recent ideas from those proposing an automaticity, or cerebellar, deficit in Nicolson and Fawcett (2019).

Another perspective is that of the relationship between working memory, dyslexia, and reading difficulties: see discussions in McLoughlin and Leather (2013); and see Knoop-van Campen et al. (2018), Peng et al. (2018), and Shin (2020). We discuss aspects related to working memory and executive functioning in much more detail later in this book (see Chapter 2). Most of these alternative perspectives incorporate a phonological viewpoint (which we discuss as part of the next element in the current framework), either as characteristics that need to be explained by the theory or as one of a number of alternative explanations. Therefore, given that this phonological perspective is part of most viewpoints, we focus on this in the current framework. If the strategies presented take into account this more likely explanation of the difficulties associated with dyslexia, then they should be useful to most of those with dyslexia.

Before we move on to discuss phonological processing, a final term needs a little introduction as it has emerged as a framework

Introduction

in which to view dyslexia and other potentially co-occurring conditions. This is the term neurodiversity (see Dwyer, 2022, for a recent discussion of related terms and their background). The use of 'neurodiversity' (and similar terms) within education has emerged due to many practitioners, and those theorising about inclusive education, being worried about terms such as dyslexia being seen in a negative way. Put bluntly, dyslexia is associated only with difficulties meaning that an individual with dyslexia should be seen as disabled in some way – to have a problem that needs fixing. If we take more of a medical perspective, then dyslexia may be considered a neurodevelopmental disability that requires intervention so that it can be 'cured' or overcome. This can be contrasted with a more social perspective where the difficulties are purely because of the way society views the difficulties: before reading became such a vital component of education and employment, dyslexia may not have been considered a problem. The focus on difficulty or disability has meant that many have tried to use alternative terms; for example, 'difference' may be used by some instead of 'difficulty' or 'disability'. The term diversity has then been linked with the idea that conditions such as dyslexia involve a specific way of thinking about something or processing something in the brain. The link to the brain leads to the term neuro, thereby leaving us with the term neurodiversity.

'Neurodiversity' can then be used to refer to any brain-based processing difference – from dyslexia to dyspraxia, to attention deficits, to autism (indeed, the term developed from those working with autism, not dyslexia). This makes for a more inclusive, and potentially a more positive, term: it suggests differences between people, rather than one group being able and another disabled – but it still links to the biological bases of such conditions. However, one of the problems with the term is that it has been used to refer to anything that might suggest a difference, and so may become over-inclusive: we may all fall within the neurodiversity label, meaning that its usefulness is questionable as a way to identify support (though see de Beer et al., 2022 for a use of the term when discussing adult dyslexics in work).

Despite the attraction of such a term, we do not use 'neurodiversity' in the current book for two reasons. The first is that dyslexia is not always seen from a negative perspective. Although the elements in our framework all start with the word difficulty, two out of the four then lead us to discussing positives and strengths. Indeed, many in the field of dyslexia use these more positive features as part of helping individuals understand the difficulties. This is a focus in this book too. And many with dyslexia see it as part of their identity – the term dyslexic is used in this book because of this feature. Hence, 'dyslexia' is not necessarily a term with negative connotations, particularly for those with dyslexia themselves. Secondly, the term neurodiversity does not specify support that well. Many of the strategies outlined in this book may be effective for any individual no matter what their neurological make-up, but some are specific to literacy and language issues, and all are based on our understanding of dyslexia (this framework) and our conversations with adults with dyslexia. Hence, the book uses the terms dyslexia and dyslexic.

### 1.1.3 Element 4: Causes and Consequences of Dyslexia

The fourth element of most perspectives on dyslexia is that it stems from problems related to the processing of language, particularly the phonological component of language. Phonological here relates to sounds within words: the word 'dog' is made up of the sound related to 'd', the sound related to 'o', and the sound related to 'g' – combine these sounds and you get something that approximates to the spoken word 'dog'. This can be particularly useful when trying

## Introduction

to read (or decode) new words with which you are unfamiliar – and for a young reader, this may be most of the written words that they encounter. Being able to efficiently recognise sounds within words may be vital to connect letters (referred to as graphemes) and sounds (referred to as phonemes), which is in turn a key component of using the English alphabet. There are other elements of sounds within a language that can also be linked with a writing system: for example, some writing systems, such as Chinese, focus more on syllables rather than the phoneme sounds that typically link with an alphabetic form. However, for an alphabet, recognising links between graphemes and phonemes seems to be key to successful decoding. Although there are varying views on the reasons why dyslexia occurs, deficits related to phonological processing, and to linking sounds with their written forms, are included in almost all models of dyslexia.

This fourth element is also important as it shows most clearly the link between language and literacy: written text is primarily a representation of spoken language. Assessments, therefore, may go beyond reading and writing to determine the level of development of underlying language skills. Additionally, there are reciprocal relationships between reading/writing and language, and so we are looking not only at the basic areas that are likely to lead to literacy difficulties, but also at those areas that may be impacted by poor learning experiences related to dyslexia. For example, reading difficulties associated with dyslexia can lead to a lack of reading practice, which can lead to less experience of certain types of vocabulary that would not be encountered in normal, day-to-day, spoken interactions. Reading can also lead to experiencing words in different sentence context. Hence, reading is associated with increases in vocabulary size and also with expanding links between words and their different meanings and uses. This lack of experience with words may then impact on language understanding and reading comprehension skills.

Hence, research that focuses on children is important in identifying learning problems early so that interventions can be implemented as soon as possible. However, we also need to consider the impact of learning difficulties on older learners and adults. Knowing what the consequences are if support is not effective is also useful to determine how best to help older individuals with difficulties. From the elements set out earlier, and based on research evidence (again, see discussions in Everatt & Denston, 2020), problems associated with dyslexia can lead to several types of consequences. The most obvious is that word-level reading/writing problems can lead to text-level weaknesses. However, this may then lead to problems across school subjects. As a simple example, if you cannot read your science textbook, then you are likely to struggle in science subjects at school. Struggling in school subjects because of a lack of access to materials can lead to poor educational qualifications. Equally, difficulties writing essays can lead to poor marks in assignments, which again may result in a lack of qualifications, which restricts access to post-school opportunities. Those with poor qualifications following compulsory education may not be able to access tertiary education courses and may not be in a position to apply for certain types of jobs. In addition, individuals' self-esteem and confidence are likely be affected. Employment prospects, therefore, may be constrained by the level of reading/writing difficulties experienced during schooling.

As we have also mentioned, less experience of reading can impact verbal skills. A lack of reading practice may impact on the ability to decipher the meaning of text. Such skills may become more practised during reading compared to spoken conversations. In verbal interactions, if you do not know what something means, you can always ask the person you are talking to. If you are reading text, you cannot ask the writer. Therefore, those who do not enjoy reading may gain less practice at working out (or inferring) what a text means. In

## Introduction

contrast, those that do see the need to put extra effort into reading may develop excellent inferencing skills. If you are struggling with decoding a word, one strategy might be to read around the word to infer the meaning of the phrase or sentence so that the meaning of the unknown word can also be inferred. This strategy, therefore, may enhance textual inferencing skills beyond those of individuals who have very good word decoding skills.

Finally, poor school experiences due to problems learning to read and write, and the subsequent feelings of failure that this might entail, can lead to poor behaviour and negative emotional consequences. Poor behaviour may manifest when trying to avoid situations where you are asked to do something that you find difficult or which makes you feel embarrassed. Being the class clown or troublemaker might be better than feeling shame when trying to read text out loud to the rest of the class. Such behaviours are likely to interfere with the individual's own learning, but can also impact on the learning of others in the class, which can then lead to problems with school authorities. Equally, the shame/embarrassment felt when struggling with what many consider the 'simple' task of reading can lead to low self-esteem and higher levels of anxiety than those felt by others. However, these negative behaviours and feelings need not afflict all those with dyslexia. Coming to terms with the difficulties and finding ways around them might lead some individuals to develop a more positive attitude towards the self and lead them to increased efforts to succeed. The type of consequences experienced can depend on numerous factors specific to the individual. Some of these are individual differences we are born with. Others are the range of positive and negative experiences we have in life. These latter experiences mean that as an individual gets older, the number of factors that impact on performance also has the tendency to grow, and these can influence the chances of success.

However, the relative dearth of research into dyslexia in the adult years has contributed to a lack of understanding of its impact and how to support adults in education or employment contexts (see also points made by Wissell et al., 2022). Increased understanding should lead to better provisions, but at present interventions for adults can often derive from ideas related to work with children: a focus on word-level reading or underlying phonological weaknesses, whereas the needs of adults are more likely focused on text understanding and report-writing coherence (Fidler & Everatt, 2012). Some may be recommended to try general literacy courses, such as those targeting speed reading courses and spelling programmes, despite the fact that these can have the potential to increase feelings of struggling and failure. Alternatively, dyslexic adults are recommended to try general support tools, such as assistive software that may help with reading and spelling; although some of these tools can be helpful in adult education contexts, they are often recommended with scant regard for the specific difficulties an individual may experience in the workplace (McLoughlin, 2012).

Achievement in the workplace requires a range of skill sets that have cognitive demands different from those required for success in education. Some jobs place heavy demands on literacy, others do not; some are office-based, others are operational. Although good literacy skills are increasingly essential in most workplaces, so are effective communication skills, planning, prioritisation, organisation skills, the ability to multi-task, to work under time pressure, to learn new skills, and to adapt to changes. Clearly, increasing literacy requirements has the potential to be a challenge for adults with dyslexia. However, many dyslexic adults do report struggling with some work-related skill sets that are not necessarily reading or writing

## Introduction

based (Gerber, 2012). Why some dyslexics struggle in these additional work-related areas is still debateable as there is little research to substantiate them as characteristics of dyslexia – they are certainly not issues that are discussed when investigating dyslexia in primary school children. Hence, a greater understanding of the impact of dyslexia in adulthood should potentially lead to a better understanding of the challenges faced, which should then lead to more effective individualised solutions. The aim of this book is to discuss and explore these additional challenges and consider the potential solutions that dyslexic adults themselves, and the practitioners supporting them, have found to be useful in reducing the impact of, or even overcoming, these difficulties.

## 1.2   Book Aims, Focus, and Methods

Overall, then, this book considers dyslexia from a literacy difficulties perspective but builds on these views to consider how it may impact more broadly on performance and ultimately success in one's chosen profession. The wide variation in the success levels of dyslexic people can confuse understanding further – and can sometimes lead to individuals questioning the idea of dyslexia in adults: the slightly odd (and hopefully outdated) view that you cannot both have a disability and be successful. However, this variation in success levels is something worthy of study and consideration: what is it that enables some people to succeed while others do not? This question is not new. For example, Gerber and colleagues (e.g., Gerber et al., 1992) investigated the behaviour patterns of successful dyslexic adults and concluded that internal control and self-understanding (potentially aspects of metacognitive skill) contributed to their success. Given that we can identify those aspects that support adult dyslexics in being successful, we may then be able to use that knowledge to support others. Similarly, Swanson and colleagues have argued that there are a range of deficits associated with dyslexia across the lifespan (see Swanson & Zeng, 2013). They suggest that, rather than focusing on developing literacy skills alone, a broader approach should be adopted to inform best practice for interventions targeted at younger and older individuals. One of the key areas that Swanson has discussed is the development of metacognitive skill (Swanson, 2012), which is one of the key proposals included in this book too.

As stated, the book focuses on dyslexia in adults, and particularly those adults in work, though we touch on issues related to adult education. Although 'adult' often refers to someone sixteen years of age or over, the ideas presented by dyslexic adults themselves are provided primarily by individuals who are aged at least thirty. The range of stories/comments are personal perceptions from individuals with dyslexia who have been relatively successful in their chosen field of employment, and so they have had to be working for some time. However, it is hoped that these experiences will be useful to all adult dyslexics no matter their age. Furthermore, most of the stories are from individuals living and working in the United Kingdom, but we have attempted to ensure that the ideas presented are applicable to a range of contexts so that everyone finds something of relevance, no matter their place of work.

All of the direct comments presented in the book are from real individuals, but we have used pseudonyms to avoid identification – we have also changed/deleted some statements for the same reason. The comments/stories presented are a sample of those we have collected over the years of working on this book. Those chosen were those we felt best presented the points made by most adults. Again, though, there is an element of selection based on our own understanding. The comments/stories fit into the framework of the

## Introduction

authors. Other authors have used similar techniques of interviewing those with dyslexia (e.g., Edwards, 1994; Gerber & Raskind, 2013; and see de Beer et al., 2022 and Wissell et al., 2022), and we feel that our interpretations of the commentaries/stories of adult dyslexics in this book do not differ substantially from the interview responses presented in these other published works. But they are our interpretations, so any errors of statements in the book are the fault of the authors. We would like to thank all of those who have spared their time to discuss some of the issues with us, including those not included in the book, as their input was as valuable to us as authors as the examples presented.

As indicated, interpretations are based on our framework for understanding dyslexia in adults. This is further discussed in the next chapter (Chapter 2), which provides more information about adult dyslexia, including the sort of assessment practices that are used with adults. Assessment is the starting point for the development of an individual's understanding of the nature of their dyslexia. Thus, we outline some of the processes that are involved in an assessment and discuss the potential reasons for it. The main rationale for assessment is to identify the specific difficulties that are likely experienced by an individual. However, it should also consider the individual's strengths as these can influence the performance of an adult in work as much as their weaknesses, particularly if the individual has chosen their profession. Equally, an assessment should help to provide explanations for the individual's experiences and make recommendations that support the individual in daily life and personal development.

Following on from this, Chapter 3 explores the theoretical concept of success. Some general, and maybe over-simple, definitions of success are covered, as well as the potential complexity of the concept: one person's view of success may be very different from another's even within the same context. This leads to a discussion of conceptualising career success in two ways: from a personal perspective and from a societal perspective. An overview of the literature provides a background to consider the relevance of these views to dyslexic people. The chapter considers some of the factors that are said to contribute to success, discussing issues related to self-understanding, internal control, and goodness of fit.

Chapter 4 then considers some strategies that can contribute to the success of dyslexic adults in the workplace. One of the key factors covered is the role of self-understanding. Self-understanding refers to the dyslexic individual's knowledge of their strengths and weaknesses, as well as their understanding of how, when, and why dyslexia affects their performance. Consistent with the theme of this book, Chapter 4 also covers the idea of individual differences; these can impact on our performance and reactions as much as dyslexia itself. Also consistent with other chapters in the book, ideas related to the development of metacognitive skills are discussed (i.e., task analysis, monitoring, reflection, and attribution). Additional ideas related to good planning, goal setting, and the importance of effective organisation are also covered.

Chapter 5 considers factors related to good communication skills, both verbal and written. The chapter explores various aspects of written and spoken language understanding, the sort of challenges that have been associated with adult dyslexia, and potential strategies for improving both written and verbal performance. Strategies for improving text reading are proposed, along with ideas for practising and supporting reading skills.

Chapter 6 focuses on literacy skills and effective communication in the workplace. It outlines a strategy (the '4 M's') that aims to help with literacy demands and the more efficient production of written work. Spoken language can also be an area where dyslexic adults

## Introduction

lack confidence and so participation in meetings and giving presentations are also considered in this chapter.

Chapter 7 focuses on the potential impact of dyslexia on performance at work. It again focuses on strategy development and how these can be put into practice to manage job demands. It explores the main areas that our dyslexia contributors have most commonly identified as challenges, in addition to the literacy challenges discussed in the previous chapter. Hence, a discussion of time management, memory and distractions, and stress is considered, along with issues related to dealing with new/novel circumstances in the workplace and preparing for reviews or promotion-related assessments or training.

Chapter 8 follows the themes covered in Chapter 7 by considering organisational aspects that can contribute to success in the workplace. These include the role of other people in the workplace, such as managers and colleagues, and additional resources, such as the role that technology can play. The chapter also discusses the role of the employer and explores ways in which managers/employers can provide an environment that 'mitigates' difficulties and enables individuals to demonstrate their strengths.

Chapter 9 then presents a range of stories/comments from dyslexic adults themselves to show some of the strategies and challenges they have faced. Contributors from a variety of professions tell us about their career journeys, and how they have achieved some degree of success. The aim of this chapter is to present these personal views so that the reader can see what others with dyslexia see as some of the key elements in their ability to perform the work necessary in their chosen profession.

The final chapter (Chapter10) overviews the previous chapters. It adds to the framework discussed in the rest of the book, and again argues for the importance of self-awareness – that the more we understand our abilities and difficulties, the more we can plan for success. We also remind the reader in this final chapter that the book contains ideas for support and the self-development of strategies. We are not expecting an individual to go through all of the strategies outlined. For example, Chapter 5 on literacy and language includes a number of activities to support the development of word-level reading skills. Someone who feels that these are not their area of difficulty may want to read these ideas and consider them in terms of interest but may be unlikely to want to practise them. The same goes for other parts of the book. If a strategy does not fit with self-awareness about difficulties, or needs, then we would not expect them to be practised. However, because of the wide variety of strengths and weaknesses that emerge from the core elements of dyslexia combined with years of experiential influences, the list of potential strategies needs to be comprehensive. The aim is that there will be something of interest for most people in the book: you do not need everything in it in order to be successful.

# 2

# Adult Dyslexia

## 2.1 Introduction

The perspective taken in this book is that dyslexia in adults develops from the same core elements that also characterise dyslexia in children (see Chapter 1). However, in addition to these, experiential differences lead to a range of consequences that are likely to differ across individuals and impact on performance to varying degrees based on the context in which an individual is learning and working. The core elements are still difficulties with certain aspects of reading and writing, along with some related weaknesses in certain aspects of language, and these can impact on any job where good literacy skills are essential as well as other areas of performance. However, experiential effects may help to overcome some of these difficulties (good teaching/intervention support or the development of effective compensatory strategies) and/or lead to additional difficulties (such as negative emotional consequences that might mean high levels of anxiety, creating problems in many facets of day-to-day life). These also interact with the type of job (or educational course) undertaken by the adult dyslexic.

In some cases, the effects of dyslexia, and these individual dyslexia-related consequences, are minimal owing to the nature of the work required. In other situations, both may impact on performance. For some, the impact is negative; for example, making it difficult to progress in a chosen profession owing to the need to take written assessments in order to be promoted, or having low self-esteem meaning that an individual never puts themselves up for promotion. Alternatively, for some the impact may be positive; for example, when an individual has had to find creative solutions to dyslexia-related barriers, leading to improving creativity-related skills that can be a bonus in certain kinds of employment. Hence, advice for adults with dyslexia should be individualised.

Given that it may be difficult for an advisor to cover all the potential changes that work-life may bring, the focus in this book is the development of self-understanding and the use of metacognitive strategies. These are covered in Part II, along with examples from personal experiences of dyslexic individuals themselves. Before we look at these ideas, though, this chapter focuses on explaining the framework of adult dyslexia envisaged in the book so that the ideas presented within Part II can be interpreted through our framework. Furthermore, although self-awareness is core to the argument presented, support from external sources can also be helpful, such as the challenges and success stories of others. Equally, support from external sources may come via an assessment that should provide a basis on which self-understanding can develop. Therefore, we discuss assessment further, with a focus on what we feel would be most useful in these assessments and for the dyslexic adult to take from assessment reports. This chapter, therefore, has two subsections, one discussing the framework we have for thinking about adult dyslexia, the second focusing on assessment practices and how these might help with self-understanding.

## 2.2   Framework of Adult Dyslexia

There have been several frameworks aimed at developing an understanding of dyslexia in adults. One of the most useful (in the view of the authors of this book) is provided by Frith (1999). This was developed to help understand key features of a range of learning difficulties, and to allow theories about these learning difficulties to be judged against the framework. Figure 2.1 presents our framework based on the original proposed by Frith (1999). In it, the middle column is that which most researchers in the field of dyslexia would focus on, and it is the closest part of the figure to Frith's original idea. The middle column is a simple representation of the view that dyslexia is related to difficulties in phonological processing. As discussed in Chapter 1, this theory proposes that dyslexia is primarily based on deficits in processing sounds within words (the phonological processing deficit in the centre of the figure). This is based on a multitude of research evidence, along with some consistent experiences reported by practitioners (see discussions in Gillon, 2018; Snowling, 2000).

Phonological processing is a theorised cognitive process. It is something that we cannot 'see' directly. We assume/infer that the brain performs such processes based on the behaviours that we see when individuals perform language tasks that require the processing of phonological information. For example, if we ask what the first sound in 'book' is, most say a sound that is represented by 'b'. Similarly, if asked what is left when you take the 'b' sound from 'bad', most individuals say something like 'add'. These sort of tasks

| environment | brain/biology | consequences |
|---|---|---|
| Learning experiences → ↘ | Genetic factors : multiple chromosomes ↓ Brain differences: left hemisphere areas | Emotional & Behavioral reactions & Self-concept → |
| English alphabet → | **cognition** ↓ Phonological processing deficit ↙ Poor understanding of grapheme-phoneme correspondences | Impacts on certain aspects of Language, Memory & Cognition → |
| ↗ Support & Intervention → | **behavior** ↓ Difficulty learning to read and write Poor scores in phonological tasks | Access to learning materials ↓ Qualifications & Opportunities → |

**Figure 2.1** Framework for understanding adult dyslexia

suggests that we can process sounds within words – if we could not process such sounds, then we would not be able to do these tasks. These tasks can also show differences between those with dyslexia and those without. Such differences suggest that those with dyslexia struggle with many such phonological tasks. Hence, measures of phonological processing are often included in assessment procedures aimed at identifying dyslexia.

Additionally, there is biological evidence consistent with the concept of phonological processing, as well as its association with dyslexia. When we perform phonological tasks, differences occur in activations in certain parts of the brain, and these activations can be found to vary between those with dyslexia and those without (see discussions in Shaywitz & Shaywitz, 2020). Similarly, the reason why these phonological processes impact on reading an alphabet is because they play a key role in linking letters and sounds (as discussed in Chapter 1), which may also be related to variations in activations within the brain. Hence, these cognitive level features related to dyslexia have a biological basis. As suggested in the middle column of Figure 2.1, there is also some evidence that characteristics associated with dyslexia may be based on certain combinations of genes, though the precise genetic combinations are complex (e.g., see Thompson et al., 2015). Although there are still some aspects that we do not understand, the phonological explanation of dyslexia has a biological basis, it fits with predictions about cognitive processes, and there are links with behavioural outcomes of dyslexia, in terms of reading and writing difficulties, as well as poor performance in phonological tasks. Hence, the middle column of Figure 2.1 provides a basis to understand how dyslexia happens.

Despite the middle column of Figure 2.1 being the key focus for most researchers, the left-hand 'environment' column of Frith's framework may be even more important for understanding how we can influence the impact of dyslexia. This shows that things can change based on what the individual is experiencing and the efforts made by educationalists to support the learning of those with dyslexia. If support procedures work, then the impact of dyslexia on day-to-day experiences should be lessened. These environmental experiences impact all three of the elements in the middle column. Experience changes how the brain processes information (again, see discussions in Shaywitz & Shaywitz, 2020), and increased practice forms more durable links between parts of the brain. Practice also impacts on the cognitive processes that are dominant when performing a task. A child taught successful decoding strategies is more likely to use those strategies and practise them so that they become more efficient. Similarly, although support and intervention are usually targeted at behaviours (improving reading performance, for example), a positive and motivating intervention has the potential to impact on the way we think about something, and so can impact on cognition and influence brain activity. We know that improving literacy can enhance language processes, so interventions that improve reading development may well support other areas of development during childhood. Hence, these are interactive systems.

Other environmental factors can influence outcomes. As stated earlier in this chapter and in Chapter 1, the alphabetic link between letters (or graphemes) and sounds (or phonemes) is not the only type of link between a writing system and a spoken language. If decoding graphemes into phonemes is not the main way to connect written text with spoken language, then other levels of phonological processing may become more developed. Hence, the precise relationship between language and reading/writing can vary to some extent, but the links need to be there for text understanding to be supported. Also as stated before, this association between language and reading/writing occurs in both directions, so that language processes support reading development, and reading practice can improve language skills.

Furthermore, given that language can play a role in many things that humans do, it may also influence how we think about things and/or how we remember things. For example, one theorised memory system is called working memory, which is a system that has been discussed in relation to dyslexia for many years (e.g., McLoughlin et al., 2002), and one which may help us understand some of the more consequential difficulties that may derive from a lifetime of dyslexia.

Although there are differing models of working memory, the main feature is the involvement in the processing of information into, and from, longer term memory systems. This requires making sense of the information for storage to be logical and efficient. For example, if information is meaningful, then storage of the meaning would be useful. In terms of written text, determining meaning typically requires the integration of already known information with details in the text, as well as connecting different parts of text. So it would be useful to store pieces of textual information while additional information is being processed from the text and while information is obtained from background knowledge about the subject of the text. Theories typically propose that this is what working memory does. It has short-term storage roles (language information might be stored in a working memory phonological system, for example) while integration with additional information is happening (which the executive system of working memory is hypothesised to support). Hence, working memory has been proposed to play a part in language development – linking new words with past words and meanings, which is a key function of a developing vocabulary system. It has also been argued to be involved in making inferences from text; that is, connecting different parts of text that provide meaning, inferring the meaning of a word from the text around the word, and going beyond the text to determine meaning via general knowledge stored in long-term memory.

Some elements of working memory are considered fairly fixed – that is, the amount of information that can be stored in working memory is limited both in terms of the amount that can be stored and the time it can be retained. However, strategies can be learnt that may support the way that working memory is hypothesised to process information. For example, chunking information can help: remembering 'two, seven, five, nine, one, eight, three, six' in order can be difficult, but 'twenty-seven, fifty-nine, eighteen, thirty-six' is easier. Similarly, asking questions about text while reading can lead to inferencing and integration processing; and using source materials efficiently without distraction can overcome weaknesses in vocabulary- or language-related long-term memory. These need to be practised to be efficient, though. Hence, many of the features associated with working memory can provide the basis for understanding the consequences that may occur owing to lack of reading practice and weaknesses in certain elements of language processing and storage.

Therefore, in the shaded consequences column of Figure 2.1, we have included the potential for consequences on a range of factors. These include the emotional, self-concept (self-esteem or self-efficacy) and behavioural factors that may be influenced by our personality as well as our experiences: as discussed earlier, difficulties with learning may have a negative impact on some, whereas others are able to shrug them off or even use them as a reason to try harder. They also include societal success-related outcomes in terms of good educational qualifications and job opportunities (again discussed in Chapter 1). The level of dyslexia (biological and cognitive) and the support provided (environmental or experiential) both influence such educational, and prospective employment, outcomes. However, we have also included a box to indicate that both the middle and left-hand columns can also impact on the development of language and memory, and hence thinking processes. These can also impact on elements of success. However, they need not be all negative. Phonological-related problems with storing information in working memory create challenges, but learning strategies to reduce these challenges should lead to self-knowledge and a set of skills that can be valuable in many contexts, including work environments: if you are the one who can think around a challenge, how much more valuable you will be as a colleague in a modern workplace.

Clearly, though, self-understanding and the learning of what we refer to as metacognitive strategies is an important part of the right-hand shaded column of Figure 2.1 being more positive than negative.

In Part II, we look at self-understanding and strategy use further. In the second part of this chapter, though, we consider another source of self-awareness that can be developed via a dyslexia assessment. The procedures and tasks used in such assessments should provide further information that can be useful in self-understanding, and lead to an awareness of areas of strength and weakness.

## 2.3    Assessment of Adults with Dyslexia

The purpose of an assessment for dyslexia is both to determine if the individual has dyslexia or not, and to provide information on which to make recommendations for support. In the case of children, this is mainly to provide support at school, such as in an education plan or an intervention programme targeting reading. For an adult, support in tertiary or higher education may be the purpose, and may involve recommendations about accommodations in class or during assignments, such as providing materials in computer-format for using text-to-speech software or providing extra time in examinations. Finally, the aim may be to provide understanding and hence support within a work context – the main focus of subsequent chapters. It could also simply be for awareness; that the identification of dyslexia explains something important to the adult. This could explain why they have struggled with some elements of day-to-day activities in the past, or why their school-life was not as successful or enjoyable as it was for others.

Dyslexia in children is usually determined via the assessment of reading and writing (often spelling), along with measures that may inform the assessor about the cause of the reading/writing difficulty (such as phonological processing). Such assessment procedures are often also used with older individuals (those over sixteen years of age). However, one difficulty faced by those assessing dyslexia in adults is that most tests of literacy have been developed for those younger than sixteen and for those in compulsory education contexts where levels of expected literacy skills can be determined against a curriculum. There are assessment tools for older individuals (e.g., see Brooks et al., 2016; Warmington et al., 2013), but there are additional challenges with assessing older individuals. For example, an adult may have experienced many years of additional difficulties that are associated with dyslexia, such as emotional consequences that can stem from reading/writing difficulties. This may mean that poor performance on assessment measures may be more because of negative emotion related to being tested, rather than the dyslexia itself. Furthermore, the adult may develop strategies for reducing the effects of their dyslexia – compensatory strategies such as slowing down reading to focus on supporting understanding. These may mask difficulties and lead to conclusions that reading comprehension is not a problem. However, such conclusions may be over-simplistic if such compensatory strategies are not taken into account. For example, a compensatory strategy may work under some circumstances and not others. Unless the assessment process considers these alternatives, then the difficulties may not be identified. Therefore, procedures for assessing dyslexia in adults should be qualitatively different from those used in schools to assess children. Both the range of assessment tools and the aims of the assessment need to be considered carefully. Reports following assessment also need to be detailed appropriately for others to understand the assessment process and its recommendations and be relevant regarding the context in which the person is working.

In the following pages, we look at some of these issues. Many follow on from the ideas discussed in Chapter 1, where we discuss the four key elements that we see as associated with dyslexia, and the first part of this chapter, where we discuss an overview of dyslexia in adulthood. These features or characteristics of adult dyslexia are the starting point to consider how to identify it and the sort of challenges and solutions we may need to consider when implementing adult dyslexia assessment procedures. Note that the following comprises the views of the authors based on our current understanding. There are alternative positions within the field, and hence not all assessors will consider the points here as important. These alternative positions often focus on differing causal theories of dyslexia that may be accepted by different practitioners: for example, if a practitioner believes dyslexia is caused by visual processing problems associated with colour, then this may be the focus of their assessment practice. The focus in this book is based on research and practice involving adults with dyslexia, and takes as a starting point the view that dyslexia can be subsumed into the four key elements that we discuss in Chapter 1.

The first element proposes that accurate and/or fluent reading and writing/spelling develop incompletely or with great difficulty. Therefore, we need to assess a range of reading and writing skills in order to understand the challenges facing the individual and in order to identify, and target, effective support. As an example, the Adult Reading Test (Brooks et al., 2016) assesses reading accuracy, speed, and comprehension while reading aloud, and then also assesses reading speed and comprehension during silent reading to give a picture of the range of skills associated with the adult's current level of reading performance. These individual elements of reading are all compared with expected levels of performance based on the average and range of performance produced by a large number of adults within further and higher educational contexts (such as those retaking school-level examinations, and those studying for degree-level qualifications).

The second element proposes that challenges are persistent despite access to effective learning opportunities. This means that an assessor needs to understand aspects of the individual's past learning experiences. This includes information on any past support or intervention that the individual has experienced and how successful these may have been. It may also consider how successful the individual felt they were in different areas of the curriculum: feelings of success can be as important as actual educational qualifications, though both should be considered. If the individual is from another educational system than the assessor (e.g., as a child, they were educated in China but they are being assessed as an adult in the UK), then the assessor may need to know more about the education systems experienced to have a better picture of the challenges experienced by, and support provided to, the individual in the past.

A further element that we have discussed as associated with dyslexia proposes deficits in processing certain aspects of language. Given this, we would expect assessments of spoken language in addition to assessments of written language. Most adults with dyslexia struggle with phonological tasks to some extent compared with those without dyslexia, though the tasks used to assess adults need to be more complex than those developed for children: for example, removing sounds from the middle of a word is harder than from the beginning or end – and reducing the time allowed to complete a phonological task can also test the efficiency of phonological processes developed into adulthood. If we accept that phonological deficits are the likely cause of the primary difficulties faced by dyslexics when learning to read/write, then identification through assessment of such deficits would be sensible. This does not mean that reading and writing difficulties are *not* caused by other things (poor educational experience, psychological problems, etc.), but many assessors take the most likely cause into consideration as part of their assessment procedures.

This link with language processes may also help us to identify additional areas where difficulties may be experienced. As discussed earlier, the reciprocal relationship between literacy and language means that processing words at the level of the phoneme (the basic unit of sound – 'cat' has three phonemes, for example) is supported by reading acquisition, and that vocabulary growth can be supported by reading experience. Hence, an assessor often uses a range of language tasks, from phonological to vocabulary to verbal reasoning skills. Each provides a picture on how challenges and experiences related to dyslexia may have impacted on language development, and hence increase awareness and provide clues to better solutions.

At least initially, literacy difficulties are unexpected in relation to typical development in non-literacy areas. Hence, a child with dyslexia can still excel in other areas of a school curriculum. However, the central role of literacy in most areas of education means that impacts on other areas of education may occur unless appropriate intervention or accommodation is implemented. Again, some interview about past learning experiences may be warranted. However, this may go further in the case of an adult and involve assessment of other areas of processing. The previous element suggested the need to assess language functioning. However, aspects of word processing (verbal or written) can also support memory functions, either in terms of the way language is stored efficiently or in the systems that working memory can rely on when processing language-related information.

An assessor, therefore, may consider a range of skills to see how these have developed. What these additional areas of assessment are often depends on the perspective taken by the assessor (what they see as the cause and consequences of dyslexia) and the context of the assessment: if in an educational context, then a focus on processes related to study skills may be important; if in an employment context, then the requirements of the job may influence the assessor's procedures.

In terms of adult assessments, this may involve measures from the Wechsler Adult Intelligence Scale (WAIS; see the fourth edition, the latest when writing this book: www.pearsonassessments.com/store/usassessments/en/Store/Professional-Assessments/Cognition-%26-Neuro/

Part I

Wechsler-Adult-Intelligence-Scale-%7C-Fourth-Edition/p/100000392.html). This reference provides general information on the tests, if of interest. Note, though, that these tests are what are called 'closed' tests, so they can only be accessed by someone with the appropriate qualifications required to use the tests. The actual tests are therefore not available at the link, just general information about them.

These WAIS measures provide information on verbal ability (measures of vocabulary and verbal reasoning) and non-verbal ability (such as building three-dimensional shapes based on a two-dimension plan – sometimes referred to as block design). They also provide information on memory, such as in tests of general knowledge and measures of working memory processes. Some measures are accuracy based, but others require the completion of tasks as quickly as possible, which can give an indication of speeded processing levels. This may be the most familiar scale for most of those assessed in the UK, but there are alternatives, such as the Woodcock-Johnson scales (for details, see www.riversideinsights.com/woodcock_johnson_iv) or the Stanford-Binet scales (for information, see https://stanfordbinettest.com/all-about-stanford-binet-test/what-does-stanford-binet-test-measure). These alternatives are likely familiar in different parts of the world, with their choice by assessors often depending on where they have been standardised (i.e., a scale that has been standardised in the UK may not have been in another part of the world, whereas the Stanford-Binet scale may have been) or the training available to assessors (training on one scale may be available within a country, but not on another). Each of these scales covers similar skills or processes, though the precise measure may vary; for example, all have measures of verbal and non-verbal processing. Hence, the points outlined here should be relevant to assessments using any of these batteries.

## 2.3.1  Reading and Writing Skills

Most assessments involve measures of reading and writing. When assessing a child in the early period of learning, this likely focuses on word-level reading and decoding, along with spelling as the word-level feature of writing. However, the older the individual, the more likely that these sort of assessments may be less dependable (owing to learning experience and compensatory strategies) and the more likely they will not be seen as useful by the individual being assessed. This is not something 'new' about adult dyslexia – it has been discussed for thirty or more years. For example, Miles (1993) suggests that reading ability may not be as accurate an indicator of dyslexia in an adult as spelling performance. Consequently, poor spelling, in contrast to reading difficulties, may more easily identify adult dyslexia. This does not mean that some dyslexic adults will not continue to show poor word reading accuracy; it is just that not all will. The skill of accurate single word reading may have been slow to develop, but it may show good levels compared with those shown by average non-dyslexics because of the effort of the individual with dyslexia or the support provided during childhood. Spelling can be more challenging a skill, and so it may be slower to develop without extensive practice or intervention. Hence, assessments of spelling may be as important as reading accuracy when dealing with adults.

Additionally, the imperfect correlation between isolated word reading and the skills required to understand written text means that some individuals with good single word reading skills may struggle with text comprehension (see discussions of why this might happen in Cain, 2010, and Cornoldi & Oakhill, 1996). This may mean that poor reading can be classified based on word-level versus comprehension level differences: some will show word reading difficulties, whereas others will show text comprehension weaknesses (see Sleeman et al., 2022). Consistent with this partial dissociation, adult dyslexics can show single-word reading performance comparable with their non-dyslexic peers but still struggle when required to comprehend text. In dyslexia, this dissociation between good word reading and poor text comprehension may be best explained by a lack of text reading practice or teaching emphasising word decoding without extending this to text reading. However, these explanations mean that any effects of dyslexia on reading comprehension are not inevitable. Some of those with a history of dyslexia may show fairly good levels of performance on measures of reading comprehension (see Brooks et al., 2016), but still struggle with word reading and spelling.

A further issue may be the type of reading comprehension task, which can influence whether those with dyslexia show worse performance than their peers. Limiting the time allowed to read and comprehend text can have a major effect on adult students with dyslexia. It is only when extra time is allowed, or reading time is self-determined, that difference between dyslexic and non-dyslexics disappears (see discussions in Fidler & Everatt, 2012; Jackson & Doelinger, 2002; Lesaux et al., 2006). This is one of the arguments for the use of extra time in assignments/examinations, and it has been identified as a strategy by many dyslexics who show good reading comprehension scores when allowed the time to use strategies. Often the reported strategy is to re-read a text several times in order to work out the gist of the text, which can then be used to fill in any gaps in word recognition during re-reading.

Furthermore, some dyslexics may struggle with factual questions in a text (the name of someone or a date) but show good levels of performance on inference questions (working out information not explicitly stated in the text), whereas others may show the opposite disparity in performance (consider Fidler & Everatt, 2012, versus Simmons & Singleton, 2000). Consistent with the argument presented in this book, the reasons for these differences may be due to the experiences of the adult, as well as their areas of strength and weakness. Those who work out the re-reading and deriving the gist strategy may develop good inferring skills over time, whereas others may use memorisation strategies to support recall of key terms in a text. Equally, given that inference making has been linked to working memory processes (see discussions in Cain, 2010), those with weaker working memory may show lower levels of use of the inferring gist strategy. Similarly, those with good long-term memories may be able to store factual information from text better than those with less reliable long-term memory processes.

Therefore, an assessment may include a range of literacy measures in order to determine whether there are continued difficulties with reading and writing, consistent with dyslexia, and also to determine what aspects of literacy are still showing weaknesses and where there are areas of reasonable development of skills. This helps with recommendations for accommodations, as well as providing a basis for best support practices.

## 2.3.2 Educational History or the Background to Learning

The second element suggests that assessments include discussion of the history of difficulties and learning experiences. The adult's own description of their challenges during literacy acquisition may indicate the types of reading/writing problems that the individual may have experienced and give clues to current needs. Equally, this may highlight strategies that they have used to support achievement or avoid failure. Again, these give the assessor an idea of what may be useful and what might have to be overcome prior to learning being successful. Consistent with the first element, as the individual gets older, a wider range of literacy-related skills may be impacted, hence assessments looking at literacy beyond the word level are useful. This needs to be taken into account in support procedures. A basic phonological decoding intervention may not be useful, or appealing, for many adults. Few adults will want to practise isolated word reading, but interventions that embed decoding strategies within procedures that can be shown to benefit comprehension should increase the chance that an adult will practise and use such strategies.

Asking adults about their educational background and experiences has formed an important component of work in the field of dyslexia for some time. Interviews can be highly informal and personal in terms of the questions asked. However, more formal questionnaires have also been developed, primarily with adults in mind. For example, a questionnaire could be distributed to adult students entering a higher education course in order to determine the likelihood that an individual student may experience problems related to dyslexia. The same could be done within a workforce; though this sort of questionnaire distribution is very rare. Such dyslexia-related questionnaires might be best referred to as a screening tool. They are likely to give relatively simple indications of the risk of dyslexia, with a higher risk meaning that further assessment may be advised. For example, Snowling et al. (2012) has developed an adult questionnaire that asks questions about levels of reading difficulties experienced by an individual. This questionnaire was developed in order to assess the potential level of family-related incidence of literacy learning problems (see also van Bergen et al., 2014). Other examples include the checklist developed by Smythe and Everatt (2009), which comprises questions related to dyslexia rather than specifically asking about reading difficulties in the past (see also Vinegrad, 1994). For example, some questions are related to reading (such as 'Do you confuse visually similar words when reading (e.g. tan, ton)?' and 'How easy do you find it to sound out words? (e.g. el-e-phant)'). Others focus more on language (e.g., 'Do you confuse the names of objects (e.g. table for chair)?'), and areas associated with skills that may require verbal memory (e.g., 'Did you learn your multiplication tables easily?') or even compensatory strategies ('How easy is it to think of unusual (creative) solutions?'). Using such a checklist as part of an interview that also includes questions about past difficulties may help the assessor determine whether a full assessment would be worthwhile.

How such interviews or questionnaire are used depends on the assessor's purpose and context. Again, a range of evidence from the adult and maybe past assessments should provide the basis on which to identify areas of continued difficulties, which may benefit from specific support. However, it can also provide ideas for strategies that can support learning: if the adult has relied on technology to access materials for learning in the past, then this may be the best area for continued support, for example.

### 2.3.3 Cognitive-Linguistic Factors

Assessments are also likely to focus on language skills, particularly phonological areas given that this may be the most likely source of dyslexia-related literacy difficulties. We have discussed such tasks earlier: those that require the person being assessed to identify and manipulate sounds within words. As also discussed earlier, we know that there are reciprocal relationships between reading/writing and language. Therefore, most assessments not only look at the language areas that are likely to lead to literacy difficulties, but also those areas that may be impacted by poor learning experiences: literacy difficulties can lead to a lack of reading practice, which can lead to less experience of certain types of vocabulary, and this in turn will impact reading comprehension skills.

Part I

The reason why phonological skills have been considered useful in reading development is that they allow the linkage between language and writing. Being able to recognise sounds in words helps in the linking of those sounds to letters. In reading, this is sometimes referred to as decoding – that is, decoding the spoken word from its written form by linking each letter or combination of letters to their corresponding sound or sounds. This is the reason why many assessment practices also include measures of non-word (sometimes referred to as pseudo-word) reading. These are word-like in that they can be pronounced by the decoding process; that is, by translating each letter or group of letters into an appropriate sound (or to put it in technical jargon, using grapheme–phoneme correspondence rules). But they are not real words as they have no meaning, so they are unlikely to have been experienced before. For example, the non-word 'sploob' can be pronounced but it has no meaning: it is not a real word in the English language. It is unlikely that you will have seen this set of letters together in this order before, which means that you will not be able to name it from memory. Therefore, naming can only be achieved by relating letters or groups of letters with sounds – by decoding the made-up word. Such a task, therefore, can be used to determine the efficiency of the decoding processes that are used when new words are experienced – which will be most words for the beginning reader. Consistent with the view that phonological processing supports decoding, and that dyslexics have problems in this area of processing, those with dyslexia typically perform worse at such tasks than those without dyslexia (see Rack et al., 1992). This dyslexia-related weakness can be found in adults as well as children, and so may be useful in assessment practices across the lifespan.

Additionally, even when adults with dyslexia have developed good decoding accuracy, there can still be a slowness to their decoding indicative of dyslexia. Hence, speeded naming of real words or non-words can be a useful additional tool in assessment practices (see Fawcett & Nicolson, 1994; Hulme & Snowling, 1997). Similarly, compared with non-dyslexics, many with dyslexia can perform poorly in tasks requiring the rapid naming of familiar objects, digits, or colours. Note that this is not a problem finding the name since these are usually highly familiar names. Rather, the problem seems to be in accurately producing the names at speed, which may be consistent with difficulties in terms of making phonological access efficient. However, the extent to which these speeded naming deficits persist into adulthood for all those with dyslexia is debatable. Whether such weaknesses persist may depend on learning experience as much as the primary cause of dyslexia. Hence, rapid naming tasks may need to be considered as part of a range of phonological tasks, rather than as the only indicator of phonological weaknesses.

Another phonology-related measure that has been used in the diagnosis of dyslexia is memory span. This requires the individual to repeat, in order, sequences of (usually) digits. These sequences increase in length, say from repeating two digits in order (a relatively easy task) to repeating nine digits (a much harder task). The items are usually verbally presented and verbally repeated. Hence, the measure assesses the ability to distinguish, store, and produce verbal (phonological) material. The length at which the individual cannot repeat all the items in the correct order is considered indicative of memory span size and related to working memory capacity, both of which have been argued to be related to problems associated with dyslexia (see McLoughlin et al., 2002; Thomson, 2009). Although there are equivocal findings for and against differences between dyslexics and non-dyslexics on memory span measures (Everatt, 1999), this is also an area that is likely to be assessed to inform further support recommendations and provide evidence for the range of phonological-related weaknesses experienced by the individual.

Part I

It may also provide evidence linked to assessments of working memory (discussed in Section 2.3.4).

## 2.3.4 Additional Areas of Assessment

For adults, and for many of the reasons we have discussed, assessing more than reading and writing may be of greater importance than when assessing children. Therefore, many assessors emphasise the assessment of cognitive abilities and individual differences, rather than simply focusing on a deficit in literacy (McLoughlin & Leather, 2013; Thomson, 2009). This can help to identify the range of the impact of literacy learning difficulties, and it can also help explain literacy assessment findings if there are areas of skill that may be used as compensatory strategies (e.g., identifying morphological units, such as prefixes, may support decoding when phonological processing is still weak – we cover additional examples in Chapter 5). We have looked at issues related to the need to assess language skills, such as vocabulary, since lower reading experience may be associated with lower vocabulary. Equally, the challenges with language and literacy faced by an individual may lead to better development of the processing of the meaning of words, such as in strategies used to determine the gist of a passage – discussed earlier. Better links between concepts and more practised inferencing skills may show in higher scores on certain verbal reasoning tasks used by assessors. Hence, assessments may identify areas of skill as much as weakness.

Despite the view of dyslexia as leading to difficulties and weaknesses, many within the field of dyslexia have also referred to its possible positive features (see West, 1991). For example, Miles (1993, p. 189) suggests that dyslexic individuals show 'an unusual balance of skills'. West (1991) refers to many adult dyslexics' creativity and visual skills, suggesting that they will excel in fields where these skills are useful, such as the arts, architecture or engineering, and the sciences. It has also been argued that measures of visual arts skills, often related to visuo-spatial processing, should be useful as a 'positive' diagnostic indicator of dyslexia (see ideas in Davis, 1997). Rather than focusing on deficiencies, these could be used as evidence for dyslexia based upon superior performance. One problem with finding consistency in these suggestions is the paucity of empirical research. There is some evidence that at least some dyslexics show better than average performance in some non-verbal areas (consider Winner et al., 2001), including those focused on creative solutions to problems (see Everatt et al., 1999); however, this is rare and sometimes inconsistent. Despite the lack of reliable evidence, such skills may be useful in the workplace. Evidence for increased creativity may be associated with individuals finding their own solutions to difficulties related to dyslexia. Although creativity is rarely assessed in formal dyslexia assessments, looking at a range of skills that might influence performance should inform recommendations and self-understanding for the adult with dyslexia.

For many assessors, therefore, assessment batteries that include a range of measures are used. As mentioned earlier, these batteries were often developed to assess intelligence, and the history of dyslexia assessments has been linked to measures of general intelligence (often referred to as an Intelligence Quotient or IQ). One of the advantages of such batteries is that they have a long development history and therefore are among some of the more reliable assessments of human abilities. This can be very important to an assessor who needs to be able to argue for consistency in their practice. However, the use of intelligence-related batteries has some controversy attached to it. This mainly relates to past perspectives of dyslexia that argued for the need to identify a discrepancy between IQ and reading levels for dyslexia to be recognised. This discrepancy practice has a lot of problems (see discussions in Ferrer et al., 2010; Kaufman, 2009; Siegel, 1988), and therefore many use these batteries more to determine areas of skill and areas of weakness across a range of cognitive factors. For example, many such batteries assess vocabulary and verbal reason – two areas discussed earlier. They also assess non-verbal areas, so that non-verbal reasoning and visual processing skills may inform statements about areas of ability. If these relate to a specific job profile, then those skills may be a positive factor in a work context. The opposite might be the case if the job profile links more to areas of weakness in the cognitive profile of the individual. Hence, recommendations about challenges and support in a work context may be derived from the range of measures used.

Such cognitive batteries also typically assess skills related to working memory. Again, the level of ability determined by these measures should provide information on which to develop support procedures: high levels of executive functioning should provide the basis on which to develop metacognitive strategies, while lower levels may require additional training support prior to strategy recommendations (see also Doyle and McDowell, 2015; Hock, 2012). For example, Smith-Spark and his colleagues (e.g., Smith-Spark et al., 2016, 2017) identify areas of executive functioning deficits in dyslexic students and conclude that these are likely to impact on performance at work. However, at the time of writing this book, we could find no research into the influence of executive function deficits in relation to dyslexia in the workplace. If we take a reasonably referenced view of executive functioning, that of Miyake and colleagues (Miyake et al., 2000; though see also Diamond, 2013; and further discussions in Miyake & Friedman, 2012), this includes processes of 'updating', 'inhibitory control', and 'shifting'.

The updating component is closest to working memory, as discussed earlier, and allows new information to be incorporated with old. This may be an important component of understanding language, and one where a short-term phonological store (potentially measured by the memory span assessments discussed in Subsection 2.3.3) may be a useful part of the processing system. The inhibitory control component allows an individual to inhibit unwanted interpretations of information and focus on a desired interpretation. This can be vital in strategy use and hence be an important part of metacognitive strategies; it may have some relationship with what Gerber et al. (1992) referred to as internal control when discussing successful adults with learning difficulties. The shifting component means that an individual has the ability to shift between ways of thinking about something in order to identify more effective ways to deal with something. Often, tasks measuring this aspect of executive functioning expect the shifting to occur quickly, and rapid processing may be an area of difficulty for some with dyslexia. Equally, though, some of the aspects of thinking of creative solutions to problems, particularly thinking between alternative solutions, may be associated with this element of executive functioning. Hence, consideration of a range of tasks associated with working memory functioning may be another area in which to look for skills and weaknesses that can then best inform support. We discuss strategy use, particularly in Part II of this book, but again the point here is that there will be a range of individual differences that means one strategy may not fit all.

Equally, non-cognitive areas have been found to be important in considering how to support those with dyslexia. A number of studies have found evidence for dyslexics demonstrating higher levels of frustration and anxiety, lower self-esteem, and lack of confidence than their non-dyslexic peers (see discussions in Everatt & Denston, 2020). Increased emotionality can be associated with task performance decrements, potentially leading to inaccurate assessment measures. If an individual is over-anxious during assessment, then performance may not be consistent with that involving similar abilities but in a different (non-assessment) context. Taking assessments may be particularly worrying for those with dyslexia who have experienced years of academic 'failure' in school. This can lead to detrimental levels of anxiety in any situation perceived as related to achievement tests. An assessment for promotion may be a good example, and may lead to a very able individual not gaining promotion because of poor performance owing to negative levels of anxiety. Similarly, poor levels of self-concept may lead to an individual never putting themselves forward for promotion in the first place. An assessor may determine the potential impact of such feelings by asking the individual about current or past experiences, again providing a basis for advice about how to overcome such challenges. Although these may not be part of all assessment practices, they can again provide explanations of performance on tasks that the individual is required to complete, either as part of some educational qualification or job performance. High levels of emotionality can influence any task where stress and worry may be involved. For those with a history of such challenges, overcoming these may be as vital as overcoming literacy weaknesses. We also discuss some strategies for overcoming these factors later in the book (see Chapters 5 and 7).

## 2.4 Overall Profile

In Figure 2.2, there is a representation of an 'average' adult dyslexic against average non-dyslexics. The line at 0 (zero) represents the average non-dyslexic on all of the measures (or tests if you prefer) on the graph, whereas the points within the graph (shaped as solid black squares) represent the average dyslexic performance on each of the areas of assessment. Note that these averages are based on the results of testing large numbers of individuals. The average performance for adult non-dyslexics is based on the results provided by at least 100 non-dyslexic adults per test and was obtained primarily from the results presented by test authors: where test materials did not present such averages, they are derived from the book authors' own research. The black square points in the graph represent results produced by more than fifty adult dyslexics per measure, and are based on the book authors' own research.

As indicated, the black squares within the graph indicate the average performance of dyslexic adults and the 0 line represents the average performance of non-dyslexic adults. This means that a black square below the 0 line suggests that an average dyslexic would show relatively poorer performance on the measure compared with the average non-dyslexic. It is important to note, however, that these averages are indicative and most individuals (both dyslexic and non-dyslexic) vary from average. Therefore, the other values down the side of the graph represent this variability. On this specific graph, these values are z-scores. A z-score is simply a way of representing performance on different tests that have different scales: they allow us to compare a measure with scores from 0 to 10 with a measure that has scores from 100 to 1,000. As long as we know the mean and standard deviation for a measure, we can convert scores on the measure to z-scores and compare performance across measures. Note that the mean is the statistical term for average, and the standard deviation is the statistical calculation for how people vary on a measure. A z-score, therefore, is basically the number of standard deviations (a standard amount of varying) away from a mean (the average). These z-scores, therefore, provide an idea of average and spread: the mean has a z-score of zero, and a score of 1 is one standard deviation from the mean, with scores below the mean represented as minus figures; so two standard deviations below the mean has a z-score of -2. Hence, the average can tell us what to expect on average when comparing dyslexics and non-dyslexics. If the black square is on or near the 0 line, then the average dyslexic would be expected to perform like the average non-dyslexic. Equally, how far away from the 0 line the black square falls indicates levels of strength and weakness expected of the average dyslexic. Given the expected distribution of abilities on most tests, we would expect only 15 per cent of individuals to produce a score below the value of -1 on the graph; and less than 3 per cent of individuals to produce a score below -2 on the graph. Therefore, if the black squares fall around or below these negative z-scores, then we would expect the average adult dyslexic to have some weaknesses related to the assessment area. We would also expect individual differences such that some dyslexic adults will be worse than the average adult dyslexic, which may be indicative of more severe weaknesses in the skills. Likewise, we would expect some dyslexic adults would do better on some tests. But overall, the graph gives us a guide to what we would expect and to interpret assessment results.

If we look at Figure 2.2, on the left-hand side of the graph, we have performance on measures of non-verbal skills. Measures of non-verbal reasoning and non-verbal memory show good performance among the adult dyslexics tested: the black squares are at or just above the 0 line representing the average non-dyslexics. Therefore, these suggest few problems in these skills areas and many adult dyslexics can use these skills as an area of relatively strength. Measures of non-verbal reasoning would include the Block Design test used in the WAIS battery (as discussed earlier). Alternatively, it may involve the ability to see how patterns relate to each other in a logical way: Raven's matrices is a good example (www.pearsonassessments.com/store/usassessments/en/Store/Professional-Assessments/Cognition-%26-Neuro/Non-Verbal-Ability/Raven%27s-Standard-Progressive-Matrices-%28SPM%

29-and-Raven%27s-Standard-Progressive-Matrices-Plus-%28SPM-Plus%29/p/100000504.html).

Overall, the graph illustrates many of the areas of processing that may be explored in an assessment. Assessments that have the aim to identify dyslexia look for those features characteristic of the problems associated with dyslexia. Hence, most measures are used to determine areas of weakness, which is why an average dyslexic profile shows most areas of assessment to fall in the lower part of this graph. However, as mentioned before, the points/squares on the graph represent averages derived from a large number of adults with dyslexia who have come from a range of backgrounds. Therefore, they should be treated as indicative of a general trend. Most people, both dyslexic and non-dyslexic, vary from the average, so an individual dyslexic adult may produce a different profile from that presented in the graph; their profile may indicate strengths in an area of processing where the average suggests weaknesses, for example. Note also that both verbal and non-verbal reasoning are near the average line for the general population, and we would expect the distribution among dyslexics to be as variable on such measures as they are for non-dyslexic people. This means that we would expect half of all dyslexics and non-dyslexics to be above the average, and half of both to be below the average line.

Non-verbal memory measures the ability to recall detailed abstract images – for example, to say which of two images you have seen a few seconds before. Alternatively, this might involve repeating a series of pointing movements in the same order as presented, which would require visual-spatial skills to follow the pointing movements as in the Corsi blocks test. (Both the Wechsler scales at www.pearsonclinical.co.uk/ForPsychologists/Wechslerrange.aspx, and the Woodcock-Johnson batteries at https://riversideinsights.com/woodcock_johnson_iv have a range of non-verbal ability measures.)

Part I

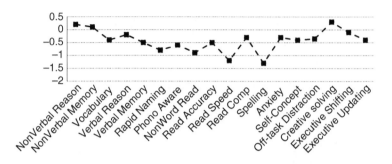

**Figure 2.2** Profile of the average performance of 100+ dyslexic adults

The following three areas of ability on Figure 2.2 relate to verbal skills. Vocabulary might involve pointing to one picture out of four that best represents a spoken word (e.g., www.pearsonassessments .com/store/usassessments/en/Store/Professional-Assessments/ Academic-Learning/Brief/Peabody-Picture-Vocabulary-Test-%7C-Fourth-Edition/p/100000501.html) or having to give a brief definition of a spoken word as in the WAIS (e.g., what does 'run' mean; what does 'democracy' mean). Note that the black square for vocabulary is below the 0 line and near the −0.5 line. This suggests that some adult dyslexics will show weaknesses compared with the average non-dyslexic in this area, which may be indicative of some of the consequences we have discussed earlier owing to lack of reading practice. In contrast, the verbal reasoning black square is closer to the average non-dyslexic line. This might assess the individual's ability to make connections between words (how are 'apple' and 'pear' related). Hence, the ability to use language may be fine, but experience of language may be more limiting. (For examples of ranges of measures of verbal ability, see the Wechsler scales at www.pearsonclinical.co.uk/ForPsychologists/Wechslerrange.aspx and the Woodcock-Johnson batteries at https://riversideinsights .com/woodcock_johnson_iv.)

The third verbal area on the graph is verbal memory. This might involve repeating series of digits as discussed earlier (and used in WAIS), though it may also involve recalling a list of words. Because of its relationship with working memory, updating procedures, and the storage of phonological information, this may be an area of weakness for some adult dyslexics, consistent with the black square being around the −0.5 line. This may also be consistent with the following black squares that represent performance on measures of rapid naming and phonological awareness (the term 'Phono Aware' is used in the graph for space). Both of these assess aspects of phonological processing, which we discussed earlier. Rapid naming is naming familiar items as quickly as possible (pictures of objects such as a chair, horse, car, tree), and phonological awareness is completing tasks involving sounds within words (such as saying the middle sound in 'cat'). Consistent with the verbal memory average, these two areas fall below the −0.5 line, suggesting a range of weaknesses in phonological areas. These weaknesses are consistent with the non-word reading performance ('NonWord Read' on the graph) represented by the following black square. Weaknesses in phonological skills may lead to weaknesses in the ability to use decoding skills (grapheme–phoneme correspondences) to name non-words, as discussed earlier in terms of the main elements of dyslexia used in the current framework. Hence, measuring a range of phonological-related skills may be worthwhile to identify weaknesses and their impact. (For an example, see the Comprehensive Tests of Phonological Processing at www.pearsonclinical.co.uk/store/ukassessments/en/Store/Professional-Assessments/Cognition-%26-Neuro/Memory/Comprehensive-Test-of-Phonological-Processing-%7C-Second-Edition/p/P100009101.html.)

Following this, there are four areas of reading and spelling represented in the graph. In this representation, the four are variable, but all below the average non-dyslexic line. Reading speed and spelling show weak performance in these adult dyslexics, both below the −1 line. In contrast, reading comprehension is not so bad, which may be indicative of compensatory strategies. Reading accuracy shows some weaknesses, but for many adult dyslexics this may not be as bad as would be expected if assessed in childhood. Hence, the range of measures of literacy can support interpretation of the variability in performance across different areas of literacy. (See examples in the Woodcock-Johnson achievement tests at https://riversideinsights.com/woodcock_johnson_iv; or the Wechsler achievement scales at www.pearsonclinical.co.uk/ForPsychologists/Wechslerrange.aspx. Maybe also look at some examples of measures specifically for adults, such as the Adult Reading Test, https://adultreadingtest2.co.uk/.)

Following this, we have some measures that are rarely used in assessment, but which are presented to support the discussion of the framework of adult dyslexia in this chapter. For some adult dyslexics, there will be evidence of negative levels of anxiety and self-esteem, and there may be some evidence of being easily distracted from task performance. This may relate to experiences in educational contexts, as discussed earlier – feelings of failure in school can lead to negative emotional consequences. Again, these are below the average non-dyslexic line but above the −0.5 line, which suggests that some will show these negative consequences whereas others will not. The 'Off-task Distraction' assessment may represent some of the strategies used to avoid situations where literacy skills are required, but can also be indicative of feelings of worry about something. Again, some may show these difficulties, but others will not. Assessments of these sort of areas usually involve asking the individual about current or past experiences or feelings; see, for example, the Spielberger State-Trait Anxiety Scale (www.apa.org/pi/about/publications/caregivers/practice-settings/assessment/tools/

trait-state), the Goodman Strengths and Difficulties Questionnaire (www.sdqinfo.org/), and the Culture Free Self-esteem Inventories (www.proedinc.com/Products/10335/cfsei3-culture-free-selfesteem-inventoriesthird-edition.aspx). They may also be part of an interview with an individual – and some assessors may determine task worries during observations of performance in other tasks, particularly if time-limited.

The final three areas are related to some of the metacognitive ideas that are discussed in the rest of this book. The black squares here show that some of these areas can be good (the 'Creativity' point is above the average non-dyslexic line), some can be average (as in the 'Executive Shifting' assessments), and some can show slightly poorer performance (the 'Executive Updating' point). Ideas for creativity measures can be found in Everatt et al. (1999), but also see the Torrance Tests of Creative Thinking (www.ststesting.com/). For a range of measures of executive functioning try Leather (2018) and Miyake et al. (2000).

## 2.5　Conclusion

The framework presented in this chapter argues that core elements of dyslexia are to be found in adults, just as they can be identified in children. However, it also proposes a range of individual differences that further influence these core elements and the performance of individuals with dyslexia in their day-to-day performance, including at work. These develop owing to underlying biological and cognitive factors, but also the experiences of individuals during learning and in everyday life. The range of work that an adult may need to perform as part of their employment may also be very different from the requirements of school work in childhood. This means that a range of strategies is needed to support adults across this range of different circumstances. The dyslexia is still there, and will influence performance through a range of direct and indirect links. However, positive factors develop through experiences, as well as negative ones, and so support needs to be individualised. Self-awareness of these issues should be helpful, and leads to recognition of the potential of some of the ideas discussed in Part II. However, the key point in this chapter is that strategies to deal with adult dyslexia can build on success rather than needing to focus simply on remediation. They can, therefore, be based on what the individual does as well as the support of those around them.

# 3

# Theoretical Perspectives on Success

## 3.1 Introduction

Success is important to us as human beings because it engenders motivation and a sense of purpose, striving for more and improving performance; it encourages perseverance, and increases the ability to take the next step forward. Success is also cumulative: people build on their previous success, and this in turn can increase self-belief and self-confidence. However, success is a complex and multifaceted construct. One person's view of success can vary greatly from another person's. This may be because people place different values on different things. For example, if we take the example of someone's career, one person's goal might be financial, to have a well-paid job in a large organisation, whereas another's might be more vocational in nature, to work in the caring professions. Others may see success as achieving a good work/life balance, and for some career may be less important in terms of their perception of success; it is just a job – to be happy and healthy is sufficient. These differences may be a result of personal beliefs, experience, and personality, but they can also be influenced by a range of factors such as family aspirations, education, gender, and cultural and social experiences.

There are many definitions of success, the simplest, from the *Oxford English Dictionary*, being 'the accomplishment of an aim or purpose'. The 'aim' can be seen from two perspectives, societal and personal. Society's perception of success may be aligned with the attainment of high grades in exams, or fame, or wealth, or social status. Personal perception of success is perhaps better understood as specific goal achievement. An individual chooses goals such as passing examinations, selecting a particular career path, or finding a job, taking a driving test, getting fit, or even just baking a cake. The achievement of these personally chosen goals engenders feelings of accomplishment, which can lead to an increase in motivation to do it again. There are also a wealth of aims and goals that span both societal and personal perspectives, such as good health, wellbeing, happiness, and a good family and social life.

Individual perspectives of success are likely to be influenced by experience. For some, gaining educational qualifications may have been straightforward, and whether this is perceived as success or simply a normal facet of life may depend simply on the importance of the qualification. For others, passing exams may be the result of a great deal of hard work and possible previous failure. When these individuals achieve this goal, they may feel extremely successful because of the effort they have put into the qualification. Alternatively, long hours of work and effort may diminish their experience of success: the hard work may temper their feelings of success. As another example, some people feel a sense of achievement when they bake a cake, whereas for others it

## Theoretical Perspectives on Success

is just something they can do quite well and so they do not think much about it. Therefore, an individual's setting of a goal within the current context of their life, along with the effort and the level of challenge involved, can result in varying feelings of personal achievement or success.

Furthermore, people can experience success in one area of their life, whereas they may feel the opposite in another area. For example, an individual may feel successful socially while struggling at work. Even within the same work context, feelings of success can vary. Some individuals may be very successful when giving presentations or networking with people but less so when writing reports; something that is a common occurrence for some dyslexic people.

Nevertheless, despite its complexity, success is something most people strive for at both a personal and societal level. Achieving personal and societal goals increases motivation, as well as positive feelings about the self, which can lead an individual to move forward to greater success and further increase self-belief/self-esteem (Bandura, 1986). Feelings of success, therefore, can be an important part of an individual's life, and also impact on an individual's contribution to society.

Given the focus of this book, the rest of this chapter concentrates specifically on career success and how this might be related to characteristics of dyslexia. For example, being dyslexic has been seen as a potential barrier to success within certain occupations. One of the arguments presented throughout this book is that as people have gained a greater understanding of dyslexia in adulthood, and the adjustments (accommodations) that have dealt with some of the challenges of dyslexia, then such barriers to success may be less evident. However, given our current less than complete understanding of dyslexia, and the variable awareness of the impact of dyslexia within different employment contexts, it is likely that many dyslexic people do struggle in work. This may limit their aspirations and engender a lack of confidence, which can lead to a lack of success. In order to help understand how we might promote success among those with dyslexia, this chapter explores the components of career success and the literature regarding dyslexic people who have achieved a measure of career success in their lives. Our aim is to develop a framework to understand the strategies discussed in Part II that can enable dyslexic people to make informed decisions and become more successful.

## 3.2   Career Success

Career or work success mirrors the complexity around the term success previously outlined. In general, career or work success can be seen as achieving successive goals and feeling satisfied with a job done within one's workplace experiences (Abele & Spurk, 2009; Hall, 2002; Judge et al., 1995). However, career success can also be viewed from an objective/societal perspective and from a subjective, and more personal, evaluation of performance (see discussions of this from Hughes, 1958, to Heslin, 2005), again mirroring the general views of success discussed earlier.

Societal career success often revolves around three extrinsic tangible measures of an individual's career. The first is financial status, or the amount an individual earns, and their accompanying wealth based on their occupation. Second is the eminence of the occupation: professionals such as lawyers, accountants, and doctors are often more highly regarded within society. Finally, there is the level that the individual climbs up the occupational ladder, with an individual deemed to be more successful the closer to the top of the profession or organisation they climb. Nevertheless, Heslin (2005) has argued that financial status may not be an accurate measure of success. In some occupations, such as nursing or academe, high performance in a job is not rewarded by a relative increase in salary. Furthermore, high pay and/or promotion do not always make people feel more successful at a personal level (Hall & Chandler, 2005). The Peter principle suggests that people who are promoted beyond their level of competence can actually feel less successful. Furthermore, people often choose a work/life balance option, or a sense of meaning, purpose, and contribution to society at the expense of a higher salary.

Therefore, an individual's perspectives of success can conflict with the standard societal measures of success, which can also lead to disparities across the three elements of societal success. For example, there is the societal perception that good academic qualifications are a forerunner to becoming successful, as they are believed to improve the chances of career success. Academic qualifications are of some importance if they are of a high level (Hogan et al., 2013; Judge et al., 1995), and some professions demand a certain academic level for entry. Furthermore, good qualifications are likely to encourage higher aspirations in individuals; their own view of their ability to succeed may be determined by the level of educational attainment. As previously suggested, though, higher qualifications are not always a route to higher paid jobs. Gaining a PhD and moving to an academic job can lead to a lower income than taking a Master's degree and working in the private sector, for example. In contrast, there are many examples of individuals who have achieved a great deal in terms of fame and income without having achieved a good education. This is potentially pertinent for a dyslexic person for whom a lack of qualifications is often considered a barrier to employment; there are a number of highly successful dyslexic individuals who have not achieved in formal education contexts.

Part I

## 3.3 Personal Perspectives of Career Success

Subjective career criteria are intrinsic to the individual. They are a person's evaluation across many dimensions in relation to the job they are performing. These include factors such as their sense of identity, the purpose of the job, and work/life balance, and most of these factors impact on an individual's perception of job satisfaction and self-efficacy. These two factors are most pertinent to the present discussion as they incorporate many of the issues related to personal perspectives on success (also see Leather et al., 2011, for discussions of these concepts in terms of adult dyslexia). Therefore, they warrant further explanation.

Job satisfaction is based on an individual's understanding of, and responses to, career experiences. Satisfaction is determined by the individual gaining what they want, and what they value, from the job they are performing (see the definition discussed in Bowling & Hammond, 2008). Heslin (2005) suggests that satisfaction includes a range of self-referent factors that can vary among individuals. Interest in the work is important, although this can sometimes be offset by financial reward. Likewise, job security and the value that they and others place on the job can contribute to satisfaction. Other factors include the potential for promotion, the opportunity to develop a career skills set, perceptions of autonomy, performing a variety of tasks, working within a good team of people, and feeling valued by a manager. Working conditions can also affect job satisfaction. These include the environment, the hours of work expected, the levels of stress experienced during job performance, the flexibility of work/life balance, and the flexibility to accommodate last-minute changes (e.g., if an individual has family responsibilities). Other considerations, such as mode of travel, the distance from home to work, and the level of difficulty and time it takes to travel to and from a place of work can affect job satisfaction if the journey is arduous.

## 3.4 Self-efficacy

Implicit in job satisfaction is the idea of self-efficacy. Bandura (1997) discusses the concept of self-efficacy as relating to an individual's own beliefs about their ability to perform and/or complete a task successfully. In terms of work, this involves aspects of the job or the whole job itself. The typical view of self-efficacy is that the more we have, the more likely we are to complete the task in hand successfully; although note that Vancouver and Kendall (2006) have advised caution about this simple relationship. Their research indicates that high levels of self-efficacy can lead to overconfidence, which may be associated with subsequent loss of concentration and effort when completing a task.

Self-efficacy is often confused with other terms such as self-concept, self-confidence, and self-esteem. They are related but conceptually different (Kanfer & Ackerman, 2005), and it is important to distinguish between them. In career research, such terms have been used in relation to success and motivation but often without clear definition (Chen et al., 2004). For example, Chen et al. (2004) maintain that self-efficacy is more strongly related to motivational and achievement processes, whereas self-esteem is more associated with anxiety and avoidance processes. Hence, the distinction between these concepts is important, particularly when it comes to pastoral intervention.

Self-esteem is a personal judgement of worthiness. It is associated with an affective evaluative judgement of how the individual perceives themselves, and whether they are satisfied with themselves in relation to others. Continually being passed over for promotion, failing examinations, or being criticised more than others can affect how you feel about yourself – hence it can impact negatively on self-esteem. Self-concept refers to how an individual sees themselves in terms of ability or competence across a wide range of domains from job performance to academic achievement to physical and interpersonal skills. Low self-concept as a learner can put an individual at a disadvantage as they see themselves as generally less competent. Self-confidence is a more general construct. It is a projection of one's overall ability to do one's job or perform to a certain level. However, it need not be fixed and can fluctuate owing to environmental factors, such as sleep deprivation or stress (Kanfer & Ackerman, 2005).

Returning to self-efficacy, this focuses on performance rather than personal qualities (Bandura, 1986). It is the way an individual feels about succeeding in a specific task regardless of previous achievements. Therefore, it is possible for an individual to have high self-efficacy in a particular task, such as problem-solving, but to have low overall self-esteem; that is, they feel that they are not as intelligent as others because of their weak literacy skills, which is a common perspective from many dyslexic adults. Likewise, a doctor may be clinically very experienced and well regarded in their job, but after several failures when taking professional examinations, their self-confidence is undermined. This may occur despite their medical expertise and clinical competence ensuring that their clinical self-efficacy remains high.

Bandura (1997) identifies four sources of self-efficacy. First, an individual's past performance and mastery of the task is important. If a task has already been understood and completed successfully, then individuals will have more confidence in completing a similar task, which should lead to higher levels of self-efficacy. Secondly, watching others do the task (referred to as vicarious experience) can increase confidence in one's ability to attempt a task, particularly if the other person

## Theoretical Perspectives on Success

is working in similar circumstances. Thirdly, verbal persuasion, or the encouragement of others, can boost one's self-belief in achieving the goal. Finally, emotional cues can influence self-efficacy. For example, too much or too little adrenaline can affect one's performance. Bandura also suggests that self-efficacy is not necessarily stable, and negative experiences within one or more of the four sources noted can undermine it.

Self-efficacy is also influenced by cognitive and motivational processes. More cognitive bases can be associated with an individual's understanding of their abilities. For example, Dweck (2017) discusses the concept of fixed or growth mindset. For individuals with a fixed mindset, success in passing exams is essential as failure would indicate that the goal (passing) cannot be achieved. Such individuals are likely to see their ability as unchangeable (fixed). Heslin et al. (2020) argue that this rigidity reduces such an individual's learning ability as they fail to experiment with strategies and are unable to listen to feedback. This may mean that they are less likely to succeed. Alternatively, individuals with a growth mindset seek the opportunity to increase their knowledge and to accept any mistakes as part of the learning process, seeing failure as expanding their experience, and their knowledge.

The motivational processes associated with self-efficacy are related to goal-setting, and how the individual's self-beliefs about their abilities inform the goals they set for themselves. These beliefs are influenced by three elements: how large and how complicated the task is, the strength of their personal belief about their own competence, and the degree to which their expectations are generalised across many tasks (Bandura, 1997). It is easy to see how taking on a huge new project in an already busy role, or studying for a promotional exam at the same time as performing a busy job, can challenge an individual's self-belief in success. However, resilience is also associated with self-efficacy. Resilience is a multifaceted construct but is usually understood to be the ability to bounce back from adversity. Even in highly challenging situations, and those where success is not achieved fully, feelings of resilience can overcome the negative impact of not meeting your own expectations. By activating motivation, and maintaining self-efficacy, people can persevere and potentially overcome challenges, which can then become a self-perpetuating strength – or what some refer to as resilient self-efficacy (see discussions in Everatt & Denston, 2020).

Lunenburg (2011) argues for the need for workplaces to build self-efficacy, and outlines how self-efficacy can affect performance in three ways. First, it influences the goals people choose for themselves. People perform at the level that is consistent with their self-efficacy beliefs (Zimmerman et al., 1992). Thus, those with high self-efficacy set higher personal goals (Bandura, 1997), thereby increasing the level of achievement. Secondly, it influences the effort that people exert on a task. Those with low self-efficacy may exert less effort when performing complex tasks because they are uncertain of achieving the goal, whereas those with high self-belief will make every effort to achieve the goal (Bandura, 1997). Finally, it influences the persistence with which people attempt new tasks, as employees with high self-efficacy are more confident that if they keep at it, they will succeed (Zimmerman et al., 1992). Overall, therefore, self-efficacy can, to some extent, determine job performance: high levels of self-efficacy more often leads to better performance and, therefore, people becoming more successful in the workplace.

## 3.5  Goal-Setting

As mentioned earlier, self-efficacy and motivation overlap with goal-setting. Goal-setting theory is another much-researched area in career success (see discussions in Locke & Latham, 2002). Authors such as Locke and Latham argue that there is a relationship between specific goal-setting and task performance as people will raise their performance to achieve a specific goal. Goal-setting also influences achievement as it serves as a standard for evaluating one's own performance. However, it should be noted that if the goal is set too high and not achieved, then this may impact on feelings of success and people's self-efficacy related to the task. Therefore, the level of the goal is important. Nevertheless, feelings of success in the workplace are increased when people see that they are able to achieve by pursuing and attaining those goals that are important and meaningful to them. This is the reason for setting clear objectives related to a job.

Realistic goal-setting improves performance in four ways. It provides a focus for attention, both cognitively and behaviourally. It energises individuals to achieve the goal. It encourages persistence and speed when an end is in sight. Finally, people increase their understanding of their behaviour as a response to goal-setting and achievement. As indicated earlier, if the goal is too complex or too hard, it is better to lower the goal or expectations as the anxiety resulting from struggling to succeed, and possibly failing, can lead to ineffective strategy use, such as working very long hours for little positive outcome. It can also lead to giving up on the task with the associated loss of self-belief. Locke and Latham (2002) suggest that goal-setting theory and self-efficacy theory complement each other. For instance, when a manager sets a challenging task for an employee, the employee should experience a higher level of self-efficacy on completion of the task, which then leads the individual to set higher goals for themselves.

## 3.6 Planning

Planning is best understood as setting a sequence of mini-goals or steps to achieve a desired outcome. It is generally seen as a higher order processing skill, or an executive function. It can be seen as a dynamic process involving a deliberate and specific sequence of actions in order to achieve a predetermined goal (cited in Reid Lyon & Krasnegor, 1996, p. 257), or the ability to map out a sequence of moves in preparation for task completion (Lezak et al., 2004). Hence, planning can be an area of difficulty for those experiencing problems sequencing activities, and strategies for overcoming such experiences may be necessary for good planning activities. Some of these sequencing strategies are discussed in subsequent chapters (see Chapter 4 for examples).

At some level, planning is inherent in all goal achievement. Arguably, there are different levels. The daily planning of activities, or a to-do list, is not the same type of cognitive activity as planning to problem-solve, to achieve a complex task, or to overcome a set of difficulties. Identification of the problem/task determines the goal and the type of cognitive processing involved. Therefore, goal-identification and setting is an initial and integral part of planning. Successful planning also involves decision-making (i.e., goal intention) and taking action (i.e., goal implementation). Goal intention is working out goals that are feasible and desirable. Goal implementation involves acting on those intentions (Gollwitzer & Oettinger, 2011). While setting goals is important, it is goal implementation, or putting those planned steps into place, that predicts successful outcomes.

There is considerable evidence for the positives of planning. Aarts et al. (1999) claim that planning encourages volition to reach the goal. They also hypothesise, as do Locke and Latham (2002) and goal-setting theory, that planning increases the chance of success as it draws upon relevant previous knowledge. Likewise, if it is a new task, planning facilitates the attainment of the goal associated with the task as it draws on previous experience and knowledge. Finally, they argue that planning increases the speed of intended action as it provides a cognitive map; it is a form of mental priming enabling people to respond more rapidly and more effectively when there is a high cognitive load. Arguably, this is particularly important for dyslexic people.

## 3.7   Executive Functions, Working Memory, and Metacognition

Planning can be considered as a complex executive function process. Banich (2009) has argued that executive functioning involves processes related to goal-directed behaviour and controls complex cognition especially in non-routine situations. Such executive functioning is critical to learning and performance, playing a central role in thinking, problem-solving, decision-making, and oral and written language processing (Reid Lyon & Krasnegor, 1996). While there are alternative perspectives about executive functioning, the perspective we discuss in Chapter 2 argues for three general processes (see Diamond, 2013; Miyake et al., 2000). Cognitive flexibility or shifting is the ability to shift between mental states or between different cognitive domains. This is important as it enables people to cope with rapid and changing environments, and when different aspects of information need to be processed. The second general process involves inhibition of one or more ways of processing or reacting to something. This can be vital to avoid being distracted from a task. We can think of this in terms of cognitive inhibition and selective focused executive attention (consistent with thinking about something in a particular way), as well as in terms of response inhibition, which may be related to issues of self-control and discipline, such as avoiding saying something that we might regret at a later date. The third general process is that of updating, and is often associated with working memory. Working memory can be defined as 'a processing resource of limited capacity, involved in the preservation of information while simultaneously processing the same or other information' (Swanson, 2015, p. 176). All three general executive processes are critical for cognitive development, and may be vital for success in school and employment, particularly where a focus on the task in hand is essential (Diamond, 2013), or where problem-solving is required to make effective decisions at work (Bailey, 2007), or where an individual must respond to rapidly-changing circumstances, or needs to plan, prioritise, organise, and juggle the demands of a job (Garner, 2009). Hence, many of the concepts related to executive functioning have been related to modern working requirements. If these processes are inefficient, then job performance may also suffer.

Although controversial, some have argued for deficiencies in some elements of executive functioning among those with dyslexia (see Smith-Sparkes et al., 2016 for an overview). This may not be universal among those with dyslexia, and it may focus on certain elements of executive functioning (see Leather, 2018); however, deficits in some of these processes may make some of the work-related skills sets outlined in the previous paragraph more challenging for dyslexic adults. If we assume that these challenges are not universal, and may be specific to certain areas of executive functioning, where might these be? The component of executive functioning that has been most widely discussed in relation to dyslexia is that of working memory, which links to the updating elements of executive processing. However, weaknesses may not be across all areas associated with working memory. Much of the work in these area focuses on verbal working memory weaknesses as being more characteristic of dyslexia. This is one of the reasons why measures of memory span (as discussed in Chapter 2) are used in assessment for dyslexia (see also Mather & Wendling, 2012). Although the relationship between dyslexia, reading/language problems, and working memory is still an area of debate, strategy development that avoids taxing working memory should increase chances of improving performance and achieving positive outcomes even in complex work environments. Again, we discuss some of these strategies in subsequent chapters (see Chapter 4 for examples).

## 3.8   Metacognition

Metacognition is another term that has been discussed in relation to self-efficacy and planning. Metacognition suggests a conscious awareness of one's own thinking about something, as well as one's own learning processes (see Ferdinand-Duque et al., 2000). As such, it should lead to improved performance in academic and work settings. It involves executive functioning, particularly related to planning and monitoring, but also suggests reflection about, and knowledge of, ways that one can complete a task.

As with many of the constructs we are discussing in Part I, there are slightly different perspectives regarding metacognition that largely depend on the background of the author, from cognitive (Borokowski & Burke, 1996; Flavell, 1979; Schraw & Dennison, 1994) to educational (Butler, 1998; Dwyer, et al., 2014; Sternberg, 2005) to clinical or neuropsychological (Shimamara 2000). However, we can consider four general components of metacognition. First, metacognitive knowledge includes a knowledge of one's self, the task to be performed, and the range of strategies that can be used to accomplish the task. It is perhaps this component of self-understanding, and the conscious awareness of the task, that primarily delineates it from other cognitive processes. If an individual can articulate what the task is, and how they might address it, then metacognition might be a better way to describe thinking about the task (see also Schraw & Mosman, 1995). The second component is that of metacognitive control, or the process of planning and regulating problem-solving, reasoning, and learning activities. This component is akin to many of the processes associated with executive functioning discussed earlier, as well as self-regulatory processes (see Schraw & Dennison, 1994). A third component may be hypothesised as feelings of confidence in monitoring performance and judgement (see Flavell, 1979), and relates to the fourth affective attributional component, or the belief about whether things are going well or badly. According to Eflikdes (2008), this latter component is the conscious or unconscious trigger to activating the metacognitive control element.

There is some debate as to whether metacognition is a general skill or specific to certain tasks. Research often focuses on metacognitive behaviour in specific tasks, such as reading (Wong, 1996), problem-solving (Swanson, 1990), or what people experience when engaged in metacognitive activities (Efklides, 2008) or when performing a complex task at work (Birney et al., 2012). Schraw and Dennison (1994) suggest that monitoring skills are general by nature, whereas others (Kelemen et al., 2000) have argued for more specific monitoring processes. Veenman and Spaans (2005) suggest that initially metacognitive skills develop in separate domains, becoming a more generalised ability with age. Similarly, Efklides (2008) argues that they develop through an individual's observation of their own and other's behaviours in specific contexts. McLoughlin et al. (2002) suggest that dyslexic adults can be metacognitive (planning and reflective) in some aspects of their life (e.g., in sporting situations), but that this does not transfer to activities such as reading, where they do not change the reading behaviour according to the task demands. For example, some dyslexic adults report reading every word and continually re-reading, even in circumstances where this does not support comprehension.

Metacognition is independent of intellectual ability. It does not necessarily involve reasoning or problem-solving, but it can improve learning and performance. Dwyer et al. (2014) and Magno (2010) have postulated that metacognition is essential in the development of critical thinking and higher order reasoning skills. Such skills include analysis, inference, synthesis, reflection, and evaluation (Dwyer et al., 2014). Such skills may also allow for the transfer of knowledge, adaptability and flexibility in new situations, and the development of expertise, leading some (e.g., Sternberg, 2005; Zimmerman, 2006) to argue that metacognitive skills are a core component of expertise. Bandura and Locke (2003) and Sternberg (2005) have also suggested that the increased use of metacognitive skills can lead to improved performance and a greater feeling of confidence and competence, which can ultimately develop into expertise. Likewise, Birney et al. (2012) suggest that metacognitive skills, and the ensuing deliberative processing, are an antecedent in the development of expertise.

### 3.8.1 Metacognition and Dyslexia

There is some evidence to suggest that metacognitive skills may develop less automatically in dyslexic children (Butler, 1998; Torgesen, 1996; Tunmer & Chapman, 1996). Butler and Schnellert (2015), Chevalier et al. (2017), and Stipanovich (2015) all also argue that these sort of skills deficits can continue into adulthood and impact on long-term outcomes. Reasons that have been proposed for such childhood weaknesses include a lack of time to process all the information effectively, the general low confidence in abilities and poor self-concept resulting in a lack of experimentation during learning (i.e., children may rigidly follow teachers' instructions), and a lack of practice of metacognitive strategies. Sternberg (2005) argues that metacognitive skills develop through positive learning situations, which may be less likely to occur for those who are struggling with learning. This may also support the argument that individuals can be metacognitive in some areas but not others. Consistent with the view that these processes are not all or none, and contrary to the idea that metacognition is a general area of weakness for dyslexics, some research suggests that metacognitive processes can be a compensatory influence for dyslexic people; that metacognitive skills may mitigate some processing problems. For example, Trainin and Swanson (2005) and Ruban et al. (2003) report studies indicating that successful dyslexic college students compensated for their difficulties through the use of metacognitive skills. Similarly, Chevalier et al. (2017) and Swanson (1990) have argued that among dyslexic students, a greater use of metacognitive skill resulted in better performance on problem-solving tasks and higher grades.

Many dyslexic people seek clarity about what dyslexia is: why they do things, or process information, differently from others, and why they might take longer or appear to work harder than others. Encouraging the use of metacognition, which involves thinking about how they do things, may enable them to work more efficiently. This may be particularly useful if they explore experiences that have been successful, thereby considering what have they been doing and why has it worked. If they apply similar processes to other problem areas, they are likely to find solutions. Indeed, this is one of the objectives of this book: to use individual experiences of dyslexic adults to inform the reader's own understanding of their challenges and the potential solutions that they might apply to support success.

## 3.9 Metacognition and the Development of Expertise

As mentioned earlier, metacognition is thought to be a component of developing expertise. An English dictionary is likely to define expertise as a high level of knowledge or skill in a particular area. Like success, it can be viewed in two ways: in respect to gaining a set of specific skills or having a collection of knowledge and skills. Having expertise is not the same thing as being an expert; it is possible that someone who is credited with expert status by society may not have expertise, or it may have diminished over time as expertise requires regular practice and updating to be maintained (see Horn & Blankson, 2005). The reverse is even more accurate: many people have expertise in specific areas but are not acknowledged as experts. This distinction between being an expert and having expertise is important, as being credited as experts can give people power and authority, and may be seen as an element of success. Ericsson (2018) takes a different approach, differentiating between expert performance and expertise. Expert performance occurs when an individual can produce a superior and frequently reproducible action or outcome, whereas expertise is a set of characteristics, skills, and knowledge that distinguish 'the master' from 'the novice'. Horn and Blankson (2005) suggest that in mastering a task, the novice builds a framework through trial and error in which they can organise and evaluate newly presented information and quickly identify relationships and patterns. Over time, this builds into expertise. Medical practitioners, football commentators, and horse racing pundits arguably have specific expertise in their jobs. Developing expertise in a skill, or a range of skills, required for a job is often a component of career progression and, hence, success.

Expertise at work means people have greater ability to analyse tasks, implement actions, and reflect on performance (Zimmerman, 2006). It increases cognitive flexibility and efficiency when dealing with novel situations (Horn & Blankson, 2005; Salthouse, 2012) and promotes the transfer of skills and knowledge as multiple representations of knowledge can be utilised (Norman, 2005; Salthouse, 2012). It means individuals can typically recall knowledge better, as there is often automatic retrieval from long-term memory (Feltovich et al., 2018).

Part I

Developing expertise at a personal specific level in everyday tasks means people do not need to devote so much conscious attention to what they are doing. This developed automaticity means that they can shift attention to other matters while completing the expert-based task. Developing automaticity means that people can work more quickly and can multitask. For example, a learner driver focuses on all the procedures when driving (such as changing gear, watching the road, looking in the rear view mirror). As they become more practised, drivers develop automaticity in some of these skills and so can perform other tasks while driving (such as having a conversation or listening to the radio). Good readers generally decode and encode words relatively automatically, meaning that their attention can be focused on understanding material (see discussions in Everatt, 1999). Developing expertise may also increase processing speed without a loss of accuracy (Kail & Salthouse, 1994), and may enhance self-efficacy and motivation.

There is a wealth of research into what contributes to expertise (see discussions in Sternberg, 2005). However, some of the key elements involve knowledge, both declarative and procedural, and being able to draw on personal resources and reflect, along with deliberate practice, which should develop automaticity. Ericsson (2018) considers the role of deliberate practice in the development of expert performance as leading to complex mental representations or schemata. These representations remain cognitively active, always seeking improvement. Deliberate practice involves setting specific goals. The task is then attempted and performance monitored. Feedback and reflection are aimed at performance improvement. Ericsson's model of deliberate practice is perhaps an enhancement of metacognitive skill as suggested by Sternberg (1999). These ideas are consistent with metacognitive processing when an individual is practising a skill; they will monitor, and seek feedback on, their own performance in the hope of correcting errors and building on progress, and thereby developing expertise.

Cianciola and Sternberg (2018) explore another aspect of expertise – that of tacit knowledge. This concept is closely aligned to procedural knowledge, or knowing how to. Tacit knowledge is defined as 'knowledge that is not usually openly expressed or stated…. It is not directly taught' (p. 773). An example is knowing what to say or what to do and when without instruction or prompting. Such knowledge is gained from experience and applied subconsciously in specific environments, making it difficult to verbalise. It develops from repeated experience in similar contexts with comparable but varying outcomes providing a strong foundation of meaningful knowledge that improves performance. Cianciolo and Sternberg also suggest that tacit knowledge is similar but conceptually different to job knowledge, which they posit is more along the lines of declarative knowledge (i.e., knowledge about facts and concepts) and which is often deliberately taught and learned on the job. They argue that tacit knowledge bridges the gap between formally educated knowledge and operational experience, and that it underpins practical intelligence.

Practical intelligence is the ability to adapt to, to shape, and to select appropriate actions in everyday life. Sternberg (1999) argues that practical intelligence is a better predictor of work success than academic intelligence. Baum and Bird (2010) argues that practical intelligence comes from doing and learning rather than watching and reading. They also argue that practical intelligence is a predictor of entrepreneurial success. Entrepreneurs are seen as willing to use their knowledge, or what they have learned, to experiment and try new approaches to improve the process or product. Many dyslexic people would claim that they learn best through doing, and Logan (2009) has argued that there are a high incidence of entrepreneurs with dyslexia. Billet et al. (2018) also suggest that occupational success/expertise is developed through daily activities and interactions with people, rather than in formal learning situations. Experience at work provides essential opportunities to learn through observation, imitation, and practice. Billet et al. argue that individuals should be encouraged to set goals, to plan, and execute and monitor their actions, then evaluate the outcomes. Learning should be incremental within the job context, which should support how to apply and modify actions, and how to respond in changing situations. As such, individuals develop their personal domains of occupational knowledge and ultimately job expertise.

## 3.10 Dyslexia and the Importance of Developing Expertise

The principles of developing expertise (experience, practice, knowledge) are important concepts for dyslexic people to consider, both at a personal level and in job-related tasks. Although perhaps not consciously, many dyslexic people are adopting such strategies: they know they have had to work harder and longer (to practise more) to succeed; they are not confident without sufficient knowledge and often prefer practical experience, not necessarily with a view of becoming an expert in the field but to achieve their goals. Furthermore, many dyslexic adults who were diagnosed in childhood and undertook a specialist literacy programme when developing their literacy expertise might recognise the underlying principles laid out here, particularly deliberate practice.

With regard to the development of reading skills, Fink (1998), in a constructivist study, reports that successful dyslexic adult participants did not develop the mastery of basic skills but used higher-level cognition skills and practised on discipline-specific texts to develop familiarity/expertise with the words and concepts, which resulted in improved comprehension and fluency. The knowledge gained, and practice-developed expertise and confidence in reading ability, was then transferable to general reading texts (see also Kintsch et al., 1999). Similarly, as people gain experience or expertise in job-specific tasks, and with the language used as part of the workplace (i.e., professional and technical jargon), it would be conceivable that they could rely on work-specific strategies that might mediate (compensate for) dyslexia-related processing difficulties. Hence, expertise or job-specific strategies allow dyslexic people to achieve equivalent success to their peers.

## 3.11 Dyslexia and Success

All the elements discussed here suggest specific job expertise allows dyslexic people to achieve equivalent success to their colleagues. This is consistent with many years of research into the success of dyslexic people by Gerber and his associates (see Schnieders, 2016). Gerber et al. (1992) investigations of successful dyslexic adults found that the primary factor contributing to success is that of control; that is, the extent to which they felt in charge of their lives and their work. There are two interrelated factors to this control construct. First are internal decisions, which are conscious decisions about organising and regulating one's life. Such internal elements include a desire to succeed, goal orientation, and planning, which can be considered as associated with metacognition and developing expertise. The second factors focus on external manifestations. These relate to being able to adapt to changing situations (arguably related to executive functioning), to persistence, and to learned creativity (i.e., having a range of strategies to become more adept at information processing). External factors also relate to goodness of fit or being in the right job, where the individual is comfortable with the demands made on them, and to social ecologies, or support systems such as partners, supervisors, and colleagues (see also Gerber, 2012; Gerber& Raskind, 2013). Other researchers (Raskind et al., 1999) have found similar results when investigating success attributes of dyslexic adults. These attributes include self-awareness, proactivity, goal-setting, perseverance, and the use of support systems and strategies. Maduas et al. (2008) argues that self-efficacy and self-regulation are essential elements of success in the workplace.

Gerber and Rashkind (2013) add a further factor to consider, referred to as 'finding a niche'. This involves being in a job or occupation where the interest factor, encouragement from others, motivation, and self-belief enable individuals to persevere and develop the skills, experience, and expertise to work well. It is potentially an environment where they can delegate tasks they find hard. Similarly, Logan (2009), in a studies of entrepreneurship and dyslexia, identifies the ability to delegate as one of the key attributes of success.

Schnieders et al. (2016) bring together the factors or attributes that contribute to the success of dyslexic adults. Table 3.1 outlines these. Schnieders et al. argue that the relatively little research that has been conducted in the area of dyslexia in adulthood has generally placed emphasis on disabilities and the emotional aspects. Although this has had the benefit of focusing ideas on improving support systems and services for adults, the authors suggest that individual needs and motivations should also be considered. Such work would then focus on ways for individuals to take responsibility for their desires and actions, to understand themselves and to feel in control. They suggest that once the internal and linking factors are in place, then the external factors drive increasing success. They acknowledge that this model requires practice and is likely to involve repeated failure,

Theoretical Perspectives on Success

Table 3.1 Internal and external factors of success (based on Schnieders et al., 2016)

| Internal factors | Linking factors | External factors |
|---|---|---|
| **Desire** to move on, to get ahead | **Coping strategies** – effective means of coping with stress frustration | **Learned creativity** – techniques to enhance abilities and learning utilising strengths |
| **Perseverance** Keep going in the face of adversity | **Reframing** can redefine difficulties into positives | **Social ecologies** Supportive people, colleagues, mentors, specific support networks |
| **Persistence** Resilient, and determined to do what is necessary – take longer to ensure task completion | **Proactivity** – has the intention to take control – explores all options – makes decisions and acts on them | |
| **Goal-setting** – setting specific flexible and achievable goals | **Goodness of fit** into environments that tap skills and interests, and minimise the weaknesses | |
| **Goal orientation** Goals selected are related to interests and desires | | |
| **Self-awareness** Awareness of strengths and weaknesses | | |

hence the persistence factor, and they state that an understanding of the developmental aspect of success is important. Implicit in this model are the metacognitive processes of self-understanding, planning, goal-setting and reflection. These processes are inherent in successful career progression moving from novice to gaining expertise, or from apprentice to master (see Moran & Gardner, 2007), and finding a niche.

Career success is rarely instant. It is usually built on hard work, good decisions, and being able to adapt to change. Table 3.1 emphasises the need for self-awareness in the decision-making process. There are many dyslexic people who have not been able to find their niche (their specific goodness of fit), as decisions have been made for them by others or by themselves based on a misunderstanding of their strengths and weaknesses. This may come from assumption that dyslexics make great scientists, architects, or artists (see discussions in Chapters 1 and 2). However, the evidence for this is limited, and while there are those who have succeeded in such occupations, this skill set is not found in all adult dyslexics. Self-understanding and good career guidance are essential to ensure goodness of fit between an individual's interests and skills and the work they are performing, rather than potentially over-simplified generalisations from relatively small groups of, or individual, dyslexics. McLoughlin and Leather (2013) argue that being dyslexic is not a barrier to success in any occupation, but that self-understanding, including the impact dyslexia has and how to manage job demands, is vital for success.

McLoughlin and Leather (2013) also outline a model, based on the work of Yost and Corbishley (1987), which focuses on self-understanding, personal decision-making, and goal-setting. This model (represented in Table 3.2) is consistent with the ideas presented by Schnieders et al. (2016). The role of self-understanding is key. For the dyslexic person, understanding the impact of dyslexia

## Theoretical Perspectives on Success

**Table 3.2 A model for working towards career success (based on McLoughlin and Leather, 2013, p. 206)**

| 1 | Initial assessment | To gather personal and employment information in order to make decisions about a feasible career goal |
|---|---|---|
| 2 | Self-understanding | To explore values, experiences and interests that relate to the goal. Re-framing is important, and essential to setting realistic goals |
| 3 | Analysing the self-understanding data | Identifying the barriers to success and how they may be overcome |
| 4 | Generating alternatives | Develop a list of career alternatives |
| 5 | Obtaining occupational information | Learn as much as possible about each option to make an informed choice |
| 6 | Making the choice/decision | Focus on the goodness of fit |
| 7 | Making plans to reach the career goal choice | Goal-setting, including how to handle setbacks |
| 8 | Implementing the plans | Short term goals – ensuring have the literacy and technological strategies in place – use learned creativities and be able to self-advocate, i.e., disclosure. Medium goals – training, etc. Longer term goals – these should be flexible and adaptable to make the best of opportunities |

on their performance, being aware of their skills, abilities, and challenges, understanding job demands, and developing a set of strategies for accomplishing tasks should help them navigate the workplace more effectively.

Part I

The world of work in the twenty-first century is one of constant change. The recent impact of the COVID-19 pandemic has clearly demonstrated the need to deal with change and flexibility, although this may be considered an extreme example of what was already happening in many workplaces. The workplace makes demands on people's ability to cope with change, with redefinition of a role, the need to retrain, to absorb information quickly, to understand job tasks and procedures, to recognise the impact of environment and work culture on their performance, to say nothing of the growing demands on competent literacy skills as a result of technology change. The development of information technology (IT) skills and assistive technology has benefited some dyslexic people, but the volume of written information to assimilate and the speed at which individuals are required to respond can be overwhelming. Strategies that can alleviate some of these challenges are explored in Part II. However, well-informed and carefully considered career choices are likely to contribute to an individual achieving levels of job satisfaction and self-efficacy consistent with becoming successful.

# Part II

# 4

# Strategies Contributing to Success

## Overview

This chapter explores how the ideas discussed in Chapters 1, 2, and 3 can be put into practice. We hope that the theories provide the evidence and rationale for strategy development. This chapter explores the positives and negatives of dyslexia. It focuses on developing self-understanding of individual skills and abilities. It also includes a model to explain the difficulties experienced by adults with dyslexia in different contexts, and the role of metacognitive skill in mitigating these difficulties. A focus on the strategies that individuals can use to support success involves outlining seven key personal strategies that contribute to success. These are:

1. Understand your dyslexia and yourself.
2. Be strategic, and use your metacognitive and executive skills.
3. Never underestimate your memory.

Part II

4. Make the most of your time through planning, goal-setting, and time management.
5. Maximise your motivation to build your self-efficacy and confidence.
6. Seek support from your social ecologies to find out how others can help.
7. Promote yourself positively, which includes disclosing dyslexia when appropriate.

## 4.1 Introduction

In Chapters 1, 2, and 3, we outline some key theories and current understanding surrounding dyslexia and how this relates to dyslexia in adulthood. We also explore theories associated with workplace success, such as ideas related to metacognitive and executive processing, including planning and goal-setting and the development of expertise. We outline the research of Gerber and his colleagues that explores the factors that can contribute to the success of dyslexic people. The aim of this chapter is to explore how these ideas can be put into practice. In this, we hope to provide an explanation for some difficulties experienced in life, providing a rationale for dyslexic adults who potentially have to work in different ways to those around them. This enables them to utilise unique skill sets and work 'smarter', though perhaps work longer and harder, than others to achieve similar goals.

However, within these general ideas, we need to remember that we are all individuals, products not only of our family, our culture. and our educational background, but also of our life experiences and individual abilities. All these aspects mean we have learned and developed differently. Additionally, dyslexia is a label for a set of characteristics (or ways of processing information) that can lead to

## Strategies Contributing to Success

difficulties of varying degrees for each person. How each person responds to all or some of these difficulties is related to their experiences – to the individual differences that have developed over their lifetime. This results in dyslexia affecting people in a variety of different ways. For example:

- Some adult dyslexics can read and write well, whereas others cannot.
- Some adult dyslexics can work fast, whereas others need to take their time.
- Some adult dyslexics can be very good at talking, but others cannot find the right word in some contexts.
- Some adult dyslexics are creative or artistic, whereas others are strategic and systematic.
- Some adult dyslexics can think quickly, but others may want to take their time and consider a problem.

This multiplicity of impact, and the common perceptions of (or misconceptions about) dyslexia, can lead to confusion both for the dyslexic person themselves and for those around them (a tutor in a college; a manager or team leader at work). The misunderstanding of dyslexia is perhaps especially true in adulthood when the demands made on literacy skills and cognitive functioning generally are very different from childhood; there may be less emphasis on literacy, for example. Similarly, adults are more likely to have developed a variety of skills to cope with the broader aspects of life, such as family responsibilities, experiences across a range of work-tasks or different occupations, and additional training or learning of tasks (e.g., driving a car or doing a tax return or changing a fuse on a plug). These varying demands can be challenging and sometimes come as a surprise, especially for a dyslexic person who was diagnosed in childhood and has developed good strategies and gained a good university degree, leading them to believe they have 'overcome' their dyslexia.

Part II

The time-bound workplace that requires multitasking, dealing with ever-changing environments, and working to tight deadlines presents them with new challenges that education-based strategies may not deal with. Likewise, they may experience changes in life outside work, such as finding a partner, having children, and caring for other family members, which can lead to competing demands on their time and energy, and lead to work performance suffering. Therefore, understanding dyslexia, and how it affects you as an individual in differing circumstances, particularly around times of transition or novel circumstances, is essential for success. Having to adapt to novel situations is part of human development, but potentially the dyslexic person is more at risk of failure, owing to potential lack of confidence or less-effective strategies, if they do not understand the forces that are working against them and the resources they have. One of the main reasons people seek coaching or advice is because their current strategies are no longer effective.

The dyslexic person is, fundamentally, the most knowledgeable about their dyslexia and its impact on day-to-day life; however, even their understanding can be incomplete. Many dyslexic people are self-aware: they have good personal insight. Some who have grown up with dyslexia have learned how it affects them as they move into adulthood. They deal with the challenges that adult and work life presents. Some people have suspicions that they might be dyslexic. This can often happen when their children have been diagnosed. However, they are quite content to leave it as a suspicion because they are dealing with things in a way that suits them. Indeed, some people deal with their dyslexic challenges without realising they are dyslexic. They just put in time and effort and assume it is 'just them', or that everyone does the same. If they face a challenge that they cannot overcome, such as in professional examinations, then these people might seek an assessment. Some people diagnosed in childhood may see it only as a reading and spelling difficulty, with little understanding of how this may impact on other aspects of life and work. Both these latter groups potentially struggle in the workplace and may then seek advice. Developing self-knowledge, such as about how they think or why they have to work in particular ways, can lead to people making better decisions in terms of work and career goals, and also in daily life.

## 4.2 Personal Contributions

As mentioned in Chapter 1, prior to writing this book we asked a large number of dyslexic people from a variety of professions to give us their thoughts about dyslexia, how it affected them, and what strategies they found most useful. Inevitably, the answers from these respondents (a term used in research to refer to those responding to a question) produced a range of answers: different things worked for different people. This is consistent with the increasing recognition that no one solution fits all. It is noteworthy, moreover, that this group of dyslexic respondents found their solutions/strategies through personal trial and error, or from speaking to other dyslexic people, or through coaching.

There were themes/trends in the responses, but the variety in perspectives and answers only emphasised the need for self-understanding. Individuals need to know what works for them and why, and to be able to advocate for themselves. This should facilitate success. Now we turn to a discussion of the range of strategies that our experience and discussions with the dyslexic respondents have led us to believe can be useful in improving the chance of being successful.

## 4.3 Strategy 1: Understand Yourself and Your Dyslexia

### 4.3.1 The Assessment Process

Arguably the starting point for increasing self-understanding is an assessment of dyslexia itself. Chapter 2 covers general ideas related to such assessments, such as what might go into an assessment. The importance of understanding the assessment as best we can should not be underestimated; it should provide a basis for people to identify answers about why things are hard for them. The aim of any diagnostic assessment, particularly for adults, is to provide more information for the individual so that they can make changes in their lives that benefit them. It should *not* be simply to diagnose dyslexia. It should begin by establishing what an individual is good at (i.e., their strengths) as well as identifying particular difficulties, and then (importantly) provide potential explanations for both. The assessment should empower people to find solutions and develop strategies that lead to success. In essence, the assessment is the beginning of more self-knowledge. For example, it should help an individual understand why they read more slowly than others; why word finding is so hard at times; why their mind can go blank; and why they take longer than others to complete some tasks. It may also explain why an individual prefers to work in quiet surroundings. Similarly, it should help to develop reasons for what an individual does well; for example, why they can find answers to some problems more easily than others, why they seem to think differently about a problem, and why they might be good at some tasks/activities (such as being highly organised or effective in team development).

Strategies Contributing to Success

## 4.3.2 Responses to the Diagnosis

The reason for seeking an assessment often affects the response. For those individuals who have worried why they could not work or achieve in the same way as their peers, a diagnosis of dyslexia can be a relief – with the realisation that their ways of working are not because they are incompetent or ineffective. They have an explanation for their difficulties. Although this new self-knowledge can be very positive, it must be mentioned that the outcomes from this knowledge involve a process of developing understanding that can take time; at least initially, confidence can remain a barrier to success.

Certainly for some, diagnosis can be an undesirable surprise, particularly those who have been sent for an assessment owing to performance difficulties at work or for those experiencing a lack of promotion or continued exam failure. They may not have thought about dyslexia as a possible reason for their difficulties. They may lack understanding about what dyslexia is. For these people, the shock of the label, and the association of the label with disability, can be overwhelming in the first instance, and it can take many months to accept and understand what it means in terms of finding solutions. Likewise, cultural implications or familial responses may make this new knowledge unwelcome. Responses of people around them can also make a big difference. Comments such as 'you can't be dyslexic because you went to university' or 'if you are dyslexic, I must be too because I forget things' or 'I think it's just an excuse, so you get longer in the exam' are unhelpful and may increase the self-doubt of the newly diagnosed person. Such comments can impact negatively on self-confidence and increase confusion.

Diagnosis in adulthood can also generate feelings of frustration and anger as to why there was not an earlier diagnosis; feelings about the loss of what might have been and the years of feeling incompetent or slower than others or feeling stupid. There is plenty of literature to illustrate the lack of self-esteem and confidence that dyslexic people can experience (see Chapter 2), which is understandable as they have been working against a previously undiagnosed difficulty. Discovering they are dyslexic can also produce feelings of anxiety and may impact negatively on their view of themselves. They can experience the imposter syndrome, feeling that they are not capable of doing the job, that they must have been just lucky up to now, and that 'they will be found out soon'. It can also generate anxiety about the future. How have they managed this far without knowing? How will it affect their career? Will they be discriminated against and overlooked for promotion because they have a disability? Each of these may need to be dealt with in order for the assessment to be a positive experience. In some cases, people who are diagnosed later in life may have achieved a great deal without knowing they were dyslexic. For them, there is now the opportunity to do even better, or simply to find life less stressful as there is a reason for having had to work so hard and put so much effort into their work. The recognition that they are the same determined person as they were prior to the diagnoses can help.

People often ask if there is a right time to be diagnosed: would it have been better to know earlier? There is no right answer to this. For some, earlier diagnosis might have meant more support; they might have made different career decisions, and perhaps not agonised so much about being different. However, for others it may have been a barrier that limited their own expectations. Those diagnosed in childhood who gained help and support and achieved good academic grades may think they have overcome their difficulties, only for dyslexia-related challenges to reappear in a different work environment. People react differently, so it is important that everyone is helped to understand the impact on them personally and what they can do about it. The ability to self-advocate, and to be able to demonstrate strengths and to mitigate difficulties, is also an important part of an effective assessment process.

## Strategies Contributing to Success

The feedback in the report is the first step to becoming successful. The chance to talk it through with the assessor or a dyslexia specialist can make a big difference. The diagnosis should be the beginning of a new stage.

### 4.3.3 Explaining What the Assessment Means

Going through the assessment results and explaining what each test is assessing can be helpful. There is often a lot of unfamiliar information in an assessment report, and many may focus only on the negatives: they will remember that their reading is very slow and their memory or processing speed weak. Again, this is something that needs to be overcome so that positives can be considered too. For example, discovering that reasoning and thinking skills are a strength can counteract feelings of poor self-concept, anxiety, and distraction. It is also reassuring that although the impact is different for everyone, the pattern of dyslexia-specific difficulties is usually very similar. This means they are not alone and points to being able to find advice and solutions.

### 4.3.4 Strengths and Weaknesses

Some reports have graphs to help identify strengths and weaknesses. It must be remembered that everyone has their own individual pattern of strengths and weaknesses. Some assessment reports include a brief description of what each test involves. Some people find this interesting and seek to understand these different aspects of the assessment better. Figure 4.1 is a typical graph of an 'average dyslexic' person; that is to say, it is a composite of results/data compiled from the individual test scores of many dyslexic people to determine an average that can be plotted on the graph (see Chapter 2 for more detail about this graph and the information it represents). Verbal and non-verbal reasoning skills are enclosed in the curved corner

Part II

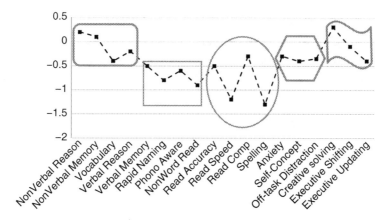

**Figure 4.1** Representation of an 'average' adult dyslexic profile

rectangle on the left of the graph, while the phonological-related skills are in the sharp corner rectangle, and literacy areas are presented in the circle, with emotion-behaviour areas enclosed in the hexagon; finally, on the right-hand side, executive areas are presented within the flag-shape. This graph displays the distinctive ups and downs of adult dyslexia. The ups are the reasoning and creative skills, and there is evidence that reading comprehension may not be too much of a weakness for many. The downs are reading speed and spelling, along with phonological skills and memory span.

The horizontal line at 0 (zero) indicate average performance for most adults, with the small squares within the graph indicating average dyslexic adult performance. Squares below the zero-line suggest the average dyslexic adult is not performing as well on this area of processing. As can be seen, there are many more scores below the zero-line. This is consistent with the assessment aiming to identify dyslexia, given that dyslexia is understood to be associated with difficulties in certain areas of processing (see Chapter 2 again): for example, evidence of weaknesses in underlying phonological processing

## Strategies Contributing to Success

that characterise dyslexia. As mentioned in Chapter 2, this profile is a composite of average scores, and so it is illustrative of the dyslexic profile – but most people, both dyslexic and non-dyslexic, vary from the average. People can demonstrate higher and lower scores on these tests, but it is the pattern that is consistent. Deficits in these weaker areas can be alleviated by good use of reasoning skills, practice on phonological tasks, and assistive technology.

One aspect that is often a source of concern is low reading speed. Frequently, people say that they knew reading was hard and they were slow readers, but they didn't realise it was that bad. Being reminded that it is performance on the day that is relevant, many people slow down their reading speed to aid comprehension (again see discussions in Chapter 2) and to support memory of unfamiliar material, which can reduce over-worrying about such weaknesses. Likewise, the reassurance that they are likely to read familiar texts much more quickly and effectively helps.

In contrast, evidence (and understanding) of their reasoning skills, and sometimes their reading comprehension abilities, as represented in a diagnostic report can help to rebuild confidence and self-esteem. Such information may provide a reason for a change in their behaviour; for example, the knowledge that reading expands vocabulary often encourages people to change their approach to reading – to do more reading, to adopt efficient reading strategies, or even to listen to audio books.

The presentation of assessment results can also help to remind dyslexic people what they have achieved. This can be used as a discussion aimed at highlighting their attainments, the attainment of qualifications, or a specific job, and may be part of discussing experiences at work or even family life that can support the development of additional ways of dealing with challenges and finding solutions. For example, parenthood requires a lot of knowledge, learning, reasoning, and negotiation, as well as planning, prediction, and anticipation, all of which are skills/strategies that are transferable to the workplace.

### 4.3.5 Reframing the Challenges

Essentially, people should feel comfortable and understand what dyslexia is to them so they can describe it positively. Gerber et al. (1992) argue that challenges should be reframed, turning negatives into positives. For example, describing slow reading might be better explained as 'I read carefully to absorb the information' or 'I take longer to do things because I like to think things through' or 'because I like to do a good job' or 'because I double check as I like to avoid errors'. The reframing promotes a positive mindset. It also helps when disclosing dyslexia and when advocating for what they need to work well. Likewise, it is essential to be able to promote one's skill set. For example, one dyslexic adult told us:

> I see things differently so come up with alternative solutions, I have to fully understand to remember things – this seems to mean I can train/induct explain things to people clearly and simply....

It is important that people can demonstrate or articulate their strengths alongside the challenges.

We asked our dyslexic respondents what they felt were the positives of being dyslexic or what their strengths were. In addition to the quote about thinking differently, these included:

**People skills:** 'I can get on very easily with all people, I read them well – I find it easier to get information from people than books.'

**Creativity:** 'Being able to solve problems creatively – I think outside the box so come up with innovative ideas. I can see the story behind things so can describe it well.'

**Verbal communication skills:** 'Being highly articulate, I can present things in a clear, logical, and concise manner as I have had to think it through.'

Strategies Contributing to Success

**Determination:** 'I never give up I know it might take me longer, but I keep going till I get there.'

**Perseverance:** 'It is not a gift, but I have learned to work longer and harder and I get satisfaction out of that and after the effort I put in I know I have done a good job.'

## 4.3.6 Explaining the Challenges

In Chapter 2, we explore the difficulties associated with being dyslexic. When we asked our contributors to describe the difficulties they experienced at work and in daily life there was a range of responses. The range covered all the common characteristics that are outlined in the dyslexia literature. However, not everyone experienced all these difficulties, but these were the six main areas mentioned:

- memory and concentration;
- taking longer to process information, to learn to do things;
- problems with literacy, taking longer to read;
- difficulties with spoken language, particularly relative to speed, word-finding, and dealing with new information;
- organization;
- confidence.

## 4.3.7 Memory and Information Processing

Difficulties with memory was one of the areas that many of the dyslexic respondents mentioned. Memory is the term given to the processes that are involved in the storage and retrieval of information. Memory allows us to draw on our past experiences and use this information in the present (Sternberg, 1999). It is essential to our lives: it allows us to function in the present, to learn through recall of previous experiences and the storage of new ones for future use. There

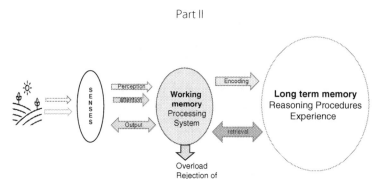

**Figure 4.2** Representation of a simple model of information processing

are three aspects to memory: encoding of information into a variety of forms, such as its meaning, to facilitate storage and learning; storage of this formatted information so it can be used to help learning and understanding in the future; and the retrieval of the information to support current learning and understanding, so that we can link new information to that which we already know.

A range of different types of memory systems have been postulated over the years. The key ones for the present discussion are working memory and long-term memory as these are hypothesised to be involved in the learning and understanding processes; and both have been discussed in terms of the effects or cause of dyslexia. In a widely acknowledged model of information processing (see an adaptation of the model in Figure 4.2), information first enters via the senses and a representation of this information is retained for a short period of time (no more than a few seconds). This information is then transferred to the hypothesised working memory system for processing. Working memory is the system that holds on to information long enough for it to be processed and transferred into long-term memory for more permanent storage. It is assumed that this system processes information in ways that allows it to 'make sense'

## Strategies Contributing to Success

to the individual – so that it fits with prior knowledge and links to other information that is being processed.

There has been a huge amount of research into, and some controversy about, working memory and how it is involved in learning. However, one of the features associated with working memory is that it is limited in capacity. This means that it can become overloaded with information, which can lead to some information being lost/forgotten or not processed as well as it might be. This is a useful concept for us to understand human behaviour, as it may explain why some things happen, particularly errors or lapses. For example, in daily life, if there is a lot going on, a lot to do, or noise and activity, some dyslexic people report not being able to 'think straight' and having memory lapses. At work, if you are introduced to someone who you have not met before, you may need to try to remember the new name and link it with a new face while listening to what is being said during a conversations and trying to remember and respond appropriately to the conversation. Again, this can sometimes overload the processing system so that things are forgotten, such as the name of the person you have just met.

These things can happen in reading and writing too. When reading subject matter that is new, you may need to work out the meaning of new words, think about new concepts and how they link to concepts you already know, and try to work out the overall ideas in the text. Trying to do all these things at once may mean that the system is overloaded, with comprehension and recall of the information being impaired. Likewise, when writing, trying to hold on to a line of thought and find the words to convey that thought, while at the same time constructing a coherent sentence with correct spelling and grammar, can be a complex processing task that may overtax the system and lead to errors (poor spelling, awkward sentence structure, or passages that are not as coherent as they should be).

These things happen to everyone. However, the dyslexic person is potentially more at risk either because of deficits in the processing system (memory may not be efficient at storing information while processing additional information) or because past feelings of failure (in school assessments, for example) makes them susceptible to heightened worry that can interfere with processing. Strategies can overcome some of these problems (many are covered in this book). For example, double-checking information can avoid forgetting or misinterpretation. However, double-checking everything can put a cumulative burden on the system and concentration may diminish, which may further undermine confidence and exacerbate processing problems. Hence, working out the best strategies to support processing in different circumstances may be useful.

Strategies can also alleviate some of the memory difficulties that individuals report. For example, a storage system related to working memory is the short-term phonological store, which is often associated with memory span – often assessed in dyslexia assessment procedures. Memory span is limited, and some dyslexic adults show lower levels of storage of verbal information in memory span tasks: recalling digits in sequence is the usual type of task used. However, strategies can be used to increase retention of such information. Chunking is an example of a strategy that can support storing more information in memory span; that is, breaking strings of numbers into groups of three: 105 – 276 – 384 is easier than those nine numbers in a row. In addition, executive functions such as planning can enhance strategy use, and may provide a basis on which information can be processed more effectively.

Planning ahead is a strategy that can support processing and reduce the impact of overloading. Thinking about how to interpret something can also support processing as it provides a basis on which to deal with information: for example, working out the gist of a passage of text, or predicting its main theme, can help with understanding and reduce

## Strategies Contributing to Success

overloading the system. The short-term phonological system within working memory is also linked to discussions of verbal working memory. The latter concept suggests that language-based processing may utilise a specific set of systems within working memory. Hence, it may be that an individual shows evidence of verbal processing deficits associated with working memory whereas non-verbal processing in working memory seems to function fine. Again, working out how to utilise your systems that are performing well may be another useful strategy.

Working memory has been hypothesised to be the gateway to long-term memory, so it is likely to be an important system for learning. It has been seen as a unitary system, but its location in the brain is unclear. Although frontal areas of the brain have been suggested as a place for the executive functioning elements of working memory, memory process may be more distributed across the brain: for example, those related to language may be within the left-side of the brain where a number of other language systems are located. Given a link between verbal working memory and phonological processing (see Chapter 2 for a discussion of phonological processing), processing of verbal information via working memory may be an area of deficit for those with dyslexia. Arguably, if there is a weakness in verbal working memory, and this supports processing to long-term memory, then verbal memory problems may be expected. This may also play a role in weaknesses related to processing written language. However, again, deficits in verbal aspects of working memory may be compensated by executive functioning systems.

The long-term memory is a relatively permanent store that is potentially of unlimited capacity. This storage system has been discussed in several ways, using different terms and concepts to explain it: we consider some of these as they may help us understand some aspects of dyslexia. One system can be considered as explicit, or declarative, memory, which can be regarded as the intentional recollection of previous experiences, factual information, and concepts.

In contrast, implicit memory refers to internalised memories that are largely unconscious. This can be useful during learning and information processing as retrieval can be automatic, allowing more conscious thought to deal with other information. Additional concepts include episodic memory, which is used to refer to the storage of experiences: the storage of an episode/event in past life. Semantic memory refers to our ability to understanding concepts by linking them with other concepts in terms of their meaning – vocabulary may fall under this label. Episodic and semantic memory may hold similar information, but it can be assumed that episodic memory does not include the level of meaning that semantic memory holds: an event may be stored in terms of what happened, but semantic memory suggests a deeper level of meaning to the event.

A final concept used in many circles is procedural memory. This may be linked to (sometimes confused with) implicit memory. Procedural memory is used to refer to the learning of procedures. This may be driving a car, playing the piano, even writing your name. With practice, some procedures can become automatic and performed without us thinking about them, hence the link with the concept of implicit memory. However, making something more automatic relies on practice – it is rarely something that happens after the first attempt unless it is a skill that is 'hard-wired' in the brain. Therefore, procedures can be effortful at first and take time to become automatic. The development of this automaticity enables more processing space for other task to be performed (e.g., having a conversation while driving).

Overall memory systems should not be considered in isolation. As mentioned earlier, the brain is a highly interactive system, so different functions of memory interact. Equally, though, problems in processing one type of information need not mean deficits in all types of information, and this is likely to be true of memory. Problems in making a procedure automatic need not mean that semantic memory also suffers. However, needing to put effort in potentially makes the processing of meaning more challenging.

## 4.3.8 Strategies to Alleviate Information Processing Difficulties

We asked our dyslexic contributors what strategies they found most useful to overcome the memory challenges they faced. There were five main themes:

- being able to explain information (use semantic memory) and ask for reminders or clarification;
- being able to take a bit longer to assimilate information or complete a task;
- being organised and planning their day;
- making notes, visual and/or written, to help them plan documents, to remember details and/or to prioritise their tasks;
- knowing they had to work harder, and being prepared for this extra effort.

As can be seen from this list, they are all doing something to help them process information effectively. The model represented in Figure 4.3 provides a possible explanation for this.

In this model, two arrows are used to represent ways in which we might support working memory processes. The first indicates that developing automaticity and familiarity can support processing. This can be a positive deliberate process that is typically based on much practice. Developing skills to an automatic level should reduce the impact on working memory and make access to long-term memory easier and quicker. This means there is more capacity for other tasks. For example, if spelling is mostly automatic, then there should be more processing-space for constructing coherent sentences.

Part II

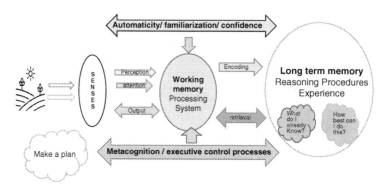

**Figure 4.3** Representation of information processing focusing on the key areas of processing discussed in the book

However, automaticity does not always develop easily, and it may not develop completely or reliably. This may be the experience of dyslexic people, particularly in relation to reading/writing and the phonological skills that underlie decoding (see Chapters 1 and 2 for discussions of the links between reading/writing, decoding, and phonological processing). Poor learning experiences can lead to errors being over-practised, making them difficult to eliminate completely. This may be the reason for feeling that a spelling error continues to recur despite great efforts to avoid it: the error has been practised, making it difficult to overwrite this memory with the correct version. Hence, problems associated with dyslexia can impact in several ways, from continued underlying deficits as well as less than perfect learning experiences that may have put down traces in memory that can interfere with new learning and task completion. Again, how these impact is variable across individuals: good learning experiences of the past avoid some of these problems, for example. However, for some dyslexic people this may mean that certain tasks, particularly those related to literacy, demand more time and effort, and/or the use of compensatory

## Strategies Contributing to Success

strategies, such as re-reading and double-checking. Such strategy use is consistent with application of metacognitive processes, which is the second major point we want to take from Figure 4.3.

The larger arrow at the bottom of Figure 4.3 represents the use of metacognitive, or executive, processes. These include planning and thinking ahead, such as forethought and asking oneself questions about what to expect and what might happen. Many of these ideas are explored in Chapter 3, but they also play a part in the processes we are discussing in this part of the book. Such strategies involve knowledge stored in long-term memory, and may be implemented through processes related to working memory. Hence, it may be necessary to utilise areas of strength in planning and thinking ahead: a planning 'picture' is better for some, though for others it could be a list recorded on an audio device. If the plan is externalised (i.e., spoken to a recording device or sketched on paper) then an additional pathway has been set up for retrieval of information, allowing other processes to support task completion. Any weaknesses in working memory processes should be reduced as they do not have to deal with problems with information retrieval, and the effects of unreliable entries in long-term memory should be overcome. Planning can also have the effect of making memory for information more reliable. If someone thinks about a task and the information needed to complete it, then analyses what has to be done, traces of these thoughts should also be placed in memory, and these are accessible in the future.

Planning also has the benefit that it provides a basis for better organisation. As mentioned earlier, when we asked our adult dyslexic contributors about their strategies, many said that being organised and planning made a difference. This is consistent with the metacognition and goal-setting literature that is discussed in Chapter 3. Hopefully, this section shows how the first general strategy (i.e., self-awareness) leads directly to many of the features of the second general strategy, which we focus on next.

Part II

## 4.4 Strategy 2: Be Strategic in Order to Mitigate the Difficulties, and Use Your Metacognitive/Executive Processes

We have already explored the theoretical construct of metacognition: this is basically understanding one's cognitive processes (consistent with the ideas of self-awareness discussed earlier in this chapter) and regulation of cognition, which includes planning and self-regulatory executive processes. Metacognition develops over time. It potentially develops more quickly when outcomes are successful. If dyslexic people have not felt successful, then these processes may not have developed as effectively, and there may be less awareness and less confidence of their own abilities. This is particularly relevant in relation to reading. Some dyslexic people are less strategic readers, often re-reading all the words in a text to answer a question, rather than scanning to find the answer within the text. (We return to issues related to reading strategies in Chapter 5.) Poor strategy use can lead to feelings that the task is impossible, and sometimes there may be an element of what might be close to learnt helplessness: that is, avoidance. However, for some, a bad strategy can be replaced through reconsideration of the task – by doing it differently, using read aloud facilities on the computer, for example. For others, a tutor or coach may be able to help by modelling more successful strategies.

Metacognitive processing is something we all do when planning a shopping trip or a holiday, going to the gym, or playing in a sports match. Often, there is a specific goal in mind and a plan to achieve the goal. Metacognitive processes are involved in making the plan, checking how our plan is going, and thinking back on how successful the plan was. This reflection or evaluation is key to the metacognitive process. It helps improve our performance and experience. For

## Strategies Contributing to Success

example, if the gym session or holiday was a success, then you are likely to do it again with improvements made. Alternatively, if it was not a success, you make adjustments for the next time or plan not to go again. Hence, this involves understanding one's own cognitive processes, and how best they can be applied to solve problems when working, learning, or doing a task. It also involves task analysis skills, which helps us to understand what the task is. This helps with selecting the best plan or strategy to use to accomplish it.

A note of caution is also needed. As with many cognitive processes, over-planning, over-monitoring, and reflecting over-critically can have a detrimental effect. It can lead to inactivity – all the time is spent thinking about something, rather than doing it. Analysing tasks can be great fun, but at some point there needs to be action to complete them. Equally, monitoring and evaluating plans and the completed task are vital components of good strategies, but these should be realistic. If a task is not accomplished as successfully as it could have been, it may be that the plan was unrealistic and hence needs refinement rather than it being a failure, unachievable and to be avoided. Talking it through with others can often help overcome this negativity.

There are many reasons why metacognitive processing contributes to success. It is a deliberate use of skills. Planning is part of the process. It enables people to feel more in control as they become agents of their learning rather than being directed to complete a task in a certain way. Furthermore, the evaluation and reflection process encourages the transfer of skills and positive personal attribution, which in turn encourages a growth mindset and builds self-efficacy and confidence.

It also makes sense for a dyslexic person to understand the way they think given that they process certain types of information differently to others: as mentioned earlier, they may prefer to draw a picture to 'look' at a problem and 'see' a solution; or they may prefer to verbalise a plan so as to make clear their stages for task completion.

Indeed, they may have been taught ways of working that don't suit them, so better self-understanding/metacognition can counteract such ineffective aspects of past learning. If told that a list is the only way to complete a solution, realising that a flow-diagram or mind map can better represent the solution for them can be a major step-forward in self-understanding and strategy use.

In addition, dyslexic adults develop their own characteristic ways of working, so it is important to consider how effective they are. For example, some people like to totally immerse themselves and focus on one piece of work at a time. Others maintain their concentration by having a variety of tasks to complete in a specified time. Some dive into a problem and scatter all information everywhere, then piece together a solution. Others are more methodical and solve the problem in a step-by-step fashion. Often, the outcomes are the same – the work is completed or the problem is solved – but the methods are different. There is some recognition of the different types of working behaviour that people exhibit in the workplace, and many organisations and companies have questionnaires and/or team-building activities designed to increase understanding of individual differences. The point is to raise awareness and encourage personal reflection, rather than these being a precise assessment tool. This can broaden everyone's perspectives and also build confidence in dyslexic people as they demonstrate that people from different backgrounds do things differently: it is not simply a dyslexia-thing.

As discussed in Chapter 3, metacognitive processing incorporates ideas of self-regulation and executive processing. Table 4.1 provides an overview of the skills that may be involved in task completion. Understanding these sorts of skills and the activities related to them provides a basis for metacognition.

As an example of different cognitive processing, many dyslexic people say they can see the solution to a problem, identify the gaps,

Strategies Contributing to Success

**Table 4.1 Skills, with activity examples, related to metacognitive processing**

| Skills involved | Activity |
| --- | --- |
| Utilising strengths | Shall I talk it or draw it or write it? |
| Task analysis | What is involved? Can I break the task into bits? |
| Task demands | How hard is it?<br>What are the barriers?<br>What resources are needed?<br>How long will it take? |
| Activating prior knowledge | What do I already know? |
| Recall and build on experience | What have I done like this before?<br>What was successful before? |
| Planning and prediction | Seeing the big picture.<br>Predicting the outcome.<br>Planning the pathway to completion. |
| Monitoring and self-regulation | How is it going?<br>Should I do more or less of some part of the activity needed? |
| Cognitive flexibility | Should I change something/direction?<br>Should I do something else for a while?<br>Can I do these two tasks at once? |
| Evaluation and reflection | Acknowledgement of what has gone well and why.<br>What needs improvement? |
| Attribution and self-efficacy | What was my role in its success? |

Part II

or predict outcomes quickly. However, they may not be able to explain the train of thought that has led them to the solution. This may mean that their comments/views are not taken seriously; others may not see what they are suggesting is valid without knowing the steps that have led to the solution. Similar experiences may be had by dyslexics who are good mathematicians (see discussions of examples in Chinn & Ashcroft, 2017). They may be able to provide the correct answer to a maths problem, but are unable to show their workings. In school/college, this may lead to the answer being marked as wrong.

Finally, word-finding difficulties may lead to dyslexic adults having to describe things in different ways: some dyslexic people use the word 'thing' or 'thingamajig' a lot while they search for the correct word. Another example is when it is raining, a non-dyslexic may talk about the need for an umbrella, whereas a dyslexic with word-finding difficulties may discuss 'one of those things that keeps you dry in the rain' (see Figure 4.4).

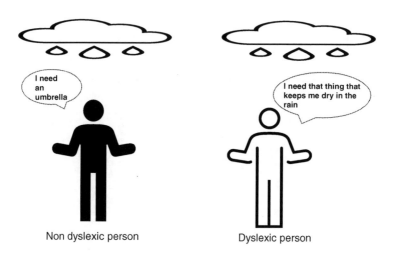

Figure 4.4 Illustration of word-finding differences

114

## Strategies Contributing to Success

This may be a reflection of the vocabulary or phonological access weaknesses discussed in Chapters 1 and 2, which may lead to the more reliable entries in long-term memory being those that provide a description of an object rather that its name. In any event, it can lead to miscommunication as both a raincoat and a bus shelter keep people dry in the rain. Hence, there is a need for clarification strategies, as well as an understanding of the differences, to avoid incorrect interpretations.

Returning to ideas related to planning (one of the key issues for this second strategy), there is a simple three-step process, based on Table 4.1, that should encourage thinking about task demands and planning accordingly:

**Step 1.** *Stop, think, and make a plan*
What really is the task? What is the goal?

**Step 2.** *Check – how is it going?*
Should I change tack?

**Step 3.** *Reflect – have I matched my skills to the task with the right strategy?*
Did I accomplish the goal? Why/why not? In what way have I succeeded?

As mentioned previously, this last reflection/evaluation step that includes an element of attribution is one of the main reasons why metacognition can improve performance. Identifying strengths, along with areas for more development, is key for personal improvement. It is especially important for dyslexic people as they often attribute success to luck or to the efforts of other people, rather than their own skills and effort. This negativity may be a result of blaming themselves for past failures because they believe, or have been told, they are not working hard enough or are not clever enough. Therefore, to clearly evaluate what their role is in a positive outcome, and being able to attribute this to something they have said or done, can rebuild confidence and improve self-efficacy. As one of our dyslexic respondents who is a sportsman said,

> I have had lots of luck and coaching and people believing in me, but it was me that won the race.

The importance of reflection in every aspect of life is increasingly recognised at an occupational level: incident debriefs, post-match huddles, 'lessons learned' on project management all ask similar questions. Notably, most of these reflections are framed positively with a view to improving performance. At a personal level, reflective practice is an essential part of professional training. This can also be the case in job appraisals, which often ask questions such as: What are you most proud of? What did you contribute to the project? What are your development areas? Such questions are aimed at encouraging people to consider their performance in order to set realistic targets for future improvement.

Overall, thinking about the way you think and how you do things enables you to make use of your abilities/skill set, your resources, and the resources of others. It should also enable making the most of your time at both a personal and occupational level. Such metacognitive practices have the potential to improve performance if they build positive reflection and attribution. The strategy-based and planning aspects should allow you to avoid pitfalls and determine reasons for success, which can form the basis for further confidence and development.

## 4.5   Strategy 3: Never Underestimate Your Memory

Earlier in this chapter, we discussed memory being an area of weakness for dyslexic people. There is little doubt that many do not have confidence in their memory skills. For example, quotes from our dyslexic respondents included:

> Sometimes I cannot remember even the simplest things such as ... even my children's names.

Such worries can lead to major misunderstandings:

> I honestly thought I had Alzheimer's

and

> It was a relief to be diagnosed as dyslexic, I thought I had early onset dementia.

Worries and lack of confidence related to remembering things may not be surprising, if processes included in verbal working memory can let dyslexics down (as we discussed earlier). However, often their memory is not as bad as they fear. Here are some important things to consider.

First, it is 'normal' to forget things often. Most non-dyslexic people struggle with remembering people's names, lose things, or forget appointments. It may be that those around you do not make these mistakes quite as often, but they do make them. And it may be that they simply do not worry about such memory lapses as much.

Second, the lack of self-belief, low confidence, and worry/fear related to trying to remember something can exacerbate the problem. If you keep reinforcing to yourself that your memory is very bad, then potentially it becomes a self-fulfilling prophecy: instead of your brain searching to retrieve information, it just shuts down in panic or you give up without giving yourself time to answer. For example, two of our dyslexic contributors said:

> I often say I don't know when I do know the answer – my mind just goes blank – my memory is so so bad

Part II

**and**

> I always say I don't know if I cannot quite remember the answer. This makes me frustrated because often a few minutes later, the answer pops into my head, but it is too late then as the conversation has moved on. I get so cross with myself and then can't follow the conversation – total downward spiral.

In both of these cases, it is more a problem of poor retrieval than poor memory. It is likely that if these people had more confidence and gave themselves more time to find the answer, they might well come up with the correct response, and might even surprise themselves. Most people, whether dyslexic or not, do not have a problem with the storage of information; it is the retrieval or the recall that is the issue.

Dyslexic people often ask if they can improve their memory skills. The answer is yes: there are many books and approaches on how to improve memory. Remembering, and how to improve it, has been debated and written about for centuries. For example, the philosopher Thomas Aquinas (1225–1274) wrote about four principles of memory improvement that underpin many of the present day approaches:

1. **Connect what you want to learn to something unusual**; a picture, an image, something funny. Be creative and multisensory, elaborate and/or exaggerate. This puts down more memory pathways.
2. **Arrange things in an order (first, second, third)**. Put them on an existing structure or system already in your head. A mind map can be an external reminder of where something is 'located' in memory. Some memory techniques involve putting information in your own home and then walking around to pick up the memories in order. Obviously, this may be best for remembering lists, but making links between well-known objects in your house and the facts that you need to remember can also help with recalling concepts.

Strategies Contributing to Success

3. **Think about information logically with focus and care**. The more you pay attention to it, the more likely it will be remembered. Similarly, if you care about something (it is more interesting), you are more likely to remember it. For example, an avid dyslexic football fan may remember vast amounts of information and detail regarding football statistics, but struggle to remember the days of the week except Saturday. For a football fan, the motivation and interest to learn football facts is high; you are gaining knowledge and confidence in that knowledge. Using things that you are interested in can help with learning and memory: How many football games are there until that job interview? If there is a game on the same day, how many hours is the interview before the game starts at 3.00 p.m.?

4. **Reflect on what you have learned** to allow important information to embed further. Repeating, reviewing, and practising can also aid retrieval and recall.

In many respects, memory strategies have not advanced much since Thomas Aquinas. But there are a few other points that can help memory efficiency.

1. Develop your meta-memory. This involves developing an understanding of your memory and its limits. Consider factors that facilitate your recall. How best do you remember things: visualising versus verbalising; linking to other information; chunking or grouping it; associating it with something you already know. Find what works best for you and use this strategically. Remember, though, that not all types of information lend themselves to one type of memory (see point 4).

2. Use personal experience and your previous knowledge base. This can help with engaging with information and putting it into a structure.

3. Be memory task-specific. Select an appropriate memory strategy for the memory task. For example, if you are trying to learn a series of unrelated numbers, such as a phone number or facts or formulae, then rote-learning (constant repetition) might be best; although additional

strategies, such as rhythm and chunking help too. If you are trying to remember a sequence of events, from beginning to middle to end, this might be best presented in a flow chart or by making up a story. Remembering a procedure, such as the stages when driving a car, is very different from recalling the meaning or definition of a concept.

4. Keep it simple. Over-complicated strategies mean more recall – it may be harder to remember the strategy than the thing you are trying to remember. And try to make it personal, so complex content is simplified into a manageable format.

If you want to read a book on memory improvement, there are many to choose from. Maybe look through those in your local library, then select one that suits your preferences/interests. Remember also to consider those that best fit with your needs: if you are studying for a qualification, for example, it may be best to look at study-skills books or go online, rather than use a general memory improvement book (see, for example, Du Pre et al., 2007).

## 4.6   Strategy 4: Make the Most of Your Time

Being able to organise and manage time is important for everyone. But time is often the nemesis for dyslexic people. Indeed, 75 per cent of our dyslexic contributors mentioned that time was the main challenge for them at work. They often take longer than others to do things, especially any written language task. They commented that time estimation was much harder for them than for their colleagues. Furthermore, they may see the big picture and so do more than is required, or have so many ideas that they don't know where to start, and therefore end up finishing much later than others or not within the time given. Therefore, the organisation of work within timeframes and time management are essential skills to try to develop further.

## Strategies Contributing to Success

Inevitably, managing time involves planning. We have discussed planning earlier in this chapter, as well as in Chapter 3. Making a plan involves making choices about the actions required and the best way to use the resources available to achieve a particular goal. Planning time is a corollary of that general planning, and it is often a precursor of success. At a personal level, how to get the family tasks done (how to ensure there is food for breakfast or clothes to wear for work, and getting the children to school with the correct kit at the right time before going to work yourself) requires a degree of planning. Likewise, to perform well at work and to get through a variety of job tasks (to answer pressing emails, to attend meetings, or to write reports) often requires time planning as much as task planning. Planning one's day is often seen as a simple task, such as writing a 'to do' list. However, good planning takes focus and energy. It is a complex cognitive task that includes understanding the task demands, estimation skills, and the resources needed to complete the task, and the time required to perform it. Without consideration of a number of factors, the plan might fail, work is not completed, things might be forgotten, and people feel increasingly stressed and overwhelmed.

A simple starting point for planning is the 5-w rule presented in Figure 4.5; though note that a sixth element, 'how', is also important. Mapping this and the answers to each question on paper can help the decision process.

### 4.6.1 Time Estimation

Estimating how long a task can take can be very hard. Time is not perceived as a constant/static experience. When you are working on something that consumes your interest and attention, time may seem to go fast, and you may be unaware of time as it passes. In contrast, if working out in the gym, or performing ten minutes of hard running, time can

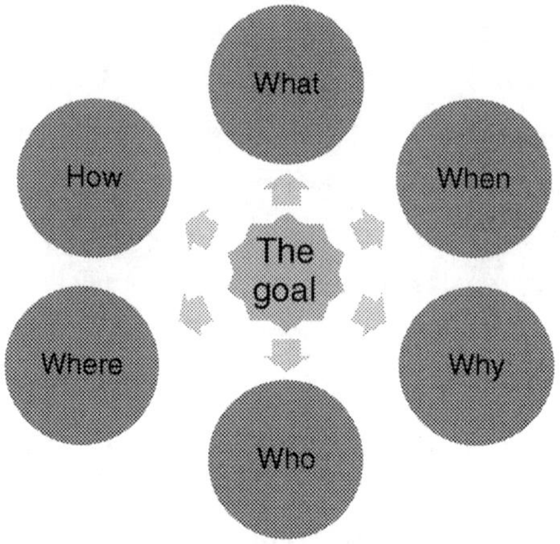

Part II

**Figure 4.5** Mapping plans to complete tasks on time

seem to go much more slowly, and the amount of time elapsed may be in the forefront of your thinking. Similarly, your current energy levels and the effort you feel you can put into running on a particular day affects the ease with which you complete the ten minutes. This can be the same when estimating how long it will take to write a report. Your knowledge of the topic, your energy levels, your previous experience writing similar reports, the relative importance of the report, and the need for accuracy all influence the time it may take to complete the work. But having a good day or a bad day may be a major influence even when all other things are in your favour. As one dyslexic contributor said,

> On a good day it will take thirty minutes to do this – on a bad day I can take up to three hours to do the same task – that is so frustrating, confusing, and demoralising.

Many dyslexic people would identify with this comment, and this variation makes time planning harder, but recognising the factors that influence performance and what might be indicative of good versus bad days means they can plan more accurately.

## Strategies Contributing to Success

There is a wealth of planning and time management tools available. These can range from physical/concrete aids, such as diaries, Filofaxes, and 'to do' lists, to software packages and apps, such as Trello, Microsoft to do, and Google calendar. Personal preference and trial and error are probably the best way to select the one that works best for you. This can take time, but it is worth the effort. In essence, all these tools are providing a structure on which to anchor information, so people can 'see' or keep in mind what needs to be done.

Practising planning and time estimation within a timeline for tasks that may be less important than some work tasks can help develop your skills and give you an idea of what you can do within a set time.

Many of the sorts of strategies discussed here were evident in comments from our dyslexic contributors. Here are some examples:

> Setting an earlier deadline for myself – for example, if something is due in two weeks' time, I have a personal deadline for a week's time.

> Prior to commencing written work or an operation, I find visualising and drawing out the steps required helps to highlight any limiting factors and aids its completion.

> Spending time organising my day and weekly calendar provides a structure to my day and week.

### 4.6.2 Organisation

The last of the previous comments focuses on being organised. This can be another area of challenge for some dyslexic people. However, there are big individual differences in organisational behaviour, and this does not apply just to those with dyslexia. Some people are highly organised; everything has its place. Others seem to operate in semi-chaos, but seem to know where everything is when needed. If you feel comfortable with your current levels of personal and work organisation, then it is probably not a problem. However, there are times when disorganisation can be distracting, demoralising, and time wasting (with precious minutes or hours being spent trying to find things). Organisation can be a way to avoid problems of forgetting things. For example,

> I tend to be quite disciplined over important things. For example, I keep my car keys and phone in the same place at home to avoid chasing around searching for them.

Being organised can help people look and feel in control. However, being highly organised can demand energy and attention, and may require constant updating. Practical strategies and routines can help, as suggested by our contributor quoted here.

Dyslexic people are best served by developing their own systems as much as possible, both at home and work. These systems can be very simple and manageable. For example, some dyslexic contributors talked about the different methods that work for them.

> Colour coded cardboard storage boxes are the system I use now I am working from home. I like hard copy to read from and my notes related to different projects are thrown in the right colour box.

> I chuck everything to do with household stuff into one drawer – that way I know where it is – I tried to file it carefully, but filing never got done and I lost too much stuff.

Routines and being organised can also make a difference to time management. For example, one contributor mentioned the following strategies:

> I now have a very strict early morning routine. I do the same thing every day at the same time – the news radio programme is my time marker and I can even fit in exercising and arrive at work with time to spare for a coffee.

The organisation system needs to be simple to maintain. Complicated methods work for some people, but they demand time and attention. Here is another example from one of our contributors:

### Strategies Contributing to Success

> I worked out a great system of planning, cross checking, sorting things out, organising everything as I went along. It was based on what I read in a self-help book and it was OK, but then I realised that was all I was doing, spending more time on that than actually getting anything done! I now have a simpler system and I am organised, but it tends to be in spurts once things get out of order.

Some people are selective about when they are organised, being highly organised at work because they have to be, but less so in their personal life. This can be a good strategy, as the effort needed to get organised and maintain an organisation system can be effortful. It may not come naturally (automatically) to some people.

In summary, organisation, prioritisation, and time management are key skills for an individual at a personal level, as well as in the workplace. Being organised and having routines in place develops a degree of automaticity and familiarity, and helps with time management and time estimation. It can also increase the feeling of being in control. However, it can be tricky to find a system that works, so persevere. Try working out the three most important things first and focus on those before moving on to others, again maybe in groups of three. As always, try to think ahead, and keep the organisation system as simple as possible.

## 4.7  Strategy 5: Maximise Your Motivation

Motivation is defined as the desire to reach a goal. It is fundamental to success. Having the desire to succeed increases determination. We discussed motivation earlier in this book (see Chapter 3); including the work of Gerber and his colleagues, who concluded that the desire to achieve goals and to be highly motivated were key factors in success (see Gerber et al., 1992). This is perhaps not surprising, as motivation increases determination and drives persistence to continue in the face of challenges.

Motivation can be seen as intrinsic, arising from within the individual. In contrast, it can also be extrinsic and a result of external factors. Intrinsic motivation is driven by the sense of personal satisfaction. This can be based on an interest or passion in a subject, or it can simply be the enjoyment of performing or completing a task. It is generally thought that those people who are intrinsically motivated are most likely to improve their skills in order to gain a sense of satisfaction, mastery, and autonomy.

Extrinsic motivation is driven by external rewards, such as to obtain money, to gain a qualification for career progression, and to gain approval based on what others or society think. Encouragement from peers, family, and colleagues, as well as positive feedback from managers, may increase extrinsic motivation. In addition, extrinsic motivation can also be driven by negative influences, such as fear of punishment or criticism. Relying solely on extrinsic rewards is often associated with less likelihood of success than when an individual has elements of personal (intrinsic) motivation.

Aspects of both intrinsic and extrinsic motivation are often at work within the individual: passing an exam may be personally motivating, but may also lead to access to a better job. The sources can also change over time: for example, you study a subject initially in order to pass an examination (extrinsic), but you end up becoming passionate about the subject (intrinsic), then become a consultant/expert on the topic and get paid for your advice (extrinsic).

However, motivation can be diminished by many things. These can include failure to achieve a goal and fear of failure. It can also be impacted by how hard a task appears to be and perceptions of how far away a goal appears to be. Motivation can also be influenced by life distractions and energy levels. Hence, if dyslexic people have to work longer and harder than others to achieve their goals, their motivation is likely to be affected. For example, there are many dyslexic people whose motivation to learn to spell has gone; wisely, they have found alternative solutions, such as using a spell checker.

### 4.7.1 Self-efficacy

Motivation can also be influenced, both positively and negatively, by self-belief, self-efficacy, and self-confidence. We explore these overlapping concepts elsewhere (see Chapter 3). Self-belief and self-confidence may be more general in nature. In contrast, self-efficacy is often associated with specific skills or tasks. It can be seen as one's own belief in having the ability to achieve a certain task. As we outline in Chapter 3, self-efficacy can be increased by previous experience of successful completion of a task (your level of mastery), by watching others complete the task, through encouragement from others to complete the task, and by your own motivation to finish the task successfully. This means that self-efficacy can be developed because you can plan to build it incrementally. For example, being able to jog 1 mile can lead to the belief that 2 to 5 miles are manageable, which might lead to feeling confident about completing 10 miles and then perhaps running a 26-mile marathon. In relation to work, people may need to improve their self-efficacy in certain aspects of their role. An example illustrates how one person developed her skills in giving presentations.

> I was advised to take a step-by-step approach first: I learnt how to use PowerPoint and design a presentation; second I practised only two slides then presented the two slides, with my manager delivering the rest, thirdly I talked through how it went – quite well actually. Having managed two slides, I felt able to do the next presentation on my own, although I had my manager alongside me pressing the buttons and I knew they would step in to answer questions if I got stuck. I then realised I could do it myself – and I do now but some go better than others.

Each step should build self-efficacy; although it should be mentioned that some people never feel comfortable when giving presentations. The suggestions about making the presentation task manageable by breaking it into incremental steps, with monitoring and feedback, all chime with the metacognitive processing outlined earlier. Mastering the task to an acceptable level, through taking a growth mindset approach, can build feelings of success and self-efficacy. It enables people to feel in control, and should lead to a decrease in anxiety.

Mastery of a task is an important element of Bandura's theory of self-efficacy (see discussions in Chapter 3, and Bandura, 1997) but it is also an essential part of Dweck's Mindset theory (also mentioned in Chapter 3 – and see Dweck, 2017). People with a growth mindset tend to keep going in the face of challenges. This has relevance for dyslexic people, as they often show a tendency to persist. However, they may also see themselves as failures as a result of having struggled with learning, which may lead some to have more of a fixed mindset. This may be apparent in their feelings about never having mastered reading or spelling and having struggled to pass examinations. These latter feelings can impact on their confidence in aspects of their job. The point here, and in the framework presented in this book, is that these areas of poor mastery are often specific to the dyslexia. They do not necessarily mean problems in other areas of life and work. Maintaining a growth mindset and exploring different ways of achieving your goal helps to decrease the feelings of failure. One's experiences in mastering a task affect self-belief and confidence for the future. If you consistently view experiences as learning and as an opportunity to become more informed, then self-efficacy and resilience should increase, and a reduction in anxiety should follow.

Strategies Contributing to Success

As we have said before, but it bears repetition, good goal-setting is also essential for maintaining motivation and self-efficacy. If you set a goal, and endeavour to accomplish it, you are more likely to achieve something. If you achieve the goal, or the major part of it, you should feel more successful and be encouraged to go further. If you do not reach the goal, it is important to look at what you have achieved, then reset the goal. Setting goals that are realistic and achievable are key. Success can be defined as goal achievement, meaning that achieving lots of smaller goals should lead to greater success than failing a big one. Mini successes lead to increased motivation, which leads to more determination and self-belief, and the potential for greater success.

## 4.7.2 Ways to Increase Self-efficacy and Motivation

Some suggestions for increasing self-efficacy that have been made by our contributors are listed here: note that we have paraphrased many. We have separated them into two parts: cognitive strategies and practical strategies. As always, not everything will work for you.

## 4.7.3 Cognitive Strategies

- Celebrate what you have achieved and look at what is to be done next.
- Plan and reflect – what went well and why?
- Have a positive frame of mind – the journey is important, not the outcome.
- Face your fears – identify the barriers – take action on them – make it safe.

Part II

- Think! Am I being emotional ? Is my response sensible? How can I do this?
- Mentally plan and rehearse the steps it takes to achieve a goal – and visualise yourself succeeding.
- Make contingency plans. Always have a Plan B – if this doesn't work, try this.
- Assess the effort you have put into what you are doing, and try to be proud of that.

### 4.7.4 Practical Strategies

- Break things into manageable chunks. Set small and realistic goals.
- Make a motivation board – a list of achievements/a list of reasons for achieving something.
- Have a mission statement of both extrinsic rewards and intrinsic rewards.
- Use mantras and self-talk: I can do this, this is good, I'm doing OK, I'm moving forward, I'm not giving up yet.
- Have a consistent approach or routine to settle yourself and then get started.
- If distracted from the beginning, do something completely different that makes you feel better; for example, tidy your desk and head, change the furniture round, go for a walk – something that you can succeed in – and then go back to the task in hand.
- Take a break.
- Take up mindfulness and practise it regularly.
- I went to my parents' place to get away from distractions and have meals cooked and get constant encouragement.
- My friend sent me a motivation box full of coloured pens to work with, smellies for the bath for relaxation, sweets for energy, and motivational stickers!
- My friend took me to the pub half an hour before closing time for a quick half-pint.

## 4.8 Strategy 6: Social Ecologies and Seeking Support from Others

An underlying element to both motivation and self-efficacy has been the role of other people. There are many reasons why being around supportive people is likely to contribute to success. Human beings are inherently social, for companionship and love, for fun and laughter, to share good experiences and bad, to share successes and failures, to educate, to learn from and to encourage and to motivate. Here is another example for our dyslexic respondents: 'We are both dyslexic, so our lives can be a bit chaotic when our organisation slips and we never know where the car keys are – but we are very tolerant about that sort of thing and generally laugh about it.'

Encouragement is the core foundation of success. In their seminal book, *Exceeding Expectations*, Reiff et al. (1997) state that in all their interviews, successful dyslexic adults credited many of their accomplishments to supportive parents, teachers, and friends. Likewise in Karen Cousins' book the majority of the successful contributors said that their family or friends had been very supportive of them when growing up (Cousins, 2020). Their parents or friends enabled them to cope with what felt like constant failure and with what may at times have seemed like a mountain ahead of them.

Alternatively, it could be one person who was there at a crucial moment in their lives and who 'stood alongside them' and encouraged them. It was these supportive people who enabled the dyslexic people to feel more comfortable with not succeeding at some tasks (such as learning to read and write as others did), and whose support improved their resilience.

Resilience provides the basis for an individual to recover quickly from difficulties, which helps them to keep going. Positive relationships with others are a contributory factor in developing this resilience. This can be by listening and encouraging, by showing belief in them, offering guidance and advice, and enabling the dyslexic person to feel more competent and in control. As such, part of resilience may be the ability to ask for help when needed.

The majority of our dyslexic contributors said asking for help was essential, although some were reluctant to begin with. They feared being misunderstood, and worried about how they might be perceived; for example,

> 'I think people will think I am stupid if I have to keep asking questions'

**and**

> 'I don't want to appear needy.'

The misperception that asking for help is synonymous with inability is common among many people, and may be particularly true for dyslexic people. This is because many dyslexic people may need help on what may be regarded as something simple, such as remembering someone's name or how to spell a word. They may also need more clarification on a procedure as part of their job, because they take a bit longer to process the information or process it in a different way. For example,

> my manager gave me the impression I should know how to do it immediately. Well, I would if she would give me a bit longer to think.

They may have got used to the 'Don't you know that?' expression on their colleagues' faces. This may make them feel that others see them as not being competent in their work.

However, more often than not, the dyslexic person is very capable of doing the harder and more intellectually challenging parts of their role. This misperception is one that can be rectified by talking with trusted others, whose opinions are valued, and who can remind the dyslexic person of their strengths and the relative values of their skill

## Strategies Contributing to Success

set – and also if the request was realistic. We talk more about seeking advice from managers in the workplace in Chapter 7.

Despite some of the points made here, many of our dyslexic contributors did refer to support from others. Here are some examples:

> Family and friends are also an important source of support and encouragement.

> I don't know what I would do without my partner – she has more belief in me than I do. When I failed my exams she was amazing and helped me see that I had to retake them.

> I find it unbearable to read instructions or guidance – and so often ask my husband to sort finances/tax/application forms. Or he reads it and then explains it to me. I know I can read it all – but I just do all I can to avoid it!

> Buying a house would be basically impossible for me (paperwork, legalese). Luckily my dad does that for a living so I have swerved that one.

> I have a reputation among my friends for being constantly late, since my time-keeping isn't particularly reliable – but this is more of a joke between us rather than a problem.

### 4.8.1 Cautionary Note on Social Ecologies

Good social ecologies are likely to make a big difference. Sadly, the inverse is also true. If the people around you are unsupportive, then no matter how good the job is or how well suited you are to it, confidence, self-efficacy, and performance are likely to suffer. The advice then is to try and move to another role or find external support systems and areas of success in life to counteract the unhelpful working environment. Likewise, sometimes families and friends are not very supportive, and here perhaps giving yourself some space for a while is the better way forward. In all these cases, maintaining one's self-esteem and confidence is paramount.

## 4.9 Strategy 7: Promoting Yourself Positively and Informative Disclosure

Finally, one of the main strategies that contribute to success is being able to ask for what you need to work well. Doing this may involve disclosing that you are dyslexic. Disclosing dyslexia is an entirely personal thing, and perhaps not surprisingly everyone deals with it differently. 'Should I tell' and 'how do I tell' are two of the most frequent questions or worries following an assessment of dyslexia.

Some people are very keen to tell everyone. They are proud of being dyslexic: they have a reason for their problems, or they feel better about not having to hide the difficulties experienced. Others are much more reluctant, and some don't wish to tell anyone. Some tell everyone immediately; others wait a while until they have come to terms with it. Many people do not disclose at work, even if they have been diagnosed in childhood, because they see it as a reading problem and don't think it would apply to work, or they have got a good degree and think the dyslexia has gone away. Others do not disclose because of the shame and embarrassment they feel, or the fear of being misunderstood and losing their job. However, all these reasons can lead to less understanding.

The positives of disclosing that you are dyslexic are that you should feel better understood, there is an explanation for why things take longer, it means not having to hide, and communication should be easier. It can also lead to accessing extra time to complete tasks, assignments, or examinations, and to getting assistive software that can be supportive. However, if people do not want adjustments at work, then there may be no need to disclose. Furthermore, it is possible to communicate how you work best without disclosing dyslexia – for example,

## Strategies Contributing to Success

> I always double-check my work or get someone to look over it as I don't like mistakes.

If the decision is to disclose, then it is important to consider who to tell. Some people tell family and friends, whereas some don't tell their family because of the difficulties it will cause. Some only tell their managers or people on a need-to-know basis.

It is also important to consider when to say something. Generally, we believe that it is important for people to be seen as individuals, and for who they are rather than the dyslexic label they may wear. So, if meeting managers, or other people for the first time, it may be better to leave disclosure and discussion until the end of the meeting, or the second meeting. It is also better to tell people from a position of strength. This may mean that it is better not to leave it too late, particularly if support or extra time is needed. Some people reveal they are dyslexic when they have been complimented for doing a good job. For example,

> My manager was giving feedback on a project I had run. He said I had some innovative ideas. I told him that was because I was dyslexic. He was amazed. I did laugh.

A final point to consider is what to say, which may also include what to ask for:

> I told my employers that I was dyslexic – they were very good about it and said that's OK but how could they help – the problem was I couldn't answer that!

Another contributor said:

> My employers said that is not a problem, we have lots of dyslexic people here. I was so relieved. Then they gave me a whole load of software which made my life even worse – they thought I would be cured but there was no way I could use it.

Part II

Whenever people decide to disclose their dyslexia, they should plan what to say – it should be brief, positive, and solution focused. Dyslexia is known as a hidden disability/difference. The individual differences between people, and this hidden nature, mean that it is particularly important for the individual to discuss what it is good for them and how they deal with it. This is especially important because other people's perceptions/experience of dyslexia will colour their judgement. As mentioned before, if a manager, or even a friend or family member, thinks it will only mean problems in reading and spelling, they may find it hard to understand that someone who can read adequately and who has largely overcome the literacy difficulties can be dyslexic. They may well be confused and not know what to say or how to help. So the clearer the dyslexic person can be, the more likely disclosure will be positive. Here are some more examples from our contributors:

> I thought you should know I am dyslexic – my dyslexia means I know I can do this job because I have these skills….
>
> I do take my time with paperwork sometimes and I might ask people to check it if I am tired.
>
> I am organised and plan my work, so I don't miss deadlines.
>
> I write my action points and so rarely forget to do things.
>
> I generally clarify what I have to do if I am in doubt so I don't waste time.
>
> I am good at talking so I prefer to discuss things than work via email – it is quicker.
>
> I prefer to work via email because then I can take my time and think things through and send a draft to be edited.
>
> I also like reminders via email as I put it straight into my task list.

However, while clarity and explanation are important, brevity helps. Too big a list of problems, even with solutions, can undermine not only the manager's confidence but also the individual's self-efficacy. Here is a salutary case study as interpreted by the authors of this book:

> AK went to for a job interview. He had ticked the dyslexic box because it guaranteed him an interview. He was very keen to get the job. It was interesting and more money, and he had some experience. The interview was going well and AK wanted to be open about his dyslexia. He had thought of all the challenges it would present him. He had a list of ten things. He began his list: he needed software – he liked to talk things through – he worked best when he could plan and organise – his work needed to be proofread – he needed a to do list to keep him on track – he liked catch-up meetings with his manager.... AK said that when he got to this point he felt the energy in the room fade. He knew the moment had passed. More importantly, he began to doubt his own ability to perform the fast-moving reactive role. He wasn't asked for a second interview. He was not surprised, but he was cross because he knew he could have done the job well once he had settled in. AK has a new job. In that interview he simply said he was dyslexic, which meant that he needed a little extra time to settle into the role and then he would be up and running. When he got into the role, in his first meeting with his manager, he was more specific about his needs and solution focused.

Disclosure and/or self-advocacy are important aspects of a dyslexic person's success. Positive disclosure is based on self-understanding. Knowing why you do things the way you do, and knowing what your strengths are and how to mitigate the shortfalls, enables you to self-advocate. Disclosure should improve the social ecology as people will better understand the reason for any inconsistency in performance and should be more supportive. It should enable people to demonstrate their strengths, which can be harder to identify than their weaknesses. However, as previously mentioned, sometimes simple self-advocacy without disclosure is all that is needed: 'This is how I do things well.'

# 5

# Literacy and Language Issues and Strategies

## Overview

This chapter explores the impact of dyslexia on effective language processing. It explains some of the underlying literacy processes that are assessed during the diagnosis (as outlined in Chapter 2). Better understanding of these processes has been helpful for our dyslexic contributors. Greater awareness of the complexity of the reading process and why it is such a challenge has decreased their frustration and improved their literacy skills and confidence.

The focus of this chapter is on:

1. Developing an understanding of the literacy processes and strategies that support the development of literacy skills (at word and text level), along with basic language skills (processing sounds and meaning).
2. Providing a range of suggestions, tasks/activities, and strategies to improve these underlying processes.

## Literacy and Language Issues and Strategies

3. Discussing working with text and strategies for improved comprehension and speed, as this is the focus of many difficulties with reading that many adults still experience.
4. Exploring some technological solutions.

## 5.1 Introduction

Good communication skills, both written and spoken, are an essential part of success at work, as well as education and everyday life. Sometimes, effective communication can present people with dyslexia with challenges. This is not surprising given that written communication is generally the area of primary difficulties for dyslexic children. And, as we have discussed before (see Chapters 1 and 2), dyslexia is not something that the individual grows out of: people learn to live with it, and develop both positive and negative strategies. The consequences of being dyslexic vary according to the individual experiences, but lack of experience with text can lead to a lack of effective techniques. Similarly, lack of practice with reading and writing can lead to poor experience of ways of interpreting language information, and possibly inappropriate strategy use.

There are also areas where the impact of dyslexia may become more apparent with age. As language becomes more complex and diverse, then difficulties stemming from weak literacy skills can impact areas of work, such as in training or assessment settings. Furthermore, people with dyslexia can demonstrate higher levels of emotionality, high levels of frustration and anxiety, low self-esteem, and lack of confidence, which can lead to poor levels of well-being and mental health issues. This can all impact on confidence in social situations, particularly those that are high pressured: going to an interview, delivering an important presentation to work colleagues, writing an urgent report for management. Although these additional problems do not occur in all individuals, particularly when good strategies have been implemented, they occur often enough for them to be noticeable. They can further negatively impact on learning, education, and performance at work.

## 5.2 Literacy and Language Issues and Strategies

As we have discussed earlier in this book (see Chapters 1 and 2), the individual differences and experiences of adults mean that simple rules for support are difficult to make. There is a range of abilities in reading and writing among dyslexic adults Some develop good word reading accuracy, whereas others continue to struggle at the word level. Some develop good strategies for dealing with text understanding, whereas others have difficulty going beyond the meaning of individual words. Equally, the literacy needs of the individual adult vary considerably depending on what they have to do at work. Some need good reading skills to progress in their chosen field, whereas others may need only basic skills. Therefore, we have outlined a set of strategies that might be useful for a range of individual differences and experiences. These vary in complexity, for the same reasons.

The suggestions here should be useful for those who are still struggling with reading, and they may also be of interest to those who have managed to develop their reading to competent level. They may be of interest to study skills tutors, coaches, and dyslexic parents who have dyslexic children. For some, the activities/tasks/ strategies may simply confirm those that they have already developed. For others, advice and encouragement from another individual (a coach or friend) may be needed before trying some of these strategies. Trying them helps in recognising where difficulties lie. For example, one of our contributors commented that

> My coach and I did some sessions on the basics of English language-morphology – and spelling and grammar – it all makes more sense now.

The ideas here include these same basics.

In discussing these ideas, we use terms such as morphology (as in the comment just quoted) as these are likely to be the terms used in other materials. We have mentioned some of these terms before, but as a reminder, a morpheme adds meaning to a word. Most words have a meaning and therefore are a morpheme, but you can add morphemes to a word to change or modify its meaning. The word 'help' conveys meaning, but 'helpful' has a slightly different meaning, and 'unhelpful' has a very different meaning. Adding morphemic units such as 'ful' and 'un' changes the meaning of the word. Another term we use regularly is phonological, which relates to sounds within words. In reading and writing, these relate to written symbols, typically individual letters. The range of written symbols that help with conveying meaning and sounds, and also elements of grammar, can be referred to by the term orthography. These three terms are used to think about ideas related to sounds (phonology), written symbols (orthography), and meaning (morphology).

## 5.3 Reading and Spelling

Reading and spelling have much in common. They are both complex learned skills involving knowledge and recall of sound–symbol associations that are supported by underlying phonological processes. Many people assume that if you practise reading, then spelling will improve, but this is not always the case. It can be useful to see reading and spelling as partially different cognitive information processing activities. In the simple input–output cognitive model, reading is largely an input activity; it involves recognising or decoding the letters in words. Highly familiar words should be recognised, but less familiar words may need the reader to access letter–sound associations (the decoding process). If the recognition or decoding processes lead to a known word, then access to its meaning should follow – just like understanding a spoken word. If unfamiliar, this may lead to producing a spoken version of the written word, but meaning may only be derived if further information about the new word's meaning is provided: the text around the word explains the meaning, as in a dictionary or someone defining the new word for you. If it is a new word in a passage, then you may be able to work out a reasonable idea of its meaning from the text around it; though this requires comprehension of most of the passage. It is important to note the text remains on the page so it can be reread, which may support the decoding of an unfamiliar word.

Spelling is primarily an output or production activity – you have to produce the word from memory. Spelling out a word is influenced by associations between letters and the sounds in the word, just as reading is, but this time we need to move from the sounds to the letters, or we have to be able to recall the precise spelling of the whole word. If spelling involves writing the word down as part of an assignment or report, then there is also be the physical process of producing the correct letter shapes, again from memory.

Most people do not think about what they are doing to process text when reading. For many, it has become an automatic skill that they do not remember learning. For a person with dyslexia, however, reading can be a difficult skill to master. Dyslexia-related weaknesses in reading experienced in childhood are likely to continue through education and into adulthood. However, as an individual gets older, the range of problems in reading can increase. At first, decoding

## Literacy and Language Issues and Strategies

individual words may be the main difficulty. However, this can lead to difficulties in the assimilation and interpretation of the text, which are more likely to be the main function of reading in adulthood. Difficulties in one domain can impact on the other: poor decoding skills can lead to poorer comprehension of the text. Equally, strengths in one aspect of text processing may support another.

One of the main strategies our dyslexic contributors referred to was slowing reading down to support the decoding of text and understanding. Slower reading can help to decode words that they are not sure about. Some of the strategies here require slower overall reading times in order to implement them. This might also mean reading parts of the text to get its gist (i.e., a general idea of what the text is about), then re-reading the same text to try to fill in any gaps in decoding (unknown words) or inconsistencies in understanding (if a word was read incorrectly or an alternative meaning of a word might fit better). Hence, slower reading is not always a sign of poor reading – it may be necessary in some instances.

Obviously, with practice, we would hope that reading speed improves, particularly when reading frequently read material: unknown words should become fewer when reading of associated material has been practised regularly. However, dyslexia is not something that goes away, so be prepared and allow yourself time, particularly when dealing with new material. As we have stated throughout this book, good planning seems the best starting strategy.

Like many dyslexic people, some of our contributors suggested they had greater problems with reading speed and word spelling (see Figure 2.2). However, sometimes some aspects of reading and writing may be under-practised; this can lead to specific difficulties with text comprehension and text production. Slow reading can be useful as a specific strategy, but if most words are processed slowly, this can take a very long time – resulting in poor comprehension or the forgetting of meaning. Similarly, focusing on spelling each individual word leaves less thought available for making phrases and sentences coherent. These difficulties with specific elements of reading and writing can impact on reading to learn and on the production of assignments, projects, or reports; and this can impact on tasks in both further education and the workplace. The lack of practice with reading and writing might mean less experience of using different strategies when reading and writing, as well as less confidence in performance, for example if reading or writing a report is something that you have never done before.

Although dyslexia is often seen as a reading difficulty, many adult dyslexics report (and show in assessment measures) more problems with accurately spelling a word than reading it. However, this is probably the case for all those learning English. For many, spelling frequently used words becomes a fairly automatic skill: it is just the way you spell the word. This 'just the way it is' perspective can get over many of the oddities of English spellings: 'monk' is just the way you spell it, even if 'munk' might seem correct based on simple letter–sound relationships. For some dyslexics, remembering that 'monks come from monasteries' may be a better way of working out this slightly odd spelling. However, the 'just the way it is' strategy can fail many, and it is one of the reasons why English spell checkers are standard in most word processors: they are needed by us all.

Certainly, spell checkers for word spelling and read-back facilities for proof-reading have helped a great deal, but poor spelling can remain a source of lack of confidence, frustration, and even shame and embarrassment for many dyslexic adults. It is particularly annoying that it is usually the frequently used small words in the language that have odd spellings. These are the ones that are most likely to show changes owing to frequency of use and the effects of accents, social language norms, or task fatigue. It can help to know why spellings are odd: for example, 'women' is likely spelt with an 'o' rather than an 'i' to avoid too many up-and-down strokes when writing with an ink pen rather than to help with the ease of linking spoken and written forms.

Nevertheless, society and people with dyslexia themselves can place great weight on spelling accuracy. This means that people are judged, and judge themselves, on this complex but basic literacy skill, rather than reminding themselves that meaning, thinking, reasoning, analysing, inferring, and decision-making are the abilities that we most value when forced to choose. However, understanding the processes and deliberate practice should lead to greater awareness, greater confidence, and, therefore, improved performance.

## 5.4   Activities/Strategies to Consider and Try

All of the examples here are intended to increase the ability to link letters, sounds, and meaning, and to increase understanding of orthography, phonology, and vocabulary. This can help to develop decoding skills in those struggling with words, which leads to better text comprehension. As such, these strategies are primarily intended to support those who show the more classic features of dyslexia and are likely to present evidence of weak reading skills. However, some of the meaning- and vocabulary-related tasks/activities may also help those with poor reading comprehension levels who have fewer problems linking letters and sounds, but show weaknesses in making links with the meanings of words. Linking these with strategies to support comprehension may also be useful (i.e., how to monitor comprehension, how to infer meaning, how to question and note-take during reading, etc.).

Part II

Language (spoken or written) is a way to communicate information, but the communication can be of enjoyment as well as knowledge. Language is the tool of most comedians, so do not neglect the humour that can be derived from practising language. Making things fun/humorous helps with practice and can also support remembering. However, also keep in mind that the goal is better reading and writing, so do not neglect practising these as well. There is no point in developing a basic skill that supports reading and writing if you do not use it to lead to better reading and writing.

These meaning-based tasks/activities should lead to improvements in vocabulary, something that is also useful for those with a second/additional language background. Trying some of these tasks/activities may also help with recognising where difficulties lie. Looking for additional examples in books or on the Internet, or developing your own, can help with further practice. If developing your own, make them fun. Many dyslexic adults will say that they actively dislike and are even frightened of language-based tasks, but more knowledge and understanding of these processes can take away the fear, increase the interest, and even lead to enjoyment.

### 5.4.1 Phonological Activities to Improve Phonological Awareness at Any Age

It helps to start with simple examples to make the task clear, then make them more complex as learning progresses. This may be particularly important for individuals who have struggled with such tasks in the past. With verbal activities/tasks, remember to take accent into account to avoid confusion. Some examples are given here, but also see Moats (2010) and Reid and Clark (2021); note that although most of the materials in the literature focus on younger learners, those targeting adolescents can also be useful for adults struggling with language and literacy skills.

> *Rhyming activities/tasks*: Think of all the words you know that rhyme with 'dog', or make it slightly harder with orthographically more complex words such as 'choice' or use made-up words such as 'doice'. Making up songs and rhymes can also be good: King Arthur singing about going to 'Camelot' can be made to rhyme with 'you have to push the pram-a-lot' (stolen from Monty Python, of course).
>
> *Deletion activities/tasks*: What do you get if you take the 'l' sound from 'lakes'? You get 'aches'. First sounds are easier, and the task can be made harder with thinking about end sounds and then middle sounds. Indeed, thinking about parts of words can be helpful when writing too: 'I found this idea of beginning, middle and end very helpful when spelling' was a quote from one of our contributors.
>
> *Swapping sounds*: What happens if the 'f' sound in 'fox' is changed to a 'cl' sound? You get 'clocks'. Again, end sounds and middle sounds are harder.
>
> *Spoonerism*: This is where we say two words, or made-up words, with the first sounds swapped around. For example, 'King John' would be 'Jing Kon'; 'mystery house' would be 'history mouse'; 'filler cart' would be 'killer fart'. Thinking of silly Spoonerisms can be fun, though you may want to keep some of them to yourself. Be creative and enjoy the flexibility of language. Watch sketches written by Ronnie Barker or read stories by Spike Milligan: both play with the sound of language in highly creative ways (though there are many others who do the same).

The point of phonological activities/tasks is to help to make recognising sounds in spoken words easier. However, for this skill to be useful in reading development, developing it still requires a linking with the writing form. As one of our contributors said,

> I am sure playing around with sounds with my children when they were learning to read helped me with my reading.

Part II

Therefore, make sure you also consider how individual sounds relate to spelling. Phonological/orthographic word activities can help to make the links, but taking this into text reading can also be useful.

## 5.4.2 Phonological/Orthographic Activities

Each of the made-up words on the left sounds like a real word. What is it?

| heet | ... | [heat] |
| gerl | ... | [girl] |
| cheaz | ... | [cheese] |
| munth | ... | [month] |
| hork | ... | [hawk] |
| stricked | ... | [strict] |
| coff | ... | [cough] |
| gaje | ... | [gauge] |
| manoover | ... | manoeuvre |

Try to think of more made-up words that sound like real words.

One of the tricky aspects of English that this exercise indicates is that we can use different letters, or combinations of letters, to represent the same sound. Being aware of this, and building up personal strategies to deal with this complexity, is one way to reduce word decoding errors and, in particular, to improve spelling. Some of the examples that follow may help with developing your own strategies, but again be creative – and make sure that the silly versions do not become the 'correct' versions. The idea is to use these activities to help with practice, and in some cases understanding.

Literacy and Language Issues and Strategies

The first task/activity comprises pairs of 'words': one is a real word and the other is a made-up word that sounds like the real word. Which one is the real one?

For example:

**Munk**      monk

(The answer is 'monk' because it is spelt correctly, whereas 'munk' is not: remember 'monks come from monasteries'.) Additional linking can help: monasteries have money and sometimes monkeys !

Now try:

| gote | goat |
| blume | bloom |
| ski | skee |
| tortace | tortoise |
| guard | gaurd |
| fude | feud |
| relevent | relevant |
| believe | beleive |
| seperate | separate |
| peice | piece |
| necessary | neccesary |

Some of these we have taken from examples of spelling mistakes made by dyslexic and non-dyslexic individuals. Note that the two versions can be very similar. As one of our contributors said,

> One of the most helpful things my coach told me was that when I spell a word wrong it is usually only one or two letters wrong, not the whole

Part II

word. Now I work out which small bit is wrong and learn that – my spelling is much better.

It may even be useful to build up an electronic list of key words that you struggle with (i.e., those you use in typical work days), noting the correct spelling alongside the incorrect forms that you use. Again, awareness of the problem can help avoid it. Some of the tasks/activities given here can also help with spelling choices, but practice with the correct form is probably the main way to avoid errors.

### 5.4.3 Morphology/Orthography Activities

Links between morphology and orthography can also help with recognising parts of words, which can then support decoding and spelling. Try making words out of the following by combining two or more. For example, 'earth' and 'worm' can be combined to form 'earthworm'. This is a compound word; a combination of two words to form a third. The list that follows also includes parts of words that are not found independently in writing but change the meaning or grammatical function of the word they are attached to. Telling the difference between these sorts of words and word-parts can be useful when deciphering text. These sort of activities can be found in most word-game books and can be useful in developing a recognition of word parts.

| re  | geo  | earth | tract |
| --- | --- | --- | --- |
| bio | port | graph | wood |
| ex  | worm | able  | ology |

Morphology is also related to grammatical (or syntactic) forms. These can also be useful in understanding and producing written text. Have a look at the pairs of words here and decide if the second word comes from the first.

Literacy and Language Issues and Strategies

| read | reader |
| bell | Belly |
| piano | Pianist |
| cat | Category |

In a similar way, follow the rule that links the first pair of words, and then complete the following pairs:

| read | reader | dog | dogs |
| bake | … | cat | … |
| art | … | mouse | … |

Here is another example. Complete each sentence with a form of the first word presented in round brackets – as in:

(four) In the race, the cyclist came in … [fourth]

The answer to the example is presented in square brackets.
Now try:

(active) The boy was tired after so much …………..
(direct) The ……………..… he gave us meant we found the hotel.
(beauty) We took photos of the …………………… sunset over the mountains.
(eat) Last night I ………………… my first home-grown tomatoes.

## 5.4.4 Word Origins (Morphology/Orthography)

The origins of English words can also help with understanding spelling. Often, inconsistencies in the links between spelling and pronunciation can be found in the word origin, which often links with morphology as much as pronunciation. For example, 'sign' and 'signature' are linked in meaning, and this link has been maintained in spelling even though the pronunciation of the two words has diverged over time. Most good dictionaries can help with examples, but there are also some websites that include information about word origins – and have a look at https://childrenofthecode.org/, as this has the facility to indicate pronunciation, meanings, and origins of words on its pages. A little bit of understanding about the difference between Old English (Anglo-Saxon) words versus Latin-based (sometimes referred to as Romance) and Greek-based (sometimes considered Scientific) words can also go a long way to explain some of the oddities that can plague our attempts to understand English spelling.

For example, why is 'ch' pronounced differently in many words in English? Well, compare the following:

Anglo-Saxon (Old English)
- ➢ 'ch' as in 'chair' or 'chief'

Latin/French (Romance)
- ➢ 'ch' as in 'champagne' or 'chauffeur' or 'chef' (more of a /sh/ sound)

Greek
- ➢ 'ch' as in 'chemistry' or 'ache' or 'orchid' (more of a /k/ sound)

Similarly, why do we use 'er' and 'or' to refer to a person doing something? Again, compare the following:

Anglo-Saxon (old English) typically use 'er'
- ➢ 'worker', 'farmer', 'baker', 'carpenter'

Latin-background words can use 'or'
- ➢ 'actor', 'professor', 'educator', 'director'

Why do we use both 'able' and 'ible'?

Old English words often use 'able'
- ➢ 'passable', 'agreeable', 'breakable'

Latin-background words can often use 'ible'
- ➢ 'edible', 'visible', 'audible', 'credible'

Although this may not help in every case (there are also a lot of English words borrowed from other languages), an understanding of these differences can help with appreciating why spellings can be awkward, and this can avoid some of the frustration often associated with this awkwardness. Having a useful resource to find word backgrounds (a good paper-based or electronic dictionary with such information – or use a search engine on your computer) can help, and although this can be time-consuming initially, the growth in knowledge and understanding can help with personal growth and literacy-based self-efficacy. One of our contributors sums this up well:

> When I started looking at the Latin meaning of words to better understand the meaning/structure of the words, I became really interested in it all – it got easier and I am more confident when I am talking to people now.

Many people with dyslexia can feel apprehensive and frustrated by words, but having the context about how and why words are formed in the way they are can change this and also the way they approach literacy tasks.

## 5.4.5  Semantic/Word Knowledge Games

Although sounding-out words may be a difficulty for some dyslexics, focusing on meaning can help with understanding and hence comprehension. There are lots of word games in books and online, and these can help with developing vocabulary that may have been weakened owing to a lack of reading practice. For example, here is a word meaning activity that can help with the development of links between words. Note that the two words on the left are related in some way. One of the four words on the right shares the same relationship to the left-hand words. Have a go at finding this word and explaining to yourself why you think it is correct.

Part II

**As an example:**

apple   pear   house   carrot   orange   tree

(Orange is correct because they are all fruits)

| items | | | options | | |
|---|---|---|---|---|---|
| car | bike | bus | cheese | shoes | lift |
| nose | eyes | mouth | leg | elbow | arm |
| bake | boil | fry | sun | cake | heat |
| − | + | x | 0 | ? | % |
| brown | orange | green | apple | blue | phone |
| dress | skirt | blouse | trousers | socks | shoes |
| horse | elephant | dolphin | snake | ant | penguin |
| 2 | 8 | 14 | 16 | 12 | 18 |
| typhoon | gale | tornado | flood | snow | breeze |
| poetry | novel | prose | play | statue | program |
| oil | electricity | gas | water | power | account |
| cod | haddock | hake | pike | salmon | roach |
| adverb | clause | hyperbole | cursive | essay | semantics |

Other good word games to help with vocabulary can be found in Clarke et al. (2014).

## 5.5 Second-Language Learning and Dyslexia

The word-based activities discussed here that aim to support first-language users should also assist second-language development

## Literacy and Language Issues and Strategies

among those with dyslexia. This is the case for adults as well as children, though again, most of the focus of work by researchers and practitioners has focused on children. There are some good books coming out on the topic, though, and even if they may target children, many of the activities can be appropriate for adults with or without revisions: see Daloiso (2017) for a good source of ideas, many of which relate to the activities discussed in this chapter.

Adults with dyslexia learning English as an additional language need to learn the connections between writing and language. This requires links with language sounds, but also with meaning. Indeed, vocabulary development is key to language learning (see discussions in Everatt & Denston, 2020). Equally, the relationship between spoken and written language can be a source of development. It is not the case that spoken language has to develop to high proficiency/fluency prior to learning to read. As has been argued, spoken and written language can support each other. Hence, developing verbal skills is still important, but the acquisition of reasonable second-language reading and writing can provide additional sources of learning.

The importance of text understanding means that you should also consider some of the strategies discussed here to support text reading. As an adult, you may have developed some of these skills in your first language, and there are many skills that develop in one language that can transfer to another. Equally, differences between the first language and the new language should increase awareness of language features, which can again provide the basis of understanding and development. Therefore, try some of the activities suggested, but consider how these may be similar or differ between first and second language. Furthermore, many of the technology tools discussed here will be useful (e.g., Košak-Babuder et al., 2019): bilingual dictionaries and listening online, even using translation aids can increase experience and support understanding. There is no substitute to language experience, so find ways that you enjoy to increase your experience and practice and to improve your understanding.

A final challenge that may influence self-understanding for the English additional language learner compared with the English first language dyslexic is the assessment practices discussed in Chapter 2. Most assessments have been developed for first-language users. Often they depend on understanding relatively complex language to complete tasks, particularly some IQ-based measures that assess verbal ability. This can lead to problems when language development has not reached a level that is expected for test completion. Moreover, few assessors have had specific training on testing additional language users. An assessment in a first language may be an option – maybe in a home country prior to moving to a new one (see Elbeheri & Siang, 2022, for information on potential dyslexia-support organisations around the world). However, this may not be an option given the lack of recognition of dyslexia in some countries or the lack of standardised measures (see Elbeheri & Everatt, 2016; Everatt, 2011). Therefore, try to find an assessor who shows evidence of experience of assessing and supporting individuals using English as an additional language.

## 5.6  Text-Reading Strategies

Strategies for decoding words within text can also be useful (have a look at Moats, 2010; and maybe see the resources files about morphemes at https://literacyinnovators.co.nz/sevenplus/). These may be particularly useful when reading longer words. The parts of words covered earlier as part of the morphology tasks/activities can be used to support the decoding of longer words. This can involve recognising familiar words within words (e.g., 'classroom' or 'housefly'; or even 'support'). Make sure that these word parts make sense in terms of meaning and pronunciation, or discuss why they don't (e.g., 'sup' and 'port' work in terms of pronunciation: given that they are said quickly, the two 'p'-sounds blend together, but splitting the word in this way does not help with meaning – 'support' is not a word that refers to the drinking of an alcoholic beverage).

Breaking words into familiar parts can sometimes also aid the processing of smaller units of sounds to improve phonological decoding strategies. Equally, the use of morphological units can be very useful in breaking a long word into smaller parts (e.g., 'dis-engage-ment') – and considering why these parts produce the target meaning can support vocabulary development. This likely includes mostly known morphemes (the 'er' in 'baker'), but it can also be used as a way to teach relatively new prefixes or suffixes (e.g., 'ex' in 'exchange' or the relationship between 'able' and 'ible', which we discussed earlier). Morphological units and their origins can then be associated with orthographic and phonological aspects of the word to provide a set of principles/strategies by which complex words can be decoded and learned (Moats, 2010).

It also helps to work on materials that fit with your needs, as using texts that are related to your background can increase interest and motivation, and facilitate understanding, Clearly, text reading is the goal for adults, and so individual word work may need to be linked clearly with this outcome. Breaking texts up can also help; very long material may seem too daunting to begin with, and so practise strategies that work for you with shorter texts before moving to longer material. It may also be best, at least initially, to select texts with which it is easier to practise strategy use. Practice takes time, so avoid making it too difficult.

One strategy is to select unknown or unfamiliar words from the text for individual word practice, which can then support decoding and vocabulary. Doing this with a new text can also provide an opportunity to apply newly learned decoding skills. If you can do this with a friend, it can provide opportunities for a discussion around the meaning of unknown words. A specific focus on morphological components within the words, especially affixes, can again provide strategies for developing an understanding of text; though typical vocabulary learning/teaching methods should also be considered with new words.

Taking time in reading can be useful (as discussed earlier, it is one of the main strategies used by many adult dyslexics). However, reading fluency can be targeted by repeated reading. Maybe try initially focusing on sentence reading before moving to paragraph reading and then longer text reading. Breaking up paragraphs into manageable chunks can also help comprehension and recall. Practice is probably the best way to support fluency of reading, but remember that word decoding strategies take time, so reading may have to be slower at times.

## 5.7 Reading Comprehension Processes and Strategies

The strategies and activities given here aim to develop understanding of elements involved in reading and writing. Implicit in the activities is the development of metacognition. Good readers often use the purpose of reading to determine how best to read a text. This can involve differentiating between types of reading, such as scanning or skimming to find an answer or fact, versus analytical reading when depth of understanding is needed, as for course texts, versus reading for enjoyment, where the focus may be more on surface detail rather than linking information with past knowledge. They read for purpose as well as meaning. Typically, good readers also question the text they are reading and monitor their comprehension. Depending on the purpose, they may record or note salient facts for later recall.

Many dyslexic people do not read in this way, tending to over-focus, with the emphasis being on decoding rather comprehension. Re-reading over-and-over again may be the only strategy even if the necessary material has been absorbed in the first or second reading. Decoding is obviously important, but the need to decode every word can sometimes be the cause of poor reading strategies. Developing a metacognitive approach and thinking about your reading habits may help refine your skills. Now we turn to some of the main areas that can support text comprehension, including decoding. We also look at vocabulary again, before focusing on strategies that can help to derive meaning from multiple words.

Decoding skills support words read in text, as mentioned earlier. Another related strategy involves pre-learning key words that appear in a text. A difficult word in a text can inhibit comprehension and enjoyment. Therefore, consider identifying and decoding such words prior to text reading. This can support understanding and fluency of reading. Both how to pronounce the key word and what it means should be considered, so as to connect text with language and meaning. This strategy can be useful in reducing the number of words misread during reading of the text. This can also be seen as a pre-reading strategy (discussed in due course) as it can also be used to help the reader to begin to think about the content of the material they are about to read (see also Thiede et al., 2003). Furthermore, some technology resources can help if word reading is a major obstacle to understanding (e.g., we mention text-to-speech software later in the chapter).

Selection of key words is important; it may depend on the level of reading already attained. Based on your understanding of your own reading levels, it may be necessary to ask for help (tutor or friend). However, words that help with the process of extracting meaning are the main focus of such a strategy. The selection of key terminology may also be important, particularly in specific work contexts – these may be vital for understanding work-based reports or papers as part of a course. Considering such words in terms of their phonetic pronunciation helps to link to spoken language. Many dyslexic adults do not attempt this, tending to focus on overall comprehension rather than pronunciation. Understanding the meaning of such terminology can be supported by discussing other sentences that include the word. Taking notes about these key words or building a glossary to have handy when reading the required text can also be useful. This should also help with future text reading within the content area.

Vocabulary used in the text is related to the last point made about terminology. Strategies for supporting working out unknown words in text can help to derive meaning from the text, but also develop word knowledge. Building up word knowledge from some of the activities described earlier in this chapter can be useful, but there are additional strategies that can be used when text reading. Dictionaries (found in books or online) can be used to support text understanding and vocabulary development. Reading with a friend or family member can be helpful in providing opportunities to discuss meanings – and sometimes reading with a child can lead to experience of words in different contexts.

Increasing experience with words can help to develop an understanding of how words can be used in different contexts and can have varying meanings across contexts. This can also help with making links between words and their meanings. Such experience

## Literacy and Language Issues and Strategies

can be increased through text reading, but listening to speech can also help. In normal day-to-day speech, vocabulary can be reasonably limited, so listening to recordings of books can help with expanding vocabulary.

Another metacognitive strategy that aids text reading is prediction, priming the brain about the information in the text. Using questions about a title, or a summary or the first paragraph, helps to predict what the text is about. This allows prior knowledge to aid understanding during reading. One way of doing this is by using a prereading strategy (see also Glover et al., 1990; Thiede et al., 2003).

First, read the title and any headings in a text, and also key sentences, such as the first sentence of each paragraph. Then review the information obtained during this process and consider the information in relation to what you know and why you are reading it. Highlighting title/headings and the first or key sentences can be helpful for focus.

Secondly asking yourself general questions related to the text in order to think about the subject area and to consider what you are about to read in more detail has also been found to be helpful. This pre-reading strategy can be particularly useful with text-to-speech software (discussed later) as it ensures some level of engagement with the text prior to the detailed reading by the computer.

Asking yourself questions about the text you are reading as you go along and using these to make brief notes about the text also help. Using questions to link the text with prior knowledge of the topic leads to increased engagement with the text and greater memory of information. Questions can be literal, about a fact in the text, or require an inference or evaluation.

A key feature of good readers is that they typically monitor what they are reading. This is an important part of developing understanding. Asking if the text makes sense, whether what is currently being read fits with previous parts of the text, can help with the development of understanding and determine if part of the text needs to be re-read so as to re-interpret it. This monitoring plays a role in making connections between parts of the text. This process can also be helped by practising making predictions about what might come next in a text. Again, if what you read does not fit with your predictions, then it may be necessary to re-read to ensure that you have fully understood what the text is about.

Making inferences, or connections from one part of the text to another also increases comprehension. Asking questions about why you are reading the text should help with making these connections and with inferring meaning. Evaluating or making personal judgements about a text can also help with making connections with prior knowledge about a topic. Again, discussing your views about a text with a friend can help. Evaluative judgements also provide a basis on which to encode information in memory for later recall.

Summarising is an important study skill. This strategy typically involves highlighting key sections of text and making summary notes at the same time as reading the text. Breaking the text down into sections, either individual sentences or short paragraphs, then either highlighting key points and/or writing summary notes down the side of the text, can be useful. This helps with the process of reviewing what has been read and interpreting it in your own words, which brings in prior knowledge again. Making a summary of the text based on the notes also aids understanding and retention. Clearly, this is a good study skill for most students, and therefore examples can be found in most study skills books (have a look at Du Pre et al., 2007, for some ideas about study skills specifically for adults with dyslexia). Again, practising this strategy can be useful when using text-to-speech software. Although the computer provides the accuracy, you still need to do the understanding bit of the reading process. Mind-maps can be useful for those who do not like a lot of writing.

Mind-maps, concept mapping, or graphic organisers (see review by Kim et al., 2004) are tools aimed at helping put ideas into an order that makes sense to the individual, and are also part of the engagement with a text and its ideas – forming a map can be as useful to some as writing summary notes. This can be when trying to take in information, as in reading, and also when trying to produce something coherent, as in writing.

There are slight differences between the three types of visual organisers referred to here, but they follow the same principle of putting key ideas into a diagrammatic form to help with understanding and learning the information in the text – and all provide a method of engaging with text. Mind-maps are the main type discussed in terms of dyslexia, as they can be highly visual in form and avoid using lots of text. However, the process of mapping may not be for everyone, and sometimes it is not always intuitively understood, so try several to see which (if any) works for you – there are many examples on the Internet.

The use of colour highlighters to structure the map and make links between key information can also be worth considering; this can also make the map more interesting and help with structuring ideas (similar colours go together). Start with shorter texts to learn the process and then move to longer texts. Although the goal is to reduce the level of writing, making written summaries of a text can help some with initial learning of how to use mind-maps or graphics. Once you get the feel for them, then the map or graphic can become the summary. There are plenty of examples of these online to play with. Some find these one-page overviews very useful for learning, and particularly for revision, though others find summary texts easier. It may be a case of trying both to see which one is preferable.

Part II

## 5.8 Technology Supports

One strategy that can help students with low levels of word decoding/recognition ability is the use of computers with text-to-speech software. This electronically reads material to the individual. Such software is often recommended as a compensatory strategy for students with weak decoding skill, such as those with dyslexia. The aim is to aid comprehension of material despite problems with decoding/recognising individual words. Clearly, this is not going to be a major strategy to help learn how to read words, as there is little explicit teaching of meaning and there is the possibility that the individual can become a passive listener. However, it can allow access to material at a time when speedy reading and understanding is necessary. Typically, it is good to try to read along while listening to the text, as this can aid word recognition skills – though this cannot replace explicit teaching of word reading strategies.

For such technology to be useful, the material has to be scanned into a computer, although increasingly mainstream packages are providing a read aloud facility that is effective for all Word documents. It is also a good idea to ensure that all words are pronounced by the software in a way that can be understood. Learning or being trained on how to use this software increases the likelihood that it will be effective. Try varying the speed at which the software reads the text until a preferred speed is obtained.

Being able to vary the text in different ways can also be useful for reading text online: for example, the text font can be made larger or smaller, or the background colour on the computer can be changed. Practice with different presentation formats (both text and speech) can help as this may not be intuitive – and starting with shorter passages before moving to longer texts is also useful. Strategies for stopping and re-reading sections should also be considered as this helps understanding and avoids passive listening. Practising ways to help with engagement in reading or thinking about text should be considered. Passive listening to spoken text is not the most effective way to understand and retain information. Therefore, some of the strategies noted later for 'questioning' the text should also be considered.

In addition to supporting reading, mapping software can also support putting ideas together to produce text. This uses the same principles as mind-maps/graphic organisers that we discussed earlier, but with the computer forming the maps for you: you have to know what key elements to put into the computer, so you have to engage with the text if reading or come up with the key ideas if writing. This sort of organising software has grown in sophistication over the years. There are now some online applications that can virtually write the text for you. Remember, though, that you still need to provide the key concepts for such systems, so you need to understand the topic – and also that if the computer writes the text for you, it does not help with memory. And how much more embarrassing if you cannot discuss with a colleague or team leader what you have submitted as your own report? However, there are a range of impressive applications around, so find one that works for you and in the context in which you are working.

Alternatively, voice-activated software can be very useful for producing text. You say what is needed, so it is your work, but the computer does the spelling for you. However, learning how to use this technology is vital – as well as the technology learning your accent. Learning dictation skills can help; you also have to plan what you want to say. In addition, it is very important to proofread what has been written, as the computer can make mistakes: it produces what it hears with no reference to context.

Therefore, don't assume that technology can replace everything. It is part of the tool-kit of strategies, and like all strategies should be based on individual circumstances. Having said that, if you are producing your own work directly into a computer, spell checkers are an important tool for most of us (dyslexic and non-dyslexic alike). Most word processing software includes spelling and grammar checking facilities, and these can be incredibly useful. Again, remember that they cannot help with some of the more unusual ways that a dyslexic adult may have learnt to spell a word, so more individualised spell checkers might be useful in addition to the general versions found in word processors. Again, get used to the system used in the relevant application and use it strategically.

One of the main challenges with technology is that it is an area where things change very rapidly. This means that there are some very useful tools out there, but keeping track of what is available would be a full-time job. Additionally, most applications are commercial products and independent assessment of their usefulness can be hard to find, as they change too quickly for reliable assessment. However, have a look at a couple of the following as examples of websites that discuss what is out there:

> https://bdanewtechnologies.wordpress.com/;
> dyslexiahelp.umich.edu/tools/software-assistive-technology;
> www.dyslexiafoundation.org.nz/assistive_technologies.html;
> www.lexdis.org.uk/guides/technology-guides/.

Given that the market changes very rapidly, and that sales are often the motivation behind producing a tool, rather than support for the user, look at a few for comparison: try to avoid information from just one website unless it is a trusted source.

Similarly, there have recently been great advances in applications on the mainstream platforms: most have a read aloud, an editor, and

## Literacy and Language Issues and Strategies

a speech to text function, and although these are not as good as the specialist software, they are sufficient for many dyslexic adults.

Having said that, there are some very interesting things happening on free web pages. Have a look at https://childrenofthecode.org/ and try the 'click on a word' ('PQ Pop-Up') feature. Make sure audio is on so you can hear the computer talk to you about the word. This sort of feature can make electronic/computer resources incredibly useful in allowing access to text even for those who have major problems with decoding. And maybe look at the 'browsealoud' feature on the IDA website: https://dyslexiaida.org/dyslexia-at-a-glance/. Finding a range of websites that fit with your needs is useful: these can be the ones you go to when they are needed, rather than trying to search for material on an ad hoc basis. A search can be time-consuming and distracting, so planning ahead is vital.

# 6

# Effective Communication

## Overview

Effective communication is an increasingly essential skill for many jobs. Chapter 5 looks at the problems experienced by dyslexic people at word and text level. This chapter focuses on how those underlying difficulties might present themselves in wider contexts, both written and spoken, in the workplace, such as producing documents, taking notes, attending meetings, and so forth. It presents an overarching metacognitive strategy, the 4 Ms, as a possible solution. It also explores the following areas:

1. Reading, writing, and proofreading at work.
2. Making notes and taking minutes.
3. Listening and speaking at work – including meetings, presentations, and interviews.

## 6.1 Introduction

The demands on literacy and language skills in the workplace are constantly changing and increasing. The technology tools we discussed in Chapter 5 were once hailed as the dyslexic person's saviour. However, for many, the increasing volume of emails and Word documents, as well as the need for speed of production, is becoming a major problem, meaning that some strategies/tools may not help. The period from 2020 to 2022, with many working from home during the COVID-19 pandemic, led to a formidable growth in virtual/online meetings, a further increase in emails, and the need for additional written documentation. People can no longer have a 'quick word' to discuss an issue – it is more likely to be formalised within an online working environment. Furthermore, working on shared or 'live' documents (working on the same document online) can increase the need for literacy multitasking, which can be extremely daunting for the dyslexic person; their literacy skills are on view for all to see.

Every one of our contributors mentioned that some aspect of written or spoken communication was a problem at work. These problems included dealing with emails, writing reports, reading documents and abstracting information at speed, taking notes in meetings, participation in meetings, and giving presentations. For some, it was a frustration. For others, it undermined their performance and their confidence, becoming a barrier to promotion. Some also felt that their managers did not trust them to do a good job because their literacy was weak. Many were aware that these language-based tasks were much more effortful for them than for their colleagues. Sometimes they found such tasks exhausting. This is not surprising, and we have discussed earlier in this book (see Chapters 1 and 5 in particular) weaknesses in reading and writing – how such difficulties

Part II

can continue into adulthood and/or how reading/spelling may not be as automatic for people with dyslexia as for others. This may mean that more effort and concentration is required when dealing with reading and writing tasks, and that more energy is expended. Taking a metacognitive approach to any literacy task, however, should make it feel easier. One overarching metacognitive strategy, which can be applied to any task but may be particularly useful for reading, writing, and revision, is described here. This strategy is a refinement of one devised by David McLoughlin (see McLoughlin et al., 2002): the 3 Ms idea that things are made **m**anageable and **m**emorable through the use of **m**emory aids. This can reduce the processing load and makes both input and output of information more effective. We have modified this idea and added a fourth element '**m**aking it **m**eaningful'.

## 6.2    The 4 Ms Principles

### 6.2.1    Make It Manageable

Ask yourself how you can best do this. One way is to break a task into manageable chunks. This involves planning and task analysis, which are executive functioning processes: analysing the task by breaking it up and identifying the easy and new/hard bits so that each can be dealt with one at a time. This sort of analysis also means that it is more likely that the information will be dealt with more efficiently. As stated by one of our contributors:

> I used to take a 'begin at the beginning and work through' approach. I now stop and think and off load all that needs to be done. I try and organise it and I try and estimate how long each bit might take. Often then I will do part of it when I have a gap – or set a time slot aside in my

day to do it … it often takes longer but at least something gets done. This also helps me get started as I am very good at procrastinating.

## 6.2.2 Make It Meaningful

This involves thinking about what you already know about a subject. Find the context for the work, make links and associations, and use questioning to help with engagement and understanding. Ask key questions such as what is my aim, what can I predict, what is relevant to my goal.

## 6.2.3 Make It Multisensory

How can I process the information more effectively? Try to make it more interesting, more memorable. Should I talk it through in my head, listen to it, use a read aloud facility, discuss with others, draw a diagram to conceptualise it; make notes or a mind map it before I start to read or write? Try to make it fun, as learning is more effective if this is the case Again, one of our contributors sums this up well:

> If I have a big project, I map it out and find the quick wins – (easy to do bits). I do those first – it helps me get started. I then look at what I need help with or things that are dependent on other people and sort that bit. Then I feel I can crack on with the rest.

## 6.2.4 Memory Aids

These are essential; we all need them – and the number of stationery shops selling to-do lists is evidence of this. We have looked at ways to aid memory previously, but a quick note in a diary, or on a phone or whiteboard or Post-it note, can be the trigger to good recall. In today's world, a mobile phone is usually to hand, and you can make written or verbal notes or send yourself a text as a reminder. Alternatively,

> I use Post-it notes for everything. Memos of course, but I even plan my reports with them. Different ideas on each note, then I can move them around and then write.

Considering the 4 Ms elements separately can make a task feel easier, especially if it is a big task. Furthermore, the increased awareness of what exactly is involved to complete the task also helps with multitasking and prioritisation as you can switch between tasks more efficiently. For example, you can make a cup of tea and butter a piece of toast simultaneously if you know to butter the toast while the kettle is boiling! The key bits to remember are what your goal is and how to make the task manageable? – how best can you do it.

## 6.3  Reading at Work

There are few jobs these days that do not require some reading. It may be reading daily rotas, lists of instructions, update texts, addresses of deliveries, health and safety instructions, emails, incident reports, correspondence, business reports, project reports, tables and graphs, or spreadsheets – and so on. Most of the contributors that we spoke to while writing this book had developed their reading skills to a competent level and were in roles that had quite a large number of administrative tasks. They all reported that reading was challenging, and that speed, volume, and assimilation of information were the main problems. We discuss elsewhere (see Chapter 5) a range of ideas related to supporting reading ability and comprehension, and potential assistive technology tools, and we discuss some of the strategies used by contributors in Chapter 7. However, to summarise these ideas, here are the thoughts of one of our contributors who works amid a high volume of written material as a university lecturer.

## Effective Communication

There are several areas of work where I am impacted by dyslexic-related difficulties. My reading speed is very slow and I lack fluent comprehension of texts, so tasks like marking essays and reading documents take me much longer than my peers. I particularly hate being asked to read and comment on something on the spot, since the pressure makes my brain 'freeze' and I stop being able to understand what I am reading.

I always used to struggle with turning around coursework marking in the required amount of time – the university sets quite tight deadlines for returning feedback to students and we get into trouble if we don't meet them. Working with my dyslexia coach I developed certain techniques for planning and approaching the marking (e.g., dividing the essays into groups depending on what topic they are on and how good they seem to be; skim reading the essays first so I can work out the gist before moving onto the detail; working on the more time-consuming essays at a time of day when I am most alert; knowing what I am looking for before I start marking an essay, etc.). I also try to set limits on how long each essay should take me – this is difficult and there are always essays that take longer than anticipated, but it does help to set some boundaries around the task.

When I write, I sometimes have a tendency to miss out or mix up small words, and proofreading takes me a long time, as I don't always seem to spot the mistakes I have made. I also struggle with multitasking as far as language is concerned – so participating in a meeting and making notes at the same time is almost impossible, as is trying to teach a class and write on the whiteboard.

I think universities can be a rather strange environment to work in, since there is often quite good awareness of how dyslexia affects students, but very limited knowledge or understanding of how it might impact on staff. In fact, there often seems to be an assumption that university lecturers, particularly in arts and humanities subjects, cannot possibly be dyslexic.

**Identifying structure in a report or article can also facilitate comprehension. For example, academic papers nearly always have an abstract,**

followed by introducing the work and providing a background; there is then usually a methodology, results/analysis, and a discussion/conclusion. The paper is already broken into chunks and people know what to expect in each section, so can find information they are looking for relatively quickly. Knowing this means that it may not be necessary to read the paper from start to finish: reading the abstract and discussion may be sufficient for the purpose of some readers. However, if the evidence leading to the conclusion is needed, then reading the results/analysis section may be necessary, along with considering the methods used to produce the results. Again, purpose of reading is vital here, or you are left needing to read everything.

There can be similar structures in reports, whether they be a diagnostic (medical or educational) or business or legal report. Nearly all have an initial/executive summary, followed by background information, then what actions were taken to produce the report, and/or an overview of the problems to solve. This is typically followed by conclusions, suggestions, and recommendations. Again, this sort of structure makes reading (and also writing) more manageable for everyone. It means each bit can be focused on separately. Familiarity of where to go in a report, the job-specific terminology used, and what to look for given your purpose in reading can significantly speed up the process.

A very good example of this and potentially a good way of practising these metacognitive skills is to read a newspaper. This is not so easy to do in the online versions but is particularly relevant for broadsheets, which are broken up into sections. It is important to note that the writing style changes according to the section in which an article is included. The first few pages are usually the headline stories. They are generally factual, and an article is often written chronologically. The next few pages have more detail and some analysis. Back pages can be factual reports of sporting events, with the penultimate back page including analysis of games or outcomes. Writing style often differs between the factual reports and the analytical sections. Writing style and phraseology also change according to the sections within the paper; from opinion columns, to lifestyle, to general interest or entertainment. For example, a lifestyle or entertainment section will often be written in the second person – it talks to you. Practising identification of these more subtle aspects of the written language can help to build reading speed and improve comprehension, as well as potentially improve writing style. Likewise, identifying signal words such as 'an important aspect', 'first', 'finally', and 'in conclusion' can provide you with a clue about what is coming up, not only helping with comprehension and focus, but also helping you to structure a line of thought when writing.

## 6.4  Writing at Work

For many dyslexic people, it is writing that is the most laborious task: the production of paperwork, documentation, reports, emails. As one contributor put it,

> After a day of report writing I can barely speak – it's almost as though I have run out of words.

Writing involves spelling, which we discuss elsewhere (see Chapters 1 and 2) as a particular area of difficulty for many. But it also requires producing correct syntactic aspects of sentences and correct grammar, both of which can also create challenges. In speaking, mixing words up may not be a problem, but doing the same in written text and getting grammar elements wrong can lead to your reader struggling to follow meaning. And precise grammar is something we generally learn through interacting with texts rather than speech. Writing also requires the recall of information and determining the purpose of the writing, and decisions about how best to present the information given; for example, a report has a very different purpose than an email. There also needs to be coherence between elements of the text: one phrase or sentence needs to be consistent with the next and all subsequent elements of a text. There is then the physical process of writing, either in terms of holding a pen and the movement coordination required to produce letter shapes/formation and other written symbols, or in the hand–eye and primarily finger–hand movements involved in learning to type. Typing is the preference for most people, as it requires less precise physical movement/coordination than writing with a pen, and it has the benefit that typing into a computer allows errors to be rectified very easily via the delete button and spelling and grammar checkers. However, typing has to be mastered, and so involves practice. Poor typing skills can equally lead to frustration when correcting typing errors. This is time-consuming and can interrupt the flow of thought.

The starting point when writing can be a problem for many (dyslexic or non-dyslexic) – it is the basis of what is known as 'writer's block'. Just starting something seems impossible. This can stem from feelings related to the size or difficulty of the task ahead. Again, breaking it up can help. Focus on producing discrete portions – one page a day may be enough – or producing drafts of the first and last paragraph. Getting over the initial worry of starting a big task just by writing something, even if it is not very good, can lead to getting the job done – it can always be revised. Employing the 5 Ws strategy from Chapter 4 can help generate ideas, maybe in the form of a mind-map. Then each section can be dealt with bit by bit.

As with reading, it is helpful to identify the purpose of writing: is it to document an action, to inform, to propose a new idea, to answer a question? Knowing the purpose can help frame the writing; and it can also lead to identifying the structure. Likewise, knowing the scope and length helps with the planning: is it an outline, an overview, a draft, or the final document? Many dyslexic people strive to write the perfect sentence or produce the perfect document, even if it is a draft. They can then become demoralised when much is changed in the document, even if their task was to start the group writing process. A draft is rarely the final product, but it can start the process and become the basis of a discussion about what should go in the final version. This discussion may lead to major changes, but would not have happened without that initial draft. Therefore, any changes should be seen as constructive and building a better document rather than criticism. Furthermore, while it has to be a good reflection of what was asked for, perhaps the extra effort and time to produce a perfect piece of written work is unnecessary.

Similarly considering the style or form of the written document can be helpful. Different types of writing have different styles/structures. For example, outlining a new process for a team might be best presented in first … second … third … steps. It is normally a descriptive piece of writing. Comparing two processes or products entails analysis and evaluation of different components. Potentially, this is more complicated and requires more planning, but again evaluation has a style. Most books on writing divide texts into different forms/styles, and these can form the basis on understanding what might go into a written document and what should be left out.

For longer emails or documents, planning and outlining the information in an order leads to a clear line of thought and communication. As we discuss in relation to reading, reports and articles often have a set of sections that can help with identifying information when reading, but they can also help to determine what should go into a section when writing. It is worth looking at work templates or colleagues' examples to help with this. There are also good student study skills books that provide advice regarding writing essays and assignments (e.g., Du Pre et al, 2007). Looking at these, or going online for tips, can also improve writing. Even a quick reply to an email can have a planned structure: for example, if answering two questions, doing this in the order of the original email is most obvious, but if the answer to the second question is more important, then perhaps it should come first.

Another example from one of our contributors:

> I make many mistakes when trying to write a quick e mail. I need to write credit reports for both new loans and annual reviews of my existing portfolio. Prior to my diagnosis, I would get agitated as my manager would often pull my first draft to pieces so it felt like I was submitting my work to a teacher. Now we both know about my condition, I am more relaxed and he is more tolerant. We both accept the first draft will need amending, which has removed a lot of pressure from the situation. I now get less frustrated when I make simple errors as I now understand why I make those errors.

Considering the audience and tone when writing is recommended. Determining the right tone may be best determined by reviewing previous similarly focused emails or documents. Should it be forthright and to the point, take the tone of a discussion, or be more informal and friendly? An email may be the latter, but a report for a manager likely requires the former. Language also changes according to role or job. There is a vast difference between medical language and legal language, but sometimes the difference can be more subtle, as between an accounts report and a policy report. Some dyslexic people have difficulty in shifting from one writing style to another, and it can be hard to unlearn habits that have taken time to learn in the first place. Looking at workplace documents with a critical eye can help: how is it phrased, why is that there? Another example from one of our contributors:

> In exec style reports, I used to make it too verbose, but I have polished that with the help of my dyslexic tutor. My workplace is very casual and since I have become a boss I have made it more so. This means the written and oral language used has effectively become how I talk

naturally in order to become an effective leader. Therefore the dyslexia is no longer hindering me in that respect. I also conduct many oral 1-2-1s so again playing to my natural strengths. I believe that the culture is on my side and all written formalities barring a few exceptional occasions will be dropped.

Grammar and spelling are both potential areas of problems for dyslexic people, and sometimes a source of shame and frustration. Once a certain level of literacy competency has been reached, then assistive technology can be a useful tool to overcome many problems. Personal strategies for spelling are suggested in Chapter 5, and going online to explore basic grammar and punctuation can make a big difference. Many websites are for pupils or students, but this makes them more accessible and informative. For example take a look at www.bbc.co.uk/bitesize/topics. Books on grammar can help (e.g., Jackson, 2005), but many can be overwhelming for dyslexic people. They are a bit like recipe books. Try and find the one that appeals to you (maybe check some out in the library). Such tools should be used for dipping in and out, rather than reading from start to finish. There is a logic to grammar, as there is with most spelling (such as the word origins we discuss in Chapter 5). Identifying the logic can take away the fear and dislike that is another prevalent characteristic of dyslexia. Learning to understand and love language (making it fun) should be the goal of any dyslexic coaching.

Proofreading is another part of writing that can present challenges, but again is a skill that can be acquired through practice. Indeed, some dyslexic people are very good at proofreading as they have had to work hard to learn to read and write, and often use an understanding of rules to make sense out of reading and writing. This can mean that they spot errors more easily than their non-dyslexic peers, who may not have the same level of understanding because reading and writing came naturally. However, for others with dyslexia, no matter how many times they check and double-check, they still don't see the mistakes. It helps to know that proofreading in any job should ideally be done by someone other than the person who wrote the original text. Risk-critical jobs, such as nursing or veterinary science, always have drug dosages checked by another colleague.

Tips for proofreading can be summarised:

- Leave at least an hour if possible after writing.
- Change the size or colour of the font.
- Conduct your own error analysis: if you always use the wrong 'their' or 'there' check them; have I left out any little words?
- Check for sentence clarity: what was I trying to say; is it clear who or what I am talking about; is the sentence too long ?
- Is the main idea of the paragraph clear?
- Check for content – have I left anything out?
- Use the read aloud/back facility on your computer.
- Don't do it when you are tired.

Proofreading should be a focus for coaching, either by a specialist or even a trusted and aware manager. Most dyslexic people remain very sensitive to a page of red ink or unhelpful comments, or even helpful comments – see the following quote.

> I have been told that my writing is always beautifully crafted, although I find this difficult to recognise myself, since I know the struggles that it took to get the words on the page. I am also a perfectionist and will not give up until I know I have got something as good as it can possibly be – I think this is partly stems from being told off or shamed as a child for making mistakes in my written work, but it is a trait that has helped me get to where I am now in my career.

Help from others, such as managers, can be beneficial, especially when both of you can see progress. Feedback should be specific and constructive. Likewise, giving oneself feedback should be constructive. What was the error? Should I have known that? How can I avoid it next time?

## 6.5 Making and Taking Notes

Reading and writing are effortful for people with dyslexia. Arguably, making or taking effective notes is more so. The cognitive demands are great, and both input and output of information is required simultaneously, sometimes at speed and often with surrounding distractions. Accuracy in spelling and writing/typing may also be required. Furthermore, sometimes people are being observed: online meetings often involve producing written notes during a meeting that all need to see.

The purpose of making notes is more personal: you need to be able to use the information again. Therefore, it helps if it is in a format that is accessible to you. Some people write bullet points or keywords, others doodle, others draw pictures. Making notes in a lecture or at a conference helps to reprocess information and to learn new information. It can be easier if there are no time barriers, but if this is not possible, determining what to write and what not is essential. Having the text of the talk or handouts in front of you can help. There is likely to be a structure to a presentation as much as to a written paper or report. Previewing by bullet pointing or mind-mapping texts/handouts prior to the lecture or study can enable information to be assimilated more easily during the talk. Using the 4 Ms strategy referred to earlier in the chapter may also make a difference. Notes for personal use can be creative, pictorial, colourful, and even enjoyable/fun.

Taking notes in the more public format of a meeting room may be more pressured as others may be able to see what you are writing and it might be time bound. Again good preparation and planning can facilitate the process. Understanding the reason for notes (to inform, to send to colleagues, or just not to forget what to do) can help in terms of knowing what needs to be recorded and what does not. Some people jot down keywords, while others try to write verbatim. The latter can be exhausting, but it is the way many dyslexic people have

> always done it as I can't work out what is important quickly enough or find the word to sum it up.

> If I don't write everything down it makes no sense and I can't remember it.

Identifying keywords/ideas can be hard particularly under time constraints, and it can be even more difficult to change a habit that has formed under situations where is may be useful, but practice and preparation can help. Another example:

> I used to take loads of notes – now I listen and write down things that make sense to me – I make sure I review my skimpy notes as soon as I can on the same day and I then dictate more detailed notes onto my laptop. I have found I can usually remember more than I think. I ask others too now when I am stuck.

There are occasions when verbatim notes are what are required from a meeting. It may be assumed that taking minutes is a task that dyslexic people cannot do, owing to the need to multitask with words. However, planning, perhaps through using an agenda, identifying speakers by their initials, looking at the last set of meeting notes and predicting what might be the outcomes from the current meeting, knowing who to go to if there are any gaps in your notes, having an action points column, and asking others to sum up can all make the task more manageable.

## 6.6  Listening and Speaking at Work

Many dyslexic people say that their listening and spoken language skills are very good. They are articulate, and can express themselves clearly. Indeed, they may prefer to gather information by talking to people. They often opt to pick up a phone or arrange a Zoom call to get information. They may volunteer to do presentations or to chair meetings as a way to ensure that verbal discussion is the way decisions and progress are made. For example:

> I have been told I speak very well. I don't really understand why I can't do this when writing. When I speak I feel free, but whenever I am asked to write something my brain just gets cluttered. What I want to write does not match what is going on in my head.

However, there are also many dyslexic people who find listening and/or speaking challenging. They may process information more slowly than others. They may struggle to find the right word or pronounce the word they have found clearly, particularly if they want to use a long word. These tongue-tied problems can have a huge impact on self-confidence, and hence performance within a work context. It may also influence how they are viewed at work. Another contributor told us:

> I often say the wrong thing or it comes out wrong. I over-explain and give too much info. I feel that sometimes it's a miracle the right thing comes out my mouth. This can be embarrassing, so most times it feels like everyone can talk better than me and explain themselves better.

People who struggle to express themselves verbally are at risk of being misunderstood. As in the quote, what they are thinking may not come out in a coherent form. These difficulties are very visible and can undermine confidence, which can then exacerbate the problem: nervousness can have a negative impact on clear speaking. Likewise, taking longer to process what is being said may mean missing out on essential information and having to ask for things to be repeated, which risks being seen as incompetent. As another contributor commented,

## Part II

> I know what I want to say, I open my mouth to speak and … blank, nothing there. Somebody else invariably jumps in and says what I was going to – I feel so stupid and so frustrated because I knew it. I now don't volunteer much in meetings.

It helps to remember that it is the sound processing system that is at fault, not thinking abilities, and there are solutions to these problems. Listening and processing require being able to identify sounds and construct meaning from them, to link and associate them, to anchor or store them for future use and retrieval. If what is being said is unfamiliar, being said at speed, and/or there is a large volume of material, then there is a great demand on the memory processes and the system can be overloaded. A solution to this is to try to slow down the conversation. It may not be a negative thing to acknowledge that you have missed a bit (others may be glad when you speak up as they probably will have too). If you have missed something, repeating what you have taken in and letting the speaker fill in the gaps can be a good way to get more information, and also to summarise it in a way that makes more sense to you. Interrupting can be hard, and many dyslexic people do not it do it for fear of being seen as silly or inattentive, but it may be vital at times. It can help to have a list of phrases ready so you know what to say. For example:

- That's very interesting – can you say something more about that last bit?
- There are a lot of interesting things here and some of it's new to me – I think I missed a bit in the middle – what did you say about XXX?
- I was busy thinking about your first comment – would you mind just running through that last bit again?

All of these statements are likely to be accurate. Clarification of what is being said is also important because as dyslexic people process information differently, they may take a different perspective. For example, without enough context, viewpoints can be equally valid but very

## Effective Communication

different: 'Can I just check which bug migration we are talking about – are we talking about computer bugs, flu bugs, or creepy crawlies?'

Again, it can help to have a list of phrases to clarify things:

- I think what you're asking is this….
- This is my understanding of the issue – do you agree?
- Can I just clarify, as I want to ensure we're on the same page?
- I like what you're saying – can I just summarise what has to be done?

You might even ask if there can be a note of key issues or ask if you can be sent an email of the key points.

Answering a question on the spot can make more demands on processing. It involves listening to what is being said, identifying the relevant parts, finding the correct information in long-term store, and then verbalising it or writing it down. There is often pressure to answer the question quickly. This often results in the answer 'I don't know', or worse, as the following contributor recounts:

> In meetings, on-the-spot-me finds it hard to come across as confident and better polished, compared to prepared-me, when I swat up in advance. For instance, I flow better when I prepare, but if I am thinking about it when I am speaking it comes across more bitty, I become self-aware of that, and my content becomes more repetitive and in myself uncertain, so eventually I lose myself and other's attention and tail off.

It is important to have a little time to think. This gives an opportunity to retrieve the answer and structure it correctly. Phrases that can gain time are:

- I know a lot about this. Let me think a minute.
- Let me think for a minute because I know this and I'll recall it.
- Oh, interesting! Let me think!
- Could you please repeat the questions?
- OK, I think you're asking this.

Part II

Thinking shows you have knowledge and confidence, so telling people what you are doing usually leads to people waiting for your answer.

Likewise give yourself time to structure your answer with phrases such as:

- Ah yes. Let me organise my thoughts on this for a moment!
- Well, two things immediately come to mind – first … second … and now as I talk, I think this last one is the most important.

Sometimes questions are very open, making it hard to know where to start. For example, answering a question such as 'tell me a bit about yourself' is actually hard to answer as it is so broad. Asking for more direction is very sensible. Statements such as 'Would you like to know about me personally, or my last job, or my skill set?' give you time to think and the starting point.

## 6.7 Lectures, Conferences, and Talks

For lectures, conferences/seminars, and information-presenting meetings/talks, many of the points already discussed should be relevant. For example, spending time looking at handouts or the agenda, and thinking about what the overall purpose is, can make a huge difference. If you are there to learn or gather information, then focus on listening and making brief notes so that you can go back and fill in the gaps at a later stage. The type of notes you make depends on your skills or preferences and the type of information presented. Note-taking may involve annotating or making bullet points, or even producing a mind map. As stated earlier in this chapter, verbatim notes can often be counterproductive as it becomes primarily a dictation exercise rather than a listening and thinking process. For many dyslexic people, listening and understanding and noting keywords is the better option. Recording is also possible, but permission has to be gained first, and time has to be found to re-listen, understand, and make notes to anchor the information presented.

Some information presenting sessions, such as workshops, interactive tutorials, and team training, can require you to participate and contribute. Again, preparation is key. Are you someone who likes to dive in and say your bit first or do you take it all in and comment at the end? Either way, you are engaging with the process, and thinking about what you are going to contribute ahead of time means that the words and phrases used, and information processes, are more accessible.

If you are chairing or leading the meeting, then you need to be prepared to listen, guide, and facilitate the conversation. This sometimes requires you to deal with opposing views and to collate and sum up what has been said. You may not have to contribute much yourself, but you may have to take in new information at speed. This may be hard, particularly if you are not confident in your knowledge base. Again, prepare by looking at the agenda, and make it manageable by breaking up what needs to be done it into sections. Think about the other people in the meeting. What are they likely to say, and either get each person to sum up as they go along or get someone to sum up at the end. Potentially, you may only have to remind people of the action points.

## 6.8   Presentations and Interviews

As mentioned earlier, spoken language can be a strength for some dyslexic people, and so giving presentations or going to interviews may be enjoyable. For others, such things are a nightmare. It is worth remembering, though, that these differences are also true of non-dyslexic people. Many people dislike what they sound like or look like and worry about how they are going to come across. Our contributors reported having the additional fear of forgetting words, mispronouncing words, their mind going blank, and not having a clear line of thought, and so being unable to express their ideas effectively. They worried about sounding muddled and therefore incompetent. These contributors had a range of solutions, from avoiding giving presentations to over-planning and rehearsing for days. They were all aware that they had to prepare and practice and had to have a set of notes to prompt them. It can be useful to observe others to pick up phraseology and ideas, but simple copying is not helpful: developing a personal style is the most important part. Here are some examples from the comments we received:

> I feel sooo vulnerable when I am speaking; it is much worse than the spelling. Everyone can see it, hear it and there is nowhere to hide. I hate it because I know I should be able to do it.

> Working from home has been great, I have developed my presentation skills online. I have everything written out all around me so I don't forget. I am not sure how I am going to manage when I have to present face to face.

> I practise and practise, but often I am still so nervous that I struggle to say long words, so I don't use them and so I sound like a baby.

In this latter case, having confidence to acknowledge that saying long words can be an issue is often sufficient for the people listening to ignore the mispronunciation. Different pronunciation does not necessarily impede communication for people who speak English as a second language, and this is the case for all. We talk in Chapter 5 about the impact of dyslexia at word level and suggest some activities to help. Breaking words into syllables, or familiar parts, can sometimes aid processing sounds to improve pronunciation: for example, 'spec–i–fi–city' = 'specificity'. Equally, breaking words up into chunks based on morphological units (e.g., un–conscious–ly), and recognising where the meaning lies can help with recall.

The 4 Ms strategy can help when going to an interview. How can I best do this? Should I get someone to help or hear me rehearse? What information and resources do I need, or could be helpful, in the planning process? We have discussed using phrases to clarify and buy time to present your answers clearly earlier. It is this sort of preparation that helps you feel more in control, and should help you find the right words and be more able to demonstrate what skills you have. Overall, being aware of your shortcomings and presenting yourself confidently are the keys to success when speaking and listening.

In conclusion, it is worth remembering that verbal language is an essential but can be imperfect tool for everyone. Being aware of your difficulties but being active and positive about the best way for you to communicate can work well for everyone. One contributor explained:

> Digital by nature is a lean and agile culture, which is document light but creation heavy. As a designer that means instead of writing a big requirements doc, I can draw a process flow and a picture and that is job done.

# 7

# Dyslexia in the Workplace

This chapter aims to explore the impact of dyslexia on performance at work. It incorporates the framework of adult dyslexia outlined earlier in the book (see Chapters 1 and 2) along with ideas for strategy development, so that the latter can be put into practice to manage job demands. In the chapter, we explore three main areas: these are the ones our contributors have most commonly identified as challenges over-and-above the literacy challenges discussed in Chapters 5 and 6. These three main areas involve the following.

1. Common challenges in the workplace.
2. New situations or novelty.
3. Workplace training and professional examinations.

The 4 Ms strategy that is introduced in Chapter 6 is something we discuss further here. We finally explore developing job-specific expertise.

## 7.1 Introduction

Dyslexic people bring many skills and strengths to their job, their work ethic and determination being two of them. However, there can inevitably be considerable challenges to deal with. The world of work is a place of continued learning and change. The demands on people to learn new procedures are high, and to change in the face of modern work practices. In addition, the arrival of the COVID-19 pandemic has highlighted the need to be able to cope with change, to adapt to new circumstances, and to develop new strategies as people have moved to working from home. Potentially, any time of transition, frequent change, and novelty can place greater pressure on the dyslexic employee because of the extra processing involved in being in a new situation. In addition, there is also a growing pressure within many work-areas for staff to gain more qualifications or participate in further training.

In this changing workplace environment, self-efficacy and job satisfaction can be undermined. Good career decision-making is important; so in this chapter, we revisit the concept of the goodness of fit and the development of job specific expertise, building on the discussions related to success in Chapter 3. The strategies and suggestions outlined in this chapter aim to build the foundations for work success.

## 7.2 Dealing with Work-Specific Challenges

The challenges our contributors mentioned were many and varied. Therefore, we address the most commonly reported ones here. From our perspective, the workplace challenges generally fell into four categories.

Part II

1. Time management – issues related to multitasking, prioritisation, work overload and organisation.
2. Remembering information – recalling instructions and procedures, as well as people's names, dealing with minutes in meetings, changes in work-roles.
3. The environment – such as dealing with distractions in the office versus working from home and the potential issues related to hybrid working.
4. Coping with stress.

### 7.2.1 Time Management

Nearly all of our contributors said time management was a big problem, particularly in relation to volume of emails or number of meetings. For some, this is only an issue during certain busy periods in their jobs or when they have sudden additional work or training to complete. For some, their time is managed for them. There is structure in the nature of their job, they have appointments and booking systems for meetings, and they acknowledged this helps. For others, time management, and working to tight deadlines, is always a problem. They have to put in extra time to work longer and harder, and then have to cope with the cumulative fatigue. Producing written work and having to double-check what they have written for content and spelling, is a predominant challenge. They also suggest they are putting in the extra time in their own time and working from home made this easier as nobody noticed. As one put it,

> I have to spend a disproportionate amount of time to get it (my work) right (or write haha). Which means I struggle to fit it all in.

As we have mentioned, time estimation can be a recurring issue for many dyslexic people. This can be an essential skill in most jobs, and for some, even getting to work on time is hard:

> I do not know why I am always late – although I put the alarm on early every day but time disappears and I end up rushing to work and arriving in a fluster and needing half an hour to recover. This is better now because I work from home most days.
>
> Some days, I am on time for everything and I fly through my work. Other days I feel as though I am walking through treacle.

This inconsistency presents a dilemma and can be demoralising. One way to manage bad days is to spend a bit longer planning on those days as you need to expect things to take longer. The 4 Ms strategy outlined in Chapter 6 can help with this, especially when considering how you feel about a task, how much energy you have, and how best you can do the task. You might need to manage people's expectations about delivery times and to structure the day with more breaks. We discuss planning elsewhere, particularly in Chapter 4. However, in relation to the workplace, several contributors said that having a designated planning half-hour every Monday morning with coffee (or even on Sunday evening) was essential. It helped to set them up for the week ahead. Here is an example:

> Every Monday morning I start by looking at my outlook calendar for the meetings I have to go to, and think about what needs to be done in preparation for them, how can I best do them. I then list the other things I have to achieve for the week, analyse what is involved, and I plot them in the calendar. This structure helps me feel a bit more in control even though I know it will change. On Wednesdays, I have another designated half hour – if I can – to review how things are going, and on Fridays I will do a washing up exercise – looking at what has been completed and what needs to roll into the next week. I try to do this methodically but when I am really tired, it slips and I will just think about stuff. I have learned since starting this that my week's work never follows the original Monday plan but I do know what I have achieved and in good weeks that is pleasing … and it is very handy as I am always well prepped for management catch ups.

This contribution is a good example of the application of both metacognitive thinking and elements of the 4 Ms.

Another popular strategy that helps with time management and concentration is the Pomodoro approach. This technique was developed by Francis Cirillo in the late 1980s. It involves task analysis and setting specific goals to be achieved within a twenty-five- to thirty-minute period, and then taking a break of five minutes. This method is consistent with goal-setting theory; people achieve more if they set realistic goals, and concentration is improved by working for short periods. Many people find this helpful when they are revising for professional exams. Some people use it to help keep to time on work tasks, but it does not work for everyone. However, the principle of having a small goal and working towards it, then taking a break, is what can make a difference to concentration and motivation.

However, it is essential when planning and managing time to set realistic goals (see discussions in Chapter 4), but it is also useful to remember that plans rarely work perfectly. A plan in this context is a guide, a map. If time slips by, consider why this might have happened and revise the goal. Managing people's expectations also helps: if time is short, do what you can as best you can, but warn your manager it may not be complete and tell them what you have achieved.

### 7.2.2 Prioritisation

One of the biggest challenges in the workplace is being able to prioritise. A quick web search will result in a multitude of techniques. Many are based on, or adapted from or similar to, the time management matrix of Covey (1991). He suggests categorising tasks into four groups that can be placed in boxes:

1. Urgent and important; that is, deadline or crisis driven. Ideally, there should be only one or two task in this box and generally they are easy to identify.
2. Important but not urgent. Arguably, this is the most useful box as it is the planning box. It also specifies time for networking, and rest and recreation.
3. Urgent but not important. This includes the bulk of daily tasks, and so may often be the largest box. Sometimes tasks in this box need to be moved into the first one; sometimes they can be downgraded to the not urgent box.
4. Not urgent and not important. This box comprises things that keep you busy but don't achieve much. They may be the sort of tasks that you need to consider if they are really helping to achieve a goal.

As with all the systems and strategies suggested in this book, it is the underpinning principles that are important to consider. In what way will this work for you – can you adapt it to work in your circumstances? It works well for some people, as it provides a structure that people can work with, and it encourages the cognitive decision-making processes that are involved with prioritising a wealth of tasks. Again, it does not suit everyone, though. Some people do a mind map instead, or 'rag' rate (red, amber, green) their tasks, but the logic underlying the Covey system does help to develop prioritisation skills. For example, one contributor commented:

> Being introduced to Stephen Covey's time management matrix changed my life and helped me achieve so much more. Regular breaks also help me reset.

### 7.2.3 Multitasking

The definition of multitasking is being able to deal with more than one task at the same time. It is an increasing aspect of most jobs, particularly with the onset of technology. We can now even sit on a Zoom-call meeting (on mute and without video) and be doing the washing up at the same time. Trying to read emails or documents while contributing to meetings is likely be much harder as both tasks require similar amounts of attention and similar language-based processes. As such, one task is likely to be done at the expense of the other. Likewise, answering questions about one project when doing another can be challenging – again, the similarities and differences may interfere with each other. It is generally recognised that some people are better at multitasking than others.

In the dyslexic world, some like to be methodical and do one thing at a time so they don't forget anything. In contrast, other dyslexics may prefer to dip in and out of tasks as the variety helps them maintain concentration. In all cases, the crucial factor is the type, and possibly number, of processes that are required for both tasks. If one task is relatively undemanding, then it can be completed at the same time as another task. If a task is new or difficult, and all your attention is required to complete it, then it is unlikely that another task can be accomplished at the same time, and attempting to multitask may not be advisable.

A strategy, or tactic, may help. For example, try directing your attention to one task for a short specific period and then deliberately switch to the other task, and then back to the first, or on to the third before going back to the first. It is this deliberate cognitive control of your attention that helps. However, such attention switching and multitasking can be tiring for long periods, so you may also need to add breaks into the routine. And it can help to make a note or use a memory trigger to remind you to go back to a task and complete it: an asterisk on a paper where you left off; or, if you are washing-up, the tea-towel on the table to remind you to go and finish it.

Task analysis is also an important part of efficient multitasking. For example, as part of the 4 Ms idea, one M is to make things **man**ageable. Task analysis can help with this by allowing you to combine tasks or parts of a task to make them manageable. Ask yourself if you can put elements together to make the whole thing more manageable: can one element be used in a number of tasks? Once you have thought through how to do something, then other important aspects to note are familiarity and automaticity. The more you do something, the more automatic it should become. Therefore, you may be able to improve your multitasking in some areas as you become more practised and expert in a role. However, if all this fails, it may be best to acknowledge that multitasking is simply not the way you work. If it is not effective for you, then try to set out a method in which you can complete all your tasks. Multitasking can undermine self-efficacy if tasks are badly done or not completed.

### 7.2.4 Work Overload

Many of our contributors felt overloaded at work. They felt overwhelmed by the emails and the volume of meetings. Feeling overloaded can lead to feeling incompetent and stressed. Some dyslexic people have said they felt more overloaded during the COVID-19 pandemic as they were working from home. The number of online meetings and emails increased as people attempted to stay connected to their jobs and colleagues. Some people struggled without the momentary relaxations/distractions that can take place in an office, the longer walk to get a coffee, or the lack of others to talk to. The feeling of being overloaded is often more bearable if it can be shared with others – and sometimes even work can be shared to achieve a goal.

One of the best ways to deal with feeling overloaded is to discuss your workload with others, including your manager. Being prepared for this conversation by reviewing your job objectives (i.e., analysing the actual task demands of the job), and maybe producing a mind map or spreadsheet so you can highlight what is realistic to achieve. Putting things on paper or on screen can relieve negative feelings by decreasing the pressure on memory. It can also reduce the fear of having so much to do, particularly if presented in a way that makes tasks look/feel more manageable: they can then be controlled and dealt with one at a time – crossing off a task on a list can lead to a sense of achievement that can make the overall burden more manageable. Considering the importance and urgency of tasks in the list, map, or spreadsheet can also help. Again, a couple of comments from our dyslexic contributors:

> When I sat down at looked at what was really essential in my job – I thought that quite a lot was duplication – so I spoke to my manager in my development meeting – she did not completely agree with me – but I did lose some bits and I felt much better.

> I was totally overwhelmed in my job – my manager suggested I try and work to SMART goals.

The SMART goals mentioned here are a framework to remind you to think about how to make goals more manageable. They are **S**pecific to what needs to be done and when; make goals **M**easurable, so you know what you are achieving and what needs improvement; make goals **A**chievable (we have discussed this several times before); make them **R**elevant to what you need to do (to your objective); and make them **T**ime-bound, so you know when the goal needs to be accomplished. The idea is that the framework is there to help you work 'smarter' with more purpose. This may be useful as a way to think about, and prioritise, tasks that need to be done. Some find this sort of framework very useful and find it helps them to focus. However, the quickest way to deal with work overload is to talk. Communicate what you can do and discuss what is realistic with your manager or colleagues.

## 7.2.5 Organisation at Work

As mentioned previously, organisation overlaps with time management and planning, and covers all dimensions of life and work. Organisation was again highlighted by our contributors as being an issue, some because they felt under pressure to be very organised the whole time:

> I sometimes think I am bordering on OCD

while others felt they worked in a state of permanent chaos:

> I lurch from one task to another and am never able to find documents be in the right place at the right time or complete the documentation in time. I have lost jobs because of it but get another job quickly as I am good at interviews. My current manager despairs of me – but I think he knows I can do the work.

The perceptions of others, such as managers and colleagues, are important here. Appearing to be well organised gives the impression of being in control, and this in turn builds confidence. Therefore, becoming better organised is a goal to aim for. However, this can be hard to achieve, and as with many tasks, it is best to keep things as simple as possible with a goal/outcome in mind. A quick win is to be organised in your work space even when working from home. Keeping desks tidy and clutter free and having a clear desk policy at the end of the day can make a big difference. In addition, when going out to work, some dyslexic people have everything they need in one bag, which is especially useful when hot-desking. They don't have to worry where things are and can concentrate on their work. It is worth making a bit of time on a weekly basis to reorganise and 'reboot' yourself. Another very important advantage of being better organised is that it can help your memory, as you know where things are both physically and cognitively. Therefore, it is worth the effort to maintain some level of organisation.

## 7.2.6 Memory Challenges

After time management, and all the associated elements just described, the next biggest area of concern for our dyslexic contributors was their memory. We explore memory from a theoretical aspect in Chapter 3 and from a personal perspective in Chapter 4. Our dyslexic contributors said that their main difficulties with memory at work related to the recall of names, remembering lists instructions, remembering procedures especially if there had been recent changes, and recalling information for professional examinations, which we address later in this chapter.

Some of our dyslexic contributors commented that they thought their memory and concentration had got worse while working from home. This may not be surprising, and may have happened to many people in similar circumstances. Memory is often triggered (cued) by situations and/or context. We often ask for prompts when talking (e.g., 'just remind me when or where') as these provide a link within memory – and memory aids often do this (e.g., a knot in a handkerchief is not the memory, but it reminds you of what you were thinking when you tied the knot). The environment around you can act in the same way. It can trigger a whole range of memories or a specific memory of what you were thinking about the last time you were in that environment. Walking into a place you have not visited for years can bring back memories. Your place of work can act as a memory jog as much as elsewhere. Being in an office can trigger what needs to be done – this may be the place itself, a Post-it on a desk, a diagram on the wall, a list in a drawer; but equally you may (subliminally) hear or notice something connected to a task that needs to be performed. These sort of memory jogs may not happen at home, which can instead cue non-work memories. Therefore, the memory strategies (Post-its, lists, diagrams) may need to be increased when at home.

Some contributors also mentioned problems with remembering dates and times. This is also likely to happen to many people. A lack of variety, the sameness in the daily routine when working from home, can mean that dates and times become merely labels. They are not necessarily connected to an activity or an actual situation or context. Equally, a timed routine at work can help with keeping track of time: the post comes at 9.30 a.m., a tea break at 11.00 a.m., the manager always looks round the office on Tuesdays. These can all be cues to times and dates that are related specifically to work. The same may not be true at when working at home.

Remembering people's names has always been a bugbear for dyslexic people. Forgetting a name can undermine confidence, with people feeling it diminishes their credibility:

> I feel so rude stupid and embarrassed when I cannot remember someone's name. It seems such an easy thing to do – why do I find it so hard?

And

> If I don't remember a patient's name how can I expect them to trust my judgement and advice?

However, as we have said before, it is important to recognise that many non-dyslexic people are bad at remembering names. This is one of the reasons for the common use of name tags at meetings/conferences or other events. The Thomas Aquinas ideas outlined in Chapter 4 can work well when trying to remember people's names. However, sometimes the best advice is to admit that you are not good with names, and maybe add that you rarely forget a face or reassure your colleague that you recognise them from a previous meeting. As one contributor said,

> Zoom calls can be very handy because the name of the person talking is on the screen in front of you.

It can also be useful to make a mind map, or similar organisational diagram/spreadsheet, of everyone (or the key individuals) at work, indicating what they do and something particular to them to help with memory. Keeping this close, in a book or on a phone, can help, especially in new situations.

Remembering instructions and procedures, especially when they have been changed or updated, can be an issue. Again, the 4 Ms strategy can help. Making it manageable by breaking it into bits, making it meaningful by using logic, making it multisensory by visualising, verbalising, or counting on your fingers, and of course making a note of it (a quick flow chart if it is a procedure or a numbered list with trigger symbols). If there have been changes to the role, then highlighting the changes in different colours can help. It is often harder to remember small changes – memory works best on difference – so exaggeration can help. A personal response can also be effective for memory – is the change better or worse?

### 7.2.7 The Environment

Another common theme for our dyslexic contributors was coping with their working environment. Some people found the distractions in the office, such as noise and constant interruptions, and even the availability of the coffee machine and being able to talk to others, meant that they found it hard to concentrate and complete the task in hand. Many of these people initially found the move to working from home greatly improved their productivity: the peace and quiet, and not having to face commuting, has been beneficial. Furthermore they have been able to develop strategies that have helped them:

> Working from home has been great as I can now manage my difficulties with meetings. I mind map all I might need to say on different coloured

post-its and stick on a board them behind the laptop. I don't need to rely on my memory – nobody realises I am checking my notes and I contribute much more to the meeting. It's going to be hard going into the office.

However, as indicated earlier, after a few months, some people began to struggle with the monotony of their environment. At home, work felt more tedious without the social aspect of the workplace, leading to struggles with motivation. The lack of boundaries between work and home has also meant that some have put in longer work-hours even though productivity may not have increased, and may even decrease through tiredness and demotivation. Here is one example:

> I was really struggling so I sought help. My coach suggested I put some structure into the day so I now have a flexible routine – I try to get up and go for a "commute walk" as if going to work. I get home have a coffee and breakfast and start.

Finding the routine that works for you can make a great difference.

### 7.2.8 Managing Stress and Poor Performance

Stress at work is an increasingly acknowledged problem in the workplace. There is a wealth of well-being advice and programmes available, and it is an area of growing focus for human resources. Stress and anxiety were reflected in our contributors' comments.

- Work overload:

  I never ever finish the day with everything done – it always hangs over me.

- Cumulative fatigue, such as when having to put more effort and time into achieving equivalent goals to their peers:

  I am exhausted by everything right now – just want to do what I have to do and get this exam.

Part II

- Lack of confidence/self-belief:

    I never believe I have done things well – I always think people are being kind.

- Focusing on the negative:

    If I have made one small mistake in a big job but the rest is good – all I worry about is that little thing I got wrong.

- Manager assessment:

    I don't take things in very quickly and my manager thinks I can't do my job, so I try not to ask questions and then I worry about getting it right, and then I get it wrong so my manager feels he is right and I start to think that too – it's a negative cycle, but I love this job and I know I can do it so I am permanently stressed.

- Exam stress:

    As a doctor I have to take loads of exams and I keep failing them. This is now impacting on my work as I and also my supervisors are questioning my competence. I am a good doctor, but without the exams I can't progress – the job is pressurised enough as it is without all this added stress.

There are often complex reasons for stress at work. The people around you, at work and socially, can increase stress levels, and it is worth trying to determine what they are so that you can then work towards solutions. Try understanding yourself and what leads to stress. What practical strategies can you take to reduce stress? Consider how others can help. Feeling stressed stems from feeling out of control. Applying the 4 Ms to your workload can help to identify the sources and what you might manage. Do what you can, but try to ensure it is done positively. Communication is essential. Talk through what is causing increased stress with someone. This might be friends or family initially, then your manager or someone in human resources; though sometimes it is necessary to seek professional advice. Self-help apps can be useful to provide ways to reduce feelings of stress, and advice can be found online in the form of practical strategies. Some are more helpful than others and it is important to do what works for you. It may also be worth trying something different: you might surprise yourself:

> I took up the saxophone – it is amazing – I now roll through the days humming, waiting till I can next play it.

However, dealing with stress can be hard, and if it becomes overwhelming, professional help (health, medical, or counselling) should be sought.

The suggestions here are things that worked for our contributors:

- Plan your day and positively tick off what you have achieved; move what you haven't completed to another time.
- Colour your day with creativity – have some fun parts to enjoy or laugh at.
- Get enough breaks.
- Be nice to yourself – you work harder than others, and you care more.
- Get enough rest and relaxation: anxiety and stress are often increased by extreme tiredness.
- Exercise is essential – run the stress off.
- Yoga or mindfulness or breathing techniques – or 'ground' yourself on a walk.
- Assault your senses with perfume or strong mint tea.
- Positive visualisation and verbalisation techniques.

## 7.3 Dealing with Novelty and Change

The world is increasingly one of change, so it inherently involves novelty. Jobs are frequently restructured, processes are updated, and career structures changed. People no longer stay in one role for most of their working life, and the job market is much more fluid. A few of our dyslexic contributors said they thrived on lots of variety and changes to their jobs. This seemed to be a way to keep them motivated. However, most were more cautious about change, or even disliked it. They did not like moving house, were reluctant to move jobs, and even smaller things such as upgrading their phone was a source of negative feelings. For example, one said

> I hate having to go through the upgrade process on my mobile – it take me ages to remember the new ways of getting it to work.

Another commented,

> I find having to cope with all the change in people and IT systems at work exhausting.

Technology can be a great source of strategy solutions, but its constant change can be a challenge in itself.

Change frequently involves facing new situations. Perhaps one of the least recognised and documented areas of difficulty for many dyslexic people is dealing with novelty, although there has long been recognition that transition to a new school or different level of education for dyslexic children and students can be hard and lead to negative consequences for the learner. However, the same may be true for the adult having to change jobs or seek new training. One possible reason for the dislike of, or caution about, change is that anything new and unfamiliar can require more cognitive processing. Novelty requires the assimilation of new information, potentially placing more demands on working memory and the storage of information in long-term memory. Change may also require unlearning old ways of working – and unlearning can be hard.

Getting a new job is a big change, and usually some planning will have gone into it when looking for and/or applying for the new job. However, it is worth acknowledging the effect that the novelty of the job can have on initial performance. During the period settling into a new role in a new environment, you are likely to feel more tired than usual. In such cases, it helps to be as prepared as possible; to analyse the job demands and identify what is already known and what will have to be acquired. Planning ahead and getting as much knowledge as possible about the work team (e.g., who likes to be helpful, who is the knowledgeable person), the work culture, and the environment is useful. If possible, visit before you start. It is a good idea to see the first week as information-gathering time. Learning new information (new terminology, new places, systems and procedures, and new people, team members and workmates, managers and colleagues) can be exhausting. The extra processing required can mean that dyslexic people take longer to cope with the change, and benefit from extra time to acquire new work skills or work-knowledge. Understanding this and allowing yourself time can make a difference to your confidence in the early stages of the job.

### 7.3.1 Promotion

All of this is relevant when being promoted; except that promotion may not involve a change in location. This is another big change, and again goes better if people can plan ahead. Consider if you feel ready for the promotion and if it is the right time: self-efficacy is an important aspect of going for promotion. Consider whether it is the promotion or your interest in the job that is the attraction: this can help with measuring goals and outcomes. Evaluate how much the job is going to change and what the gaps in your knowledge and skills are. Be realistic about how you are going to be able to fill those gaps. You may need to give yourself (and perhaps ask for) a little longer settling-in time. Knowledge and interest in the job content will improve your job satisfaction. Overall, consider if it is a job that will suit you.

Part II

If you have been working at the level related to the promotion, then it is likely to be easier in terms of understanding the role and having the skills ready to perform the tasks required. If there is not a change in organisation or location, then there may be even less novelty. However, promotion may still present challenges or unexpected consequences. As one contributor reported:

> 'I had been doing the job at that level for months, so originally saw promotion as getting better paid for the same job. However, I quickly realised there was much more accountability – I was totally responsible – the buck stopped with me – my confidence wobbled dramatically until my manager who is also a friend told me to pull myself together.'

Another contributor gave a longer view of the challenges of promotion. Having had the experience of not being prepared for a new job, not passing probation, and losing confidence, a second opportunity allowed him to plan more successfully. Here is what he told us:

> 'I was asked to move to this new role with little warning on temporary promotion – different people – different projects -it felt daunting. But I focused more on me, and how I could prepare myself for moving into it. I thought about:
>
> 1. Understanding the role I was moving to. I asked myself, What do I know – who do I know to get info from – how is it going to be different – what is really important to know in this role.
>
> 2. Making the time to meet and catch up with my new colleagues; I thought ahead about what to talk about.
>
> 3. Being more prepared to ask questions with my manager to ensure I understood what was expected of me.
>
> In the first couple of weeks, I spent time putting together a strategic plan which would allow me to structure my work and provide a framework for the team. This I agreed with my manager, so I felt more able to be on top of the work, one step ahead, rather than in a position where I might have been on the back foot, catching up.

## Dyslexia in the Workplace

On the back of the strategic plan, I have then focused on delegating the work in the plan and drawing on my leadership training to help coach my team, resisting the temptation to get directly involved and understand the details myself.

Within the first month, this has helped me to feel confident in the role; to feel that I am setting a level of direction for the team; and through the supporting tools of OneNote and my project notebook, feel that I am on top of what needed to be done.

In some jobs, part of professional training can involve short rotations between four and six months in a range of different locations. Likewise, some jobs involve short-term project work lasting between six and twelve weeks. This constant change can be very demanding, as one contributor said:

> I didn't realise how hard it was going to be. I hated it. Just as I got used to the environment, felt I knew what I was doing, I was on to the next place. I did learn a lot but it was a struggle. I only survived because my supervisor was very supportive. I finally developed a personal toolkit, everything I needed to work well was in my bag – I had a laptop with all my software and notebooks, pencils, and technical stuff. I also developed checklists of good questions to ask on arriving in the new place. I even tried to do a recce the week before so I knew where I was going – it was less scary.

Changes within a job tend to be smaller than those experienced when changing job or taking promotion (though there may be exceptions when one business is taken over by another, which can lead to larger changes). Small constant changes of procedure or processes are increasingly part of the workplace now. These may involve changes in work-knowledge (updating information) or work routines. An example of this is where a company is bought out – in theory your job can remain the same, but roles/attitudes change to align with a different company ethos/work practices. Again, some planning ahead as discussed earlier can help reduce the negative aspects. Changes within a job can also involve changes of personnel.

These can make the workplace better, but in some cases they can make things worse. In all cases, an understanding of how parts of the job might change because other people do things differently can help. Similarly, good communication (talking things through) makes a difference.

The biggest recent change to the workplace has been the move to working from home because of COVID-19. As mentioned earlier in this chapter, working from home has been really helpful for some people and more worrying for others. It is likely that more types of work will move to a hybrid pattern, with a few days in the office and some days working from home. This will bring a new set of challenges. Most of our dyslexic contributors can see the benefits, but acknowledge that they will have to become better organised. For example, one contributor admitted that they

> spend most of my days in the office chatting and have to work really hard when at home to catch up!

Another strategized their home–office balance:

> I try to arrange most meetings for my office days and the write-ups for my home days, but it's quite a juggling act and I lose track of what is where.

This sort of planning can increase work-efficiency but can also bring challenges, at least initially.

## 7.4   Workplace Training and Professional Examinations

Workplace training is an inherent part of any job. Training can be defined as being taught new skills and procedures through instruction and practice over a period of time. There are many different types of training. Some can be accomplished one to one. Some may be performed in groups both large and small. Training can take place on the job, during face-to-face training courses, or as part of online training courses. Sometimes there is a combination of all three. Training in the workplace aims to ensure that employees have the skills to do their job effectively. However, training is also essential to the individual as it should enable personal growth and career progression. For training to be effective, there has to be active participation by the individual. All too often, workplace training is seen as something to be got through, becoming quite a passive activity. However, the corollary of training is learning, and for that to be effective there has to be interaction with and the reprocessing of information. This is particularly important for dyslexic people as they learn and process information differently.

There are three key principles for learning: preview and preparation, effective processing and reprocessing of information, and positive evaluation. Preview and preparation is a useful tool to use in training. We talked earlier in this chapter about the challenges dyslexic people can have with novelty, because it demands extra attention and processing. This is also true of training courses and learning new information. One way to minimise these challenges is to be well prepared for the training. This involves thinking about its aim. Often, there are course aims and objectives, and it is worth considering these to determine the purpose of the training. Ask yourself what you already know, as well as what don't you know, so you know what you will need to learn. This consideration activates a knowledge base on which the new learning will build. Such previewing should make the course more familiar, as well as making the processing more effective and the listening more interactive. Overall, previewing and preparation should lead to you interacting with the information more effectively, which will lead to better learning and memory.

Part II

The second element is the effective processing and reprocessing of information. People acquire knowledge and skills in different ways, and this can be influenced by the context in which acquisition occurs. This difference may be particularly relevant when considering dyslexic adults as they are likely to have dealt with learning differences through education. We talk in Chapter 4 about why it is important for dyslexic people to know how they learn best. One way is by using all your senses to make more pathways into long-term memory, and hence cues to access memories. Many people just read and hope to absorb sufficient information. This rarely works for most people, and probably even more rarely for those with dyslexia. Some people feel they can understand information better through pictures or diagrams. Others feel they learn best when they are listening to material or even reading it. However, engaging with information creatively is essential. Try reprocessing information into a variety of different formats that are personally accessible – for example, bullet point notes, mind maps, annotated flash cards, cartoons. Putting the information in a form that works for you should make learning, and the application of what is learnt, more effective. Reprocessing information at the end of the day also has a place, particularly if the volume of work is high, and can be a valuable reminder. Brief notes or personal jottings or a type of study log can make a difference, as a brief review and summary of what has been learned helps recall.

The final point is evaluation of learning. Again, consider the ideas presented earlier in this book (see Chapter 4) about positive personal evaluation when working out how to evaluate your own learning. Personal evaluation of how well you have learned what you need to on the course, what skills have you gained, and how you are going to apply/use those skills is important to you as an individual. Monitoring your understanding can be useful to determine what needs to be revisited, and reflection and evaluation can cement the learning. It identifies what went well and what gaps there might be, which may or may not be important to fill. The emphasis in this evaluation is on the positive. If it went well, pat yourself on the back. If it did not, then try to shrug your shoulders and work out how you can assimilate the key information. This may be done with the help of others. A daily personal evaluation can help as it allows you to refine your skills as you go along.

Workplace training is perhaps the best way to learn for many people. Apprenticeships can provide a practical learning environment, and generally everything learned has some relevance to the job. This makes it easier to see the importance of what you need to know. It provides the experience and the practice that are important for developing job specific expertise. Typically with on-the-job training, there is more opportunity to ask questions and clarify. A couple of quotes from our contributors:

> I chose to do an apprenticeship scheme because I did not like school and knew I would learn better on the job. I learnt more from my friends than I did at school. for me it was great – I could work at my speed and ask lots of questions, then I would go home and study the manuals – it was easier because I could see what I was learning. It was still hard work but I made it in the end.

> I had a great manager and she talked me through everything and then let me make my mistakes ... I was embarrassed but I did good learning and my confidence is OK now.

Face-to-face training is often done in groups, which may be different from experiences in an apprenticeship. However, many of the principles already outlined are still relevant. An additional concern for some, though, can be the interaction between the trainer and the dyslexic person. For example, one contributor told us:

> The last training I went on was a waste of time. The trainer kept saying there was a lot to get through. I was embarrassed to ask him to slow down. Everyone else seemed OK with it, so I learnt nothing. I felt as

though I was sitting under a waterfall and drowning. I got my attendance certificate and that was all.

Some dyslexic people love group work. They find talking things through helps to anchor the knowledge. Others, who are articulate and competent in their job, may become tongue tied and shy in a learning situation. As one put it:

> I nearly always ask a silly question … soo embarrassing…. I did it at school too…. Everyone seems to get things better than me Now I feel it's amazing when I say something sensible.

In both the scenarios here, preparing as much as you can for the training can help, but another strategy is to work with another person: going to such a course with a study buddy. Alternatively, finding another participant who looks to be at sea can help: two brains are better than one.

Online training is becoming increasingly popular. This can come in many forms: workshops, presentations, webinars. Some formats are more interactive than others. Once again, the preview and preparation principles are likely to make learning more effective. Workshops are likely to be the most interactive, with chat rooms and breakout rooms giving the chance to talk in small groups. Interactive e-boards and the chat function can give an opportunity for participants to contribute 'live'. Trainers are becoming more adept at designing such workshops to be as interactive as possible. However, online learning may not be for everyone – as one contributor told us:

> I have got so many qualifications over the years – I know I work harder than others and it takes me longer but I get there in the end but this last QA was something else. I had no idea what was going on, the jargon was unreal – why they couldn't use plain English I don't know. I did an assignment and did OK, but I can't follow anything online. I spoke to my old dyslexia coach – he said to try and make sense of it all in my own way before the course and then discuss, but I argued the whole way through – I did and I passed – but never again.

As with everything we say throughout this book, what works for one person does not necessarily work for others. Some people love being able to train themselves using online courses, then submitting a test paper or writing a mini-thesis or portfolio. Others prefer workshops and group work as it gives the chance to bounce ideas around, reprocess, and gain a good understanding. Try to find what works for you and try to make the best of it. Gaining knowledge is the goal: have confidence that you can achieve the goal.

## 7.4.1 Professional Examinations

Success in examinations is much more likely if some revision is done. This can mean increased pressure and hard work, often out of office hours. Juggling the demands of a busy job and having time to revise effectively as well as having a personal life can be tricky. This can often be the time people find out that they are dyslexic. A lack of time to revise, and competing demands, mean that they resort to inefficient ways of revising, and potentially run out of time. The curriculum for many professional examinations can be very broad, and it is often not possible to learn and revise everything – so it helps to be strategic. However, strategies that worked at school or university may not work in the context of a professional examination. There can be too many competing demands on your time and not enough energy for effective learning. It is at this point that some people experience unexpected failure, as they are very competent and knowledgeable in their job. If this happens more than once, it can be the trigger for a dyslexia assessment.

Revising for professional examinations involves revisiting information. Its purpose is to make learned knowledge accessible so that it can be demonstrated in the examination. However, revision can also involve new learning and gaining new knowledge. We have talked about information processing earlier: this is essential for revision because the information is better understood and can be applied to answer the exam questions accurately. In addition, revision should build confidence in your memory to retain and recall the information when answering questions. Again, we have discussed memory several times. However, in this case, the key features are that good memory involves effective information processing, storage, retention, and recall. Usually, we remember best if we understand the information we are trying to retain. Similarly, if we remember things in different ways, this can increase understanding and provide different ways to access the same information. In terms of revision, the following may be useful: classification (grouping information); association (linking information together); elaboration of a topic, for example, by adding other dimensions or making up a story; and exaggeration, using humour or outrageous associations. All can help with retention. Performing these strategies personalises the learning, which again should make it more memorable. Rote learning (learning by heart) can be effective when there is little understanding needed. However, it is limited in its application.

Knowing how you revise best is important, but planning is another essential part of the revision process. We have talked about the value of planning in many other contexts within this book, but it is particularly important for revision. In this context, it means you can decide what to do, when and how best to do it; what strategy to use to best accomplish the goal. We all plan to some extent as part of our daily lives; for example, what to wear or what to eat. Many of us will have a plan or outline of the day ahead, but many people do not plan their revision. They feel it is a waste of time, or they don't know where to start, or they are too frightened as it may reveal how much have they have to do. Some people make a rigid plan but don't stick to it, and it makes them feel anxious. However, planning revision ensures the best use of time, energy, and resources. It is usually ineffective to revise when tired, for example. Planning typically ensures that knowledge is refreshed and accessible. It should improve recall and therefore increase confidence. Flexible planning can decrease anxiety as people feel more in control. They can see they are building their knowledge base if they tick things off as they go along. If planning seems too daunting, try and see it as a map or a guide through a forest of knowledge.

Be metacognitive. It is important that you make a plan that suits you and how you work best. Using the 4 Ms strategy can help. Similarly, ask yourself what you have to learn (maybe develop an overview). Why am I learning what I am? When is the best time for me to learn? Where is the best place for me to learn? Who can help? How can I make it meaningful, multisensory, and what memory aids shall I use? What is the best strategy for this topic? Make a list of topics and have a variety of resources available. Make a flexible timetable: maybe daily and/or weekly.

Start any study session with a quick mental preview: what you already know about the topic, what you don't know, and what you need to know. Then you can fill in the gaps and build your knowledge base. As we have said before, activating prior knowledge promotes efficient learning and also improves retention and recall of information. It is important to tick something off when you have covered it, but also evaluate how well the learning went: it is the learning that is the goal, not just completing a chapter. Keep a log of what you have achieved rather than over-focusing on what hasn't been done. Build in enough rest and relaxation, and exercise if possible. Try not to work too late, as a tired brain and body do not function well. Remember the plan is a guide and will inevitably change with life events, but it is a structure on which to anchor the learning and a revision activity in itself. Plans should be fun, flexible, achievable, creative, evaluative, and effective.

Reprocessing information into a different, shorter format can make it more accessible. It also typically develops a deeper understanding of the topic. If you understand a topic fully, then you will remember it, and you will also be able to use logic to work out answers. Reprocessing information also means you avoid the recognition trap. This occurs when people look at flash cards or read a paragraph and think they know it. However, do they really, or are they just recognising what is on the page in front of them? If the information can be recalled independently without looking at the text, then it has been learned: for example, try a mini-self-test (verbal or written) to check that you can recall the information without it being in front of you.

Practising exam questions is clearly important as a form of preparation for the exam itself. It helps to be familiar with the format, so that you know what to do on the day. If your exam is a mixture of question types, try to work out which ones you like the best and think why. If you really find multiple-choice formats hard, why is this? Is it knowledge, or reading and interpreting the question, or trusting your judgement to find the correct answer? Look into where the challenges may be as these can be the basis of finding a solution.

An examination can be likened to a mental marathon. As with running 26 miles, it is a good idea to build up your stamina for the day. In the weeks before the exam, practise doing a certain number of questions in thirty-minute batches and take a mini-break. Then do the next set of questions for thirty minutes, and build this up to the exam time-equivalent. This is to familiarise yourself with the actual examination process as well as a self-test. When reviewing your answers, try and work out why you got them correct. If you got one wrong, consider whether it was lack of knowledge, misinterpretation, or misreading the question, or was it poor recall? Then address the problem, so that you increase the chance it will be correct the next time. Remember you are likely to do better in the exam as your adrenalin will be higher, although hopefully not too high!

An examination, whether oral or written, is a performance, so rehearsal is good. Many people like to do a mock examination. This can be useful as it allows you to practise your time management and exam strategy. But it should be viewed with caution. A mock examination usually does not take place under real examination conditions, so performance will not necessarily be the same as on the day. It should be used as a familiarisation process, rather than a test of how the real event will go. If you are going to do a mock, it is advisable to do it at least two weeks before the actual examination, so that you can refine your performance. In oral examinations, many people find practising with others is the best way to be ready for the actual day.

Thinking about the actual day and deciding what you are going to do before, during, and after the exam can give you confidence. It can relieve the pressure and stress you may be feeling. Some stress is good as it can help focus the brain. But too much stress should be avoided as it can get in the way of performing the task accurately – you focus more on the stress than the task. Know the route to the exam venue and what you need to take with you. Think about what you are going to wear, as it helps get into the exam mindset. Be strategic and pragmatic.

People and society place a huge value on exam success, and it can be important for career progression. However, an examination does not always determine whether people are good at their job or not. Some people are just good exam-takers. In contrast, many dyslexic people are often not good at written or spoken examinations. This is not down to a lack of knowledge or ability. Often, it is more a lack of self-belief, bad past experiences in examinations, and the challenges placed on the processing skills. The more comfortable people feel about their revision and exam preparation, the more likely they are to succeed. As one contributor noted:

Part II

> I actually enjoyed my revision in the end – I liked the learning, doing it my way, and it was good when I went into work and could give people advice – it gave me more confidence in doing my job even though I had to resit it twice.

## 7.4.2 Developing Job-Specific Expertise: Goodness of Fit and Finding Your Niche

The whole purpose of any type of workplace training or examination is gaining work-related knowledge and improving your work skill set; that is; developing job-specific expertise. We have touched on expertise in various places through the book, though particularly in Chapter 3. Metacognitive thinking is a prerequisite or antecedent of developing expertise and it is inherent in many job roles. Those involved in sports plan tactics ahead of a match or race. Actors plan how they are going to interpret a script. Hairdressers think ahead about the weight of hair and shape of face. Successful business people engage in planning through a business strategy, and then usually conduct a 'lessons learned' activity. Similarly, those in the emergency services and the army engage in planning, monitoring, and debriefing (or reflecting) at a personal and team level after an incident. This cognitive deliberation is aimed at minimising risk and achieving better performance in the future. Furthermore, reflective experiences mean that when something unexpected happens, it is more likely that an immediate solution will be found.

However, we are talking here about job-specific expertise – becoming expert in the individual tasks that make up a job role. Arguably, it is more important for a dyslexic person to embrace the concept of task-specific expertise, as once a task has been mastered, it demands fewer cognitive resources. This increases the chance of multitasking and means a task may be done more quickly. An experienced nurse taking a blood sample is likely to be quicker and more adept than a nurse in training. Such expertise can mean that reading of frequently read documents or notes will be faster, the production of written work should be quicker, even sending emails can speed up. However, there may be some areas that never become completely automatic. For a dyslexic person, this may focus around written outputs and/or reading quickly. Understanding this may mean finding other ways of dealing with such job tasks. As we mentioned previously, expertise is based on three elements: knowledge, experience, and practice. The latter two build up self-efficacy, and this in turn can lead to increased determination and motivation. Therefore, developing work-specific expertise in as many aspects as you can in your job is part of becoming successful.

Gerber et al. (1992) –again, see discussions in Chapter 3 –advocate that goodness of fit is a factor in people's success. This is of course a concept that works for everyone. Goodness of fit involves being in a job where you can demonstrate your strengths to a greater degree than your weaknesses. The ideal split should be 70/30 strengths versus weaknesses. However, this may not always be the case. One of our dyslexic contributor who works in the civil service illustrated this:

> If managers obsess over measuring your performance based on rigid processes or 'marking your work' based on basic things like spelling, grammar or sentence construction I tend to struggle. When managers create the space for my creativity, ideation and problem-solving skills to flourish, I flourish too.

This example indicates that it can be quite hard to find the goodness of fit, and may well demand some perseverance and self-awareness. Understanding your skill set and strengths, and knowing what to do about your weaknesses, helps to maintain motivation and determination.

Part II

A passion to do something is often the start of finding your niche. This provides the fuel for determination and perseverance, as well as job satisfaction. Interest in the job can make the extra work, training, and effort worthwhile. Understanding yourself, and the demands of the job, is important. The following contributions illustrate many of these points.

> I know I want to work in acute medicine or trauma surgery. Medicine especially surgery is my life but I couldn't work in something like orthopaedics which often requires long-term planning, intervention and documentation. I really thrive on the immediacy of trauma. A solution for your patient has to be found very fast but it is done and you move onto the next patient, and there is not so much paperwork.
>
> I am aiming to be a GP. I have always wanted to do it. The more I train the more I realise I can do it even though the exams and curriculum are tough. I like the huge variety of patients I have, many of them have very complex conditions. I generally have the time to work out the best management plan for them.
>
> It was a massive revelation to realise that I was 'only as dyslexic as the job made me' – in that I've done some jobs where my dyslexia did not factor at all. Others it is a massive struggle each day. It has been important to see that I choose whether to engage in this daily battle to adapt and that equally, I could choose not to. At the moment, for many reasons, I've opted to work in a role where I would put my dyslexia at 'code red' (!) as it can feel overwhelming and stressful. But the work meets my intellectual needs – it is challenging, valuable and interesting and my brain enjoys the stretch – so at the moment I'm happy to take this on. Knowing that my difficulties are not 'me' but the environment I'm in has made me feel more confident and able in my career.

In Chapter 9 we present a series of personal stories of people who have found their niche. They reiterate many of the points discussed here and some additional ideas about finding what works for you.

# 8

# Organisational Influences on Success

## Overview

In Chapters 5, 6, and 7 we explore the skills and strategies that the individual can personally develop to become successful. This chapter looks at organisational aspects that can contribute to success in the workplace. It explores ways in which managers and employers can provide an environment that mitigates the difficulties and enables individuals to demonstrate their strengths. We will, of course, include comments from our dyslexic contributors. However, when starting this book, we also asked for ideas/comments from other people who play a part in the success of a dyslexic person; such as assessors, coaches, and managers, as well as staff in personnel or human resource departments. Therefore, we have included some of their comments in this chapter.

This chapter comprises four main areas:

Part II

1. The workplace ecology, including managing dyslexia at work.
2. Compensatory resources, strategies, and information technology (IT).
3. Work based adjustments including extra time.
4. The employers' responsibilities – examples from the UK.

## 8.1 Introduction

As the understanding and identification of dyslexia in adults increase, it is evident that there are dyslexic people working in all occupations. Some people say nothing about being dyslexic; for a variety of reasons they do not wish people to know. Others disclose, but do not need support and adjustments as the dyslexia does not impact on their performance at work to any significant degree; for them, the understanding alone is enough. Still others have a minimal or temporary amount of support, often in specific circumstances. Finally, some may have ongoing adjustments. One coach has described it to an employer as 'like wearing spectacles – some people wear them all the time, others only when they are reading, and others don't need them at all at this stage'.

If people are in a job that suits them and they have the skill set required to work effectively (i.e., there is 'good fit'), then adjustments and support may not be necessary. Hence, disclosure is not an issue. However, for some people, aspects of their role may present challenges that with some understanding and support can be mitigated or overcome, and so work more effectively. These challenges are often literacy related and impact on performance and productivity on a daily basis or present themselves under particular circumstances. Everyday challenges might include getting through emails or producing reports to tight deadlines. For these people, some adjustments or technological solutions will be required regularly, and any technology support (spell checkers, grammar software, speech-based applications) often becomes part of the individual's personal working toolkit. Even if a person is accustomed to their job, written aspects of the role may always be more of a challenge than for a non-dyslexic person, particularly when tiredness or change/novelty is involved.

Challenges can also be related to particular occurrences, such as taking professional exams or applying for promotion, or when participating in training or while on probation. In such cases, adjustments might be temporary, while the individual gains experience and develops their skills. One often-used adjustment or accommodation is the use of extra time. As we have discussed before (particularly in Chapters 4 and 8), this can help assimilate and process information, and in the case of written information this can make the difference between success and failure. But the general point here is that there are likely to be a variety of requirements across different circumstances. This variety in a person's specific requirements and their responses to a set of circumstances emphasises the need for an individual approach with each dyslexic person. The one size fits all solution (some assistive technology and maybe a bit of coaching) does not work for many people. In fact, it can be counterproductive if the adjustments are not person-specific: technological aids can go unused and are a waste of money. However, and more importantly, the dyslexic person is no better off than before, which can further undermine their self-efficacy, confidence, and performance.

Increasingly, though, organisations are recognising their responsibility to develop all their employees. Hence, more are supportive of their dyslexic employees. Many organisations are starting actively to promote their commitment to supporting dyslexic/neurodiverse people, as they realise the skills and benefits that such people can bring to their job. As one contributor put it,

Part II

> In essence, roles which require following processes, or writing documents at pace I struggle with. Roles where I get to exercise my judgment and lead in creative ways I flourish in. I have also found as I have become more senior, work weirdly gets easier because that seniority gives me more freedom to define my role.

This is not always the experience of an adult dyslexic; some organisations are less helpful. Nevertheless, all employers have a duty to create an environment in which all their employees can thrive and develop. We will touch on this in the rest of this chapter.

In previous chapters (see Chapter 7 in particular), we have explored the importance of 'goodness of fit' for dyslexic people – being in a job that they have an interest in and which taps an individual's skills more than their challenges, thereby enhancing job satisfaction. We have also mentioned social ecologies, which includes the people at home and work who provide encouragement. Both goodness of fit and social ecologies underpin, and have a symbiotic relationship with, the development of self-efficacy. If someone is in a job that fits their skill set, they are likely to have high self-efficacy. Likewise, the encouragement of others is also likely to increase motivation, which can lead to success and increased self-efficacy. This of course has particular relevance for the workplace, as high self-efficacy generally improves people's performance and productivity. As we discuss in Chapter 3, the elements of self-efficacy, which involve past experiences, vicarious learning, verbal persuasion, and emotional cues, are intrinsic to workplace performance. Past experiences are likely to impact on an individual's belief in their ability to perform a task, both positively and negatively. Perhaps this is why in most job interviews, it is past experiences or evidence of competencies that are asked for when completing a job application. Similarly, the annual job appraisal/review system often aims to encourage individuals to recognise what they have achieved and identify their own development goals and objectives. If someone believes they can do the job, then they are likely to be more motivated and will set themselves higher work-goals; they will be more committed to the job, which is what the employer is seeking in any employee.

The other elements of self-efficacy are equally important to consider. Vicarious learning involves learning from others and can occur when being able to observe how others do things. This can lead to an individual trying it for themselves. This type of learning may be particularly relevant for dyslexic people as many learn better through interaction. This implicit learning that goes on in the actual workplace should not be underestimated. Similarly, verbal persuasion involving the encouragement of colleagues and managers can make a positive difference. Verbal encouragement may involve face-to-face smiling encouragement, nods of the head from a colleague, and other positive cues that come from personal interactions. These may be harder to communicate online, although managers and colleagues can say 'well done' or 'good piece of work' in a video meeting. Sometimes this sort of positive feedback can have less impact and may even go awry:

> I really like my manager – I thought she knew me quite well before lockdown. I found WFH [working from home] very isolating and I know I didn't work well. She kept saying I was doing brilliantly – I knew I wasn't – it was all a sham. I think she was trying to help but it made me feel worse – there was no one I could talk to.

As this last contribution shows, responses can vary. If there is an expectation of failing at a task or not reaching the level required, then there can be a degree of self-fulfilling prophecy. This can lead to negative emotional responses that can become physiological, leading to high levels of anxiety that can make performance even poorer. These emotional cues can become a major challenge to self-belief and job performance. However, with the correct sources of support and advice, and adjustments and coaching in place, this can be mitigated.

> I started my first job full of excitement. I was very keen to learn, my manager was really helpful in the beginning. I told her I was dyslexic and she became even more helpful, she had previously worked for HR. I think that's why she micro-managed me – she didn't want me to fail but I kept having to rewrite or redo everything. She didn't trust me to work on my own and I so did not trust myself and my work got worse. I failed my probation and had it extended, but I started to get frustrated and angry. I got referred for coaching and we all sat down and discussed it. Things got much better, not sure if I got better or she let up a bit – probably both, but I passed and have been promoted twice now!

For dyslexic people, it is important to remember self-efficacy is also task specific – people can be very good at some aspects of their job, such as managing a team of people, but less good at tasks involving literacy. Negative experiences of failing to meet deadlines, not working at pace, and struggling with administrative tasks, however, can undermine self-efficacy, which can then impact on overall performance. Often, dyslexic people do not excel in administrative roles so their confidence, and also their manager's confidence in them, can be undermined. As one contributor put it:

> It is often hard for dyslexics to progress beyond entry level roles, and they are often at risk of being dismissed ... too often access to the more senior roles where dyslexics can show their strengths are denied to them. This is because organisations view it as a prerequisite for employees to 'prove themselves' in more junior admin roles ... before moving on to senior ones.

We will touch on each of these points in the rest of this chapter, detailing ideas that facilitate goodness of fit. However, we will also outline how organisations can support their dyslexic employees, primarily allowing time to develop the skills they need, and maybe to provide informal and perhaps formal coaching/mentoring – we will use the example of legislation in the UK to support this discussion. The goal for both the individual and the workplace/employer should be to increase self-efficacy and job satisfaction.

## 8.2   The Workplace Ecosystem

The workplace ecosystem can be defined as the relationship of people to their environment (both physical and virtual) and to each other. Every workplace has its own culture and structure. This will likely have developed around the demands of the job and the end product or service that the organisation is providing. This culture and structure is important when looking for both the goodness of fit and the social ecologies:

> I found the corporate world of large organisations hard, there was a lot of competition and politics – and constant change. I am better in smaller companies. There is more of a community atmosphere and it is easier to see who is accountable for what. Ultimately I would like to be self-employed, though, where I can be myself.

The influence of the people around them can be a major factor in the success of individuals. These people are colleagues, team members, and, perhaps most influentially, managers.

## 8.3   Managing Dyslexia and the Role of the Manager

Being a manager is now inherent in most jobs. Indeed, it is often generally part of the promotion system. However, very little specific training is provided in the workplace for managerial roles.

Part II

Sometimes it is left to the individual to learn to do it on the job or through the vicarious process of watching others perform the role. There is the expectation that everyone can manage people, though arguably this is unrealistic. Managing people can be a tricky task: it is a role that some people are intuitively good at and others less so.

A manager's job may be described as twofold. First, they are tasked with ensuring their team works at the level required for the job – that targets are reached and the job gets done. While doing this they may have to accommodate a huge range of individual personal issues within their team, which may impact on performance at work at times. This may include new starters to the job, single parents/carers, those with long-term illnesses, and of course people who are dyslexic. A manager's second task is completing their own workload and being successful at their job. Many managers are able to cope with these competing demands well, but some find it more difficult, and it is important to recognise this, as misunderstanding can occur and communication can break down quite quickly.

There is a wealth of literature about effective leadership/management and management styles. Some organisations run in-house workshops or training events or even awaydays to help develop management skills. Such events can present an opportunity for everyone in a team to consider how different people are; to recognise that we all work, learn, and react to situations in different ways. Similarly, they can provide an opportunity to consider one's own personality and work traits. Perhaps the most important aspect of such events is that they offer time to discuss preferred ways of working in a non-threatening environment. Potentially, they can give an explanation for why relationships are not working and suggest solutions. For example, some managers are taciturn by nature and so may not see the need for ongoing feedback to their colleague. This aloofness

## Organisational Influences on Success

may be interpreted by the dyslexic individual as them not doing the job well or a lack of manager support or interest.

A dyslexia trainer contributor said:

> in my experience a change in manager is one of the most common factors in the performance of an individual, the whole system and ways of working and culture can change. The dyslexic person either benefits from the new regime or struggles to deal with it because their confidence is quickly undermined.

Managing people who are dyslexic, and being managed by someone who perhaps has little or incomplete knowledge of dyslexia, can be equally challenging for both parties. If managers go online to find out more, it is possible it will increase their misconceptions because much of the information available about dyslexia focuses on children, and it focuses on the negatives rather than the positives. A manager reading lists of problems can easily feel that a dyslexic colleague will not be capable of doing the job. We asked managers to contribute to this book. Here are a couple of their comments:

> When she came to me and said she was dyslexic, I immediately panicked and went online to find out what it was and how to help. I was totally confused by what I read. Was she like Einstein or was she going to delete all the files by accident? I thought she was definitely going to need a lot of help. I was wrong about her as it turned out – a few bits of technology and plenty of rethinking from me did the trick: she settled in well and does a good job.

> I was worried when he first told me he was dyslexic. I had heard of how much help I was going to have to give him. My own job and managing other members of the team was hard without this. It did get harder for a bit but he was such a nice person – keen, and worked so hard – we talked a lot in our weekly catch ups about how he wanted to do things – we both found better ways of coping with our inboxes! I learnt a lot from him and was sad to see him move to another role. I think I can manage other people better now.

## Part II

Many managers ask what they can do to support their dyslexic colleagues. However, it is not always helpful if the dyslexic person is not ready for the question and does not know. The following is a list of advice compiled from our contributors that may help with supportive strategies:

- Allow extra time to learn new procedures.
- Listen to how and why I work in a certain way.
- Give me early deadlines.
- Enable people to ask questions without being misunderstood – often I am just checking.
- Extra catch-up meetings so I know I am on track.
- Any meeting notes in advance of a meeting, so I am better prepared.
- Highlight key areas of documents for me to read so I can find the information more quickly.
- Give me a heads up.
- Ask me to reflect back my ideas when asking me to do something so I know I have interpreted the information correctly.
- Give me time to think and come up with my ideas and talk them through.
- Find out about me and then ask about dyslexia.
- Be more reassuring or openly positive about what I am doing – I take silence as a negative.

Not everybody would find all these suggestions helpful. Generally, the best advocate for a dyslexic is you, yourself. This may be particularly true when speaking to your manager. As before, self-understanding, confidence, and planning what to say are the keys. We have talked about disclosure previously in this book (see Chapter 4). Telling managers and colleagues what you need to work well requires some thought as it is not always easy: it is important to give it some consideration. It is also important to consider what might work for them. They too might have particular ways of working that might be hard for them to change.

## Organisational Influences on Success

Establishing a good relationship with your manager involving respect, trust, and confidence is important for everyone as it makes the working environment more enjoyable, and potentially much more productive. However, it can take time:

> At the start of my career as a policy advisor, when unaware of my dyslexia, errors in grammatical errors in written work were viewed as me 'not concentrating enough'. It led to some difficult conversations with my line manager, but now that I am aware this is a result of my dyslexia I've developed ways to work around it, e.g. printing out work in blue and reviewing on paper. I ensure that I discuss this with any new line managers at the start of projects and they are fine with it, I think.

Many of our contributors have said that their managers get irritated or ignore them if they ask too many questions. Talking to your manager and asking for advice or help can be uncomfortable at times, but it is worth remembering that it is a sign you want to improve your knowledge and skills. Furthermore, the way in which advice is sought can dispel the idea of incompetence and emphasises it is clarification that is being sought. Here are two examples from our contributors:

> I always tell my manager what I can do before asking for help – for example, I will say I can do three-quarters of this report but I am stuck on this part.

> Instead of saying I need help, I talk to my manager about what I think is needed or required and ask what she thinks. I don't mind if what I thought was wrong, at least I get the information I need and it's right – she doesn't seem to mind, in fact she said she quite likes my ideas. She says it makes for a more interesting conversation and a better document!

Both of these examples show how the contributors are making communication easier both for their manager and themselves. Saying what you think first when clarifying information is important for two reasons. First, you are demonstrating that you have knowledge and ideas rather than not knowing. Second, you are providing a framework for your manager to answer specific questions so they can give you the answer more quickly and in a way that you are more likely to understand.

## 8.4  A Personal Work Passport

Talking to managers can be hard, and knowing what and how much to say is often a question asked of coaches and assessors. There is also the challenge that frequent changes in personnel can be a feature of the workplace today. In some organisations, it is expected that people change their role regularly: in project management jobs, a role in a specific project may last from two months to six months. Again, this can make the issue of what to disclose, and to whom, particularly challenging. In such cases, the issue of disclosure can arise constantly, and having to continually outline how you might do things differently, have trouble with certain tasks, and need extra time can be demoralising. Here it is essential for the dyslexic person to identify what they need to work well and find positive ways of expressing it – see some of the advice in Chapter 4.

Some large companies have realised that discussing personal difficulties can take its toll on an individual's self-esteem, so they have introduced a document that people with specific needs compile themselves and can take to any new role. This has been called an enablement document or a working passport. In it, an individual has to consider and explain their preferred ways of working. Interestingly, this system was adopted by some organisations during lockdown during the COVID-19 pandemic. Employees could have a virtual working passport in which they specified their best working hours to accommodate

## Organisational Influences on Success

the additional family needs of home schooling and family caring. This system has recently been extended for use with hybrid working. This work passport document should be designed as a starting point that facilitates discussions with managers and colleagues in order that any working differences can be accommodated quickly and easily. Here is one contributor's view of the use of such a document:

> I find it very useful and I update it if I go to a new role as the job changes. I am not sure all my managers like it or pay much attention to it, but I think I talk better about my dyslexia, and I am reassured as I can point to it if I have to.

In Table 8.1, there is an adaptation of an individual's personal working passport. As ever, the challenges are detailed more than the skill set, but it is still important to be solutions focused when explaining to others.

Some people do not like the formality of this system as they feel it emphasises their problems. Nevertheless, it can be a personal tool, particularly if it enables you to be a bit more assertive and ask for what you need to work well. Here is one contributor's view about how to deal with problems by becoming positive about their needs and best practice strategies.

> In terms of day-to-day work activities, I have become much more assertive recently about managing my manager's and other people's expectations – e.g. telling them how long I need to read and respond to a document, or insisting that I have materials for meetings provided in advance. I don't often disclose my dyslexia, except to close work colleagues, but I will say things like 'I have a lot on my plate right now, so I'm going to need a week to get back to you on that', or 'I really struggle with multitasking and need to contribute to this meeting rather than writing things down, so would you mind sharing your notes with me afterwards?' Being so assertive was tricky at first, but I have found people tend to take it very well and don't question why I need to make such requests.

Part II

**Table 8.1 Example of enablement document or a personal work passport**

| Topic | Example | Solution or reason |
|---|---|---|
| Preferred working pattern | 9 a.m.–5.30 p.m. with thirty minutes' lunch and other short coffee breaks<br>I can work longer hours on specific occasions | Aids concentration and focus<br>Would help if someone proofreads the work |
| Times to avoid a meeting | First thing in the day<br>Last thing in the day | I am planning<br>Too exhausted to take more information in |
| Meeting preferences | Face to face<br>Or Teams with video | I remember better if I see people |
| How I like to communicate with managers and colleagues | Please text and then flag any urgent emails | I am not always in my email box |
| Assistive technology | Claro read<br>Dragon | Speeds my reading up<br>Helps with producing written documents |
| Other adjustments | Early drafts reviewed<br>Proofread if very important | I don't miss the real one<br>The document is accurate |
| Specific current difficulties | Takes me longer to settle in<br>Coping with overload | Extra time<br>Break workload into manageable chunks |

| Preferred working environment | Hybrid: three days in the office two days at home | I need people to bounce ideas off and motivate me The structure of the office day helps too Better paperwork when quiet and not distracted |
|---|---|---|
| My skills | Good at problem-solving | Think differently |
| | Good at editing documents other than my own Good visual reasoning skills I double-check everything | I find it easy to see if it reads well and very easy to fill in the gaps and see what is missing I use diagrams to help explain my line of thought I like to do a good job |

## 8.5 Constructive Feedback

Feedback on one's performance is integral to improvement, the development of task specific expertise and self-efficacy. Verbal feedback is powerful. It influences effort: positive feedback typically motivates people to do better. It influences persistence: people are more likely to keep going when encouraged. And in most situations, it builds confidence. However, the converse is also true. Negative feedback can quickly undermine confidence, self-belief, and performance. Many dyslexic people struggle with feedback, often focusing on the negative aspects. They struggle with hearing positive feedback and tend to think that their managers are being 'nice'. Here is one example from a contributor:

## Part II

> Writing a book sounds exciting! I'd love to contribute if I can. I've been looking at the questions you've sent but as you may remember, I'm not the most positive individual, so writing about how I've succeeded is proving really hard. Really really really hard. Trying to do this prompted a conversation with my manager which involved many tears (you remember I cry a lot, right?). She knows me well and is a great manager too, so she kindly wrote me some very encouraging feedback which I would never believe or write but I can copy and paste.

**What she sent us was the following from her manager:**

> I just wanted to reiterate something we spoke on briefly earlier, and put it in writing for you. You've been in a newly created job for barely a year, bringing together your skills and knowledge around an absolutely enormous and extraordinarily fragmented institution, to somehow enable two very, very different departments work together cohesively. That is not easy. Your stakeholders are a) huge and b) complex.
>
> I cannot stress how much you were the obvious and natural and only choice for this job – and you are absolutely smashing it. I really wish it was easier to measure impact for these things because I know you like to see evidence, and that's hard to gather for things like 'improving understanding' and 'creating pathways and connections' and even 'managing expectations' and all of the other masses of things, big and small, that you do. But you do all of those, and to a very … high standard, which is particularly high.
>
> I really hope that you manage to see that more and more, because I think it's really important that you be as kind and generous to yourself as you are to your colleagues.

**Asking for feedback can be a hard thing to do, especially if the relationship is not an easy one. Try and remember that asking for feedback indicates that:**

- You want to learn and improve your performance – you are motivated.
- You know that you don't know something – this shows you are thinking about it and interested in it.
- You want to do the job well.

## 8.6 Seeking Advice from Others

Another piece of advice from our contributors was to know who to go to when things became hard to cope with. It does not necessarily have to be a busy manager. Chatting with a colleague or co-worker or someone from another team may be best. The opportunity to do this has been missed by many people when working from home during the lockdown periods of the COVID-19 pandemic. Even talking things through with someone outside your work, such as a family member or friend, can give another perspective and can provide clarity. However, when a job gets very stressful and the workload feels overwhelming, or when there is something specific that is causing a problem or blocking promotion, then seeking help is essential. Likewise, if your performance is inconsistent (some things are well done and others are effortful and undermining), it is important to seek advice.

Help can come from human resources, or work counsellors or coaches. It can also be given by private organisations or found online. Sometimes discussions with such people can lead to a diagnostic assessment, if one has not happened already. While talking to good friends, family members, managers, or colleagues can be extremely helpful, our dyslexic contributors often mentioned that specific professional advice made a big difference. Input from those who have knowledge and expertise can be essential in helping people make sense of their experiences/history as a person with dyslexia. The following quote is from an assessor. A diagnostic assessment will have given her an insight into the cognitive functioning of her client, which may make her the best placed to present potential solutions.

> I will make suggestions about coping strategies such as: ensuring they do not get behind with work, that they allow more than the expected time to undertake a written task, not to hot-desk, to take work home if

feasible (this was pre-COVID), to get work-based support if necessary and to write lists of jobs needing to be done to reduce memory load. However, my job is mainly to assess it is not to support, suggestions are made post-assessment and in the written report that follows an assessment.

But by helping the client to understand their difficulties I can offer them insight into how to manage them. For example, by explaining how their brain might process things differently, I can encourage them to write notes, spider diagrams, take regular rest periods, use mnemonics, memory joggers. Specific strategies will depend on the individual's particular specific profile, difficulties and goals.

Many assessors give feedback and an explanation at the end of the assessment. In addition, diagnostic assessment reports can recommend specific assistive technology and often recommend coaching. For some newly diagnosed people, the explanation at the time of diagnosis and the report with recommendations is sufficient for them to move ahead with their lives. For others, it is the beginning of the next phase of understanding.

## 8.7 Coaching and Mentoring

One of the main suggestions from our dyslexia contributors regarding what had helped them was to seek dyslexia coaching or mentoring. There is often confusion about the terminology regarding coaching interventions. Table 8.2 outlines the differences.

Coaching and mentoring are increasingly being seen as valuable interventions, particularly in the workplace. The purpose of both is similar, as they aim to take an individual from where they are now to where they want to be, helping them to be the best of themselves. There is a wealth of literature about the different coaching theories/practices, but one of the most widely adapted is the GROW model (Whitmore, 1992). This focuses on:

Organisational Influences on Success

**Table 8.2 Training, coaching, mentoring, and counselling (adapted from McLoughlin & Leather (2013))**

|  | Teaching Training | Coaching | Mentoring | Counselling |
|---|---|---|---|---|
| Focus | Often curriculum or literacy skill based | Self-understanding development of strategies to improve skills | Personal development aimed at overall/career development | Self-understanding, including psycho-social issues |
| Programme setting | Determined by the organisation and teacher | Determined by client's priorities and influenced by organisation | Determined by client and influenced by the organisation | Determined by individual's difficulties |
| Content | Literacy or workplace knowledge | Specific goals/ strategies to improve | Broad view of performance Advice based | Often great depth on specific issues |
| Timing | Structured and regular meetings | Usually structured | Informal but with some structure | Regular Meetings |
| Duration | Dependent on content | Flexible length may vary according to individuals needs | Ongoing and can be long term | Usually short term and fixed number |
| Professional qualification | Professional trainer or teaching trained (e.g., SpLD) | Coaching and/or SpLD qualifications | Experienced and knowledgeable about career prospects | Professional psychosocial counselling training. |

**Goal**: What is your goal related to this issue? What are the benefits for you in achieving this goal?
**Reality**: Where are you now? What is getting in the way?
**Options**: What can be done?
**Will**: What will you do? Do you have the desire?

This is a general coaching model, but, perhaps unsurprisingly, it chimes/overlaps with many of the cognitive concepts we have discussed previously. It may also be adapted and used effectively by individuals on their own. However, it is the theoretical/professional understanding of dyslexia that differentiates dyslexia strategy coaching from other coaching. Being able to discuss the nature of dyslexia, its cognitive impact, and its potential effects on the individual provides a rationale for strategy development. Similarly, as dyslexia affects people differently, dyslexia coaching should be personalised for the individual, though we can summarise the purpose within the following aims:

1. Develop understanding of dyslexia and its impact on learning and working, explaining the individuals particular difficulties.
2. Identify skills and abilities, and explore how they think and can learn and work more effectively, thereby building confidence, motivation, and self-efficacy.
3. Explore a range of planning, literacy and work-related strategies to improve performance.

The duration of the coaching often varies in length depending on individual needs. For some, it may be two to six sessions, whereas others might need ten to eighteen. It should conclude when the individual feels their problems have been addressed, they have some tools and strategies to find their own solutions when challenges arise, and they feel more able to move forward, closer to their goals. As with managers, each coach has their own style, and the better the rapport, potentially the more effective the coaching. Most coaching involves an element of practical strategy development, including literacy skills, time management and organisation, memory techniques, and specific areas of workplace difficulty (such as managing information overload in meetings). They often (should) also have an element of personal development, self-understanding, and cognitive strategies to increase confidence. Sometimes, according to individual needs, it is more of a mentoring process.

Here are three contributions from our coaching contributors:

> As a coaching practitioner, my main starting point is the issue or concern that is currently being presented. We work on this, exploring strategies and solutions. Beyond this, there is often lots of discussion about how they may differ in their processing to other people. This builds confidence and assists in their self-awareness and understanding. We may spend time discussing reframing and how they can explain their ways of working to others. Understanding a range of management theories often assists. We also discuss planning, and SMART goal setting. I like to create a range of options of how to achieve something.
>
> The overall aim is to support the individuals in building their confidence, becoming more self-aware and able to create strategies as difficulties present themselves.

The second coach said:

> I use a combination of targeted emotional support supplemented with delivery of strategies. For example, I encourage the person to talk about their perceived weaknesses. These may be areas where they feel anxiety in relation to specific tasks, for instance presentations, or exams. We then find ways of overcoming these.
>
> I also work with the person to identify what steps and actions are involved in achieving their goals. Once they have broken a big goal, which may be completion and submission of a large project, down into a series of smaller, time framed achievable goals, they begin to see that with each small step accomplished, the bigger goal becomes more achievable.

Part II

**The third contribution was:**
> I focus on developing the individual's skills, most frequently their literacy skills; slow reading speeds remain a big problem in today's world and I most often work on strategies to improve reading comprehension. I also do a lot on writing skills from basic emails to big reports or briefings – this includes some planning strategies, audience, purpose, tone, and structure. I also do some basic grammar and sentence structure, but many people use Grammarly. Spelling is less of a problem these days because of Siri and suchlike, but if people are interested and we have the time we will do morphology and language derivation. I also do some work on memory skills if my client asks.
>
> I think if people improve the skill they are most worried about, then their confidence and self-esteem increases.

## 8.8 Support Groups

In addition to coaching, another area of support and advice is the internal networks found in (at least some) workplaces. These take various forms from focused training schemes to WhatsApp groups, or intranet website groups, depending on the size of the organisation. As mentioned previously, some organisations are actively promoting dyslexia/neurodiversity because different ways of thinking and problem-solving is increasingly valued in the fast changing world of work. As part of this, some large organisations have mentoring schemes, dyslexic champions, and high-level role models. Many public sector employers have interdepartmental groups that run development and leadership schemes for people to gain the skills required for promotion, such as the Future Leadership Schemes. Some of these have a particular focus on disability, such as DELTA (Disability Empowers Leadership TAlent). One of the goals of such a scheme is for the participants to become role models for others who have disabilities. Other organisations have differential attainment programmes to monitor and boost equality of opportunity for those individuals who may face barriers for a range of reasons; this may be because English is a second language, through differences in educational attainment, or of course disability.

Some organisations also have in-house support groups that run awareness training or brown bag/lunchtime briefing sessions to provide the opportunity for managers to become better informed. A good example of this is where a manager and their dyslexic colleague sit down and discuss the knotty problem of the implementation of adjustments. Some organisations have dyslexia champions, such as a dyslexic CEO or manager, who not only provide role models, but also give advice and guidance to others. In smaller organisations, the human resources representatives may give advice about other dyslexic people in the organisation who can be approached. One of the most effective ways to get advice is to say you are dyslexic; this can often prompt others to talk, leading to experiences and advice being swapped. This can have a snowball effect, with other dyslexic people joining, such as in a WhatsApp or social media group.

If there is little support or advice in house, or you prefer not to disclose, then it is worth looking outside your workplace. There is a wealth of information available in the form of TED-talks and podcasts online. There are also local, national, even global support groups, and it is generally best if people look these up and choose what works best for them. All advice is most effective if it is constructive, positive, and solution focused. The following quote is advice from one of our dyslexic practitioners:

> Develop an understanding of your dyslexia. Develop a knowledge of the technologies, funding and support that will enable you to reach your full potential. Explore disability disclosure within the workplace.

Part II

Seek out a dyslexia mentor/work coach who can help you through the maze of employment-related issues. Be proud of what you have achieved so far. Do not be deterred by other people's opinions and realise you won't be the only dyslexic in the room.

## 8.9  Compensatory Resources, Strategies, and IT Skills

The first part of this chapter has focused on the social ecology of the workplace. This section looks at the practical and assistive technology solutions available that can support task completion in the workplace.

## 8.10  Practical Strategies

There are many quite simple and practical things that can make a big difference. We discuss some in Chapter 4, but we also asked our dyslexic contributors to identify some solutions. Unsurprisingly, they came up with a variety of solutions for the workplace, such as the following:

- Filing and inbox management at work has been key – I keep everything and like a magpie I store helpful bits of information that I can lift text from.
- Making lists features a great deal, lists using everything from diaries and Filofaxes to bits of paper and Post-it notes.
- Keeping lists of things to do, using mind maps to plan my work, and having daily catch-ups with the team to make sure I'm accountable for my work really help.
- A whiteboard: this has made me so much more efficient in my personal and professional life.
- A printer and coloured paper so I can read from hard copy.

Whiteboards and wall planners, to-do lists, and Post-its all help to support memory. They provide memory cues/prompts, which can facilitate recall and/or processing of new information. The kinaesthetic aspect of writing things down seems to help some dyslexics. Likewise, the use of colour coding can help. Many dyslexic people will say they comprehend better if they can read from a hard copy, leading them to print what needs to be read. Additionally, extra 'urgent and important' in-trays or files can help with prioritising. Hard-copy resources work for some:

> I am a stationer's dream customer. I absolutely love shopping for all things to help me feel better organised at work. Some work, some don't but it is fun trying and my workmates think it is hilarious.

Others use their mobile phone for everything:

> The phone in your pocket is an essential tool you need to help address dyslexia.

Spending a bit of time thinking about embracing the need to be better organised, and exerting some cognitive control to become more focused and finding creative, but practical, solutions can enable people to mitigate their memory and executive function difficulties.

## 8.11   The Environment

There is little doubt that the working environment has an impact on people's performance. If the atmosphere is positive and conducive to working, then people are often less distracted. Distraction can be a big problem for some dyslexic people. Once the attention goes, the line of thought goes, and people have to go back to the beginning. Some workplaces can be highly distracting (such as open-plan offices, which can be noisy), and constant interruptions can significantly undermine the speed at which people produce work – for a dyslexic, written work may be a particular challenge in such circumstances. For example,

> I really quite like the WFH setting when I have heads-down work to do so I can focus and minimise the time spent on dealing with others' distractions.

As discussed previously, working from home can bring solutions, but also its own challenges and distractions. However, many dyslexic people seem to be managing these and are happy with hybrid working: for example, meetings and face to face two to three days a week and paperwork on the other days. Some of the tips given by our contributors include the following

- headset – cuts out the noise and people can see I don't want to be disturbed;
- getting in early – get the admin done early before the noisy bunch;
- staying later to catch up in the quiet of the day;
- have a desk away from the human traffic;
- switch off your notifications or equivalent for most of the day.

## 8.12  Assistive Technology

Technology was once proclaimed as the potential saviour of the dyslexic person. In many ways it is. Word processing packages with spell checkers, and voice-activated software such as Alexa or Siri can reduce many of the spelling problems associated with dyslexia (though homophones and unusual spellings may still trip these systems up). Computers and applications have made reading much more accessible for many people: text to speech software and audiobooks can be vital components in the strategy toolkit of the dyslexic. Increasingly, it is worth looking at what the mainstream packages

## Organisational Influences on Success

can provide as they constantly develop and improve their systems; for example, the edit function checks spelling and grammar and conciseness of language. There are also many programmes that help with planning and the organisation of ideas (mind-mapping software), and there are also memory and organisation packages that help people plan their day.

There are also drawbacks to technology. It has increased the speed of working immeasurably. This has led to increased expectations from colleagues, clients, and customers: an answer to an email should be returned immediately, potentially placing increased stress on the dyslexic person and putting them at a disadvantage. The expectation is that assistive packages can 'cure' dyslexia is also a major negative, as this is by no means the case. As one contributor put it:

> There is no silver bullet of technology to cure dyslexia. Software is not the only answer. You can purchase a toolbox with a saw, hammer and nails; this does not make you a joiner. A software package does not make you literate, successful or intelligent.

**Table 8.3a Type of computer-based resources used by contributors (text)**

| Software Package | Name | Used for | Comments |
|---|---|---|---|
| Text to speech | Claro<br>Text-help read-write gold<br>Read aloud<br>Reading pens | Reading comprehension<br>Proofreading | *I use it all the time – it helps me process the information much more naturally and quicker*<br>*I use it but only when I am tired* |

Part II

| Software Package | Name | Used for | Comments |
|---|---|---|---|
| Speech to text | Dragon Dictate M/S Google | To write emails reports etc | *I love it* *I can't get on with it – it makes too many mistakes – quicker to write* *I use it make my own notes after meetings* *I use it to make to do lists* |
| Spelling and writing | Text help auto correct Spellcheckers MS-editor | Spelling and proof reading | *THRWG is great for homophones* *Editor is easy as it is on my laptop* |
| Grammar | Grammarly | Improving my writing | *It stops me writing long sentences* |
| Note-making | Audio note taker Evernote One note | Making concise notes (e.g., presentations) | *Great for presentations, I learnt it at uni* *I can integrate all my work on it – worth the learning how to use it* *Can use with iPad pen* |

However, there are packages that our contributors found helpful, though responses varied in terms of the level of use and the type of apps considered useful. Again, finding those that work for you is the obvious advice. Some 'techy' people use everything they can find, whereas others tend to use what is recommended and then fairly selectively, perhaps when they are tired. In Tables 8.3a and 8.3b are the main ones they used, with their comments.

Organisational Influences on Success

### Table 8.3b  Type of computer-based resources used by contributors (general)

| Software Package | Name | Used for | Comments |
|---|---|---|---|
| Planning | Mind jet<br>Mind view<br>Inspiration<br>X-mind<br>Mind manager<br>Excel | Getting ideas on paper<br>Big-picture stuff | *It is useful at times*<br>*I plan my daily work and meetings*<br>*I plan projects and reports*<br>*I plan my presentations*<br>*Works well with my dyslexic brain* |
| Organisation | Google calendar<br>Microsoft 365 calendar<br>Trello<br>One note | Diary planning<br>Meetings | *Essential so I can see what I have to do in a day and a week and month*<br>*I can tick off what I have done*<br>*A posh Post-it to help organize my plans* |
| Memory | Dictaphones<br>Google note | Recall in meetings | *Very good but have to find time to listen to it*<br>*Easy way to remember the key points of a meeting* |
| Other visual planners | The G suite iPad sketching<br>Miro<br>Axure<br>Visio<br>Mindnote<br>One note | | *Single source of collaboration –*<br>*Digital prototyping tool*<br>*Draw into text – all my notes are readily accessible* |

Part II

# 8.13 Reasonable Adjustments

Reasonable adjustments are a recognised and valuable asset for many dyslexic people. Although as mentioned previously, not everyone will need them, it is important that they are available if required. The philosophy underpinning reasonable adjustments is that there is equality in the workplace if someone has a disability. This can make the concept of adjustment controversial, as what may be reasonable for one person may not be for another. Therefore, they should be arranged on an individual basis. However, it is not easy to be equitable. It involves legislation, rules, evidence and criteria, all of which are inevitably rigid in nature, although in some cases there is some flexibility.

There are five principles underpinning reasonable adjustments.

1. They should be evidence-based. Adjustments require evidence of the need to adapt the workplace or routines. They also need to be based on the specific individual needs. Being dyslexic is not enough. There needs to be documentation for the particular difficulty, such as problems with verbal and written communication or memory and concentration. This information is usually included in the diagnostic assessment report.
2. There is the principle of inclusion. Any reasonable adjustment should be integrated into the work role so that the individuals are included.
3. There is the need for equity and fairness. Adjustments aim to level the playing field. For example, extra time in an exam is to compensate for slow reading rates, and the purpose of an exam is usually to demonstrate knowledge, not to test reading skills.
4. Adjustments are not allowed to compromise the essential requirements of the job. Therefore, the questions to be asked are: Does the individual have most of the key competencies? What impact is dyslexia likely to have? What adjustments will make up the difference? Reasonable adjustments may need to be considered on more than

one occasion, as the job requirements can change. Nevertheless, the legislation is not designed to support people in jobs who do not have the required skill set. This is particularly important in risk-critical jobs where there may be a threat to the public.

5. Finally, there are financial and administrative considerations. Adjustment should not place an undue financial administrative burden on the organisation in terms of costs of training or equipment or workplace support. To mitigate this, the cost of training/coaching and equipment can be supported through government schemes such as the Access to Work scheme.

## 8.14 Extra Time

The most important and effective adjustment in the workplace is that of extra time. We have explored difficulties with time – speed of processing, time estimation, and management – elsewhere in this book (see Chapters 4 and 7). In this case, the focus is on using extra time to accommodate these difficulties. The need for extra time for dyslexic people is probably the only area of agreement in the dyslexia world – although how much time should be allowed is more contentious. Generally, in an examination, a figure of 25 per cent extra time goes unchallenged. However, some assessors recommend more based on evidence they find during the diagnostic assessment process; for example, 50 per cent extra time is possible in some examinations in the UK. Asking for much more time may potentially exclude the individual under the criteria for adjustments mentioned earlier, and there may be a problem with tiredness in exam situations.

Although there is no substantive research to support the 25 per cent allocation, it seems to be sufficient to give the majority of dyslexic people the time they need to succeed in exams. However, in other settings, it is much harder to establish the percentage of extra time needed and the duration of the time adjustment. Sometimes extra time is needed on a long-term basis, but sometimes it is needed to learn new skills and develop expertise, and once this has taken place there is less need for the adjustment. On occasion there are specific events, such as selection and recruitment or the completing of training or professional examinations, where extra time is needed. However, again, once the event is completed, then the adjustment may not be needed.

Professional examinations can be a barrier to a dyslexic person's success. Most dyslexic people are at a significant disadvantage in these assessment settings. They can come in many formats, such as written papers, long or short answer tests, multiple choice question exams, or practical and oral examinations. They can often tap into dyslexia-related weaknesses, especially when requiring reading or writing, or processing large amounts of textual information, needing to identify questions at speed, searching (skimming) for the relevant information and answers, the recall of information often with little context, or formulating an argument at speed. Such processing can place huge demands on verbal working memory. While they may aim to test knowledge, examinations are not necessarily a good measure of an individual's ability to do a job, as they also test reading and specific processing skills. Moreover, many dyslexic people lack self-belief and confidence in these settings. Some become anxious, particularly if they have experienced failure in the past (perhaps in school), and this can further undermine their performance. This anxiety, lack of self-belief, and lack of confidence can be specific to the examination/assessment setting, and may not impact on practical or operational experience.

This dyslexic disadvantage is recognised, and extra time in written examinations is now commonplace. However, it is harder to allocate

## Organisational Influences on Success

extra time in some assessment settings. For example, the following is an email to a dyslexia coach:

> I have just received this email regarding 'Reasonable Adjustments' for my clinical exam. I wondered what your thoughts are? Given I should be granted 25% extra time, just 10 minutes at the start seems very short to read through **all** 13 stations briefs? What is your experience with this?

The response was:

> Their reply is the standard one and I think it is unlikely they will change it. They will argue that the 10 minutes is 25% extra for just the reading part of the exam i.e. reading the cases, and it is not needed for the clinical part. So it is not 25% of the whole exam time.

How extra time is calculated, as this example shows, can vary, and it is also difficult to provide evidence for extra time in practical or oral examinations. In the past, examiners have argued that the job requires people to be able to work at a particular speed, which means that extra time may go against the criteria for the assessment process. While this may be correct, assessment and workplace settings are not the same, hence people perform differently, which may make this argument less convincing in many cases. Therefore, examination/assessment decisions need to be made on a range of criteria, evidence-based and if possible specific to the individual

Indeed, examination boards are increasingly being asked to review their criteria. Other adjustments that are now being considered include:

- a quiet room to read the questions aloud and/or to facilitate concentration;
- paper and pencil to make notes;
- being allowed to sit a written paper in a paper format rather than online;

- the examination either online or paper being in a specific colour and/or font;
- taking notes into an oral exam – or making brief notes to plan a spoken answer;
- acknowledging the dyslexic person may take a bit longer to find the correct word;
- being allowed to ask questions to clarify what is being asked.

There is also a move by some examination organisations to allow additional attempts to sit an exam if the candidate has been recently diagnosed and is now entitled to 25 per cent more time. For example:

> If I hadn't been given a bit more time in the exam, and to work out better ways of revising and another two resits, I wouldn't have passed. What a waste of ten years of training and what a waste of the money spent on my training. I am so glad I passed.

## 8.15 Recruitment and Selection

Adjustments at the recruitment and selection stage should be implemented, as being dyslexic should not be a barrier to an occupation. Clear job descriptions help people make informed decisions regarding the goodness of fit: is the job right for them; do they have the skill set; what might be the problems and do they have solutions? Dyslexic people benefit from having as much information as possible made available to them. They may also benefit from talking to human resource people, whether the hiring manager or someone who works in the organisation. The demands of different jobs vary considerably. If the job is very reactive and involves rapid processing of written information with very short deadlines, then the individual needs to consider their skill set. Extra time to get their knowledge up to speed may be an option, but working in that environment may prove very stressful in the long term. A more proactive job, involving seeing the bigger picture, with time to plan, maybe a better option.

Some dyslexic people will take advantage of the disability schemes; for example, at the time of writing this book, there is the disability confidence interview scheme in the UK. In this, ticking the disability box should mean an interview is automatically given. Other applications just have a 'do you have a disability?' box. In these cases, some people will not tick the box for fear of discrimination or unconscious bias. Here are a couple of examples from our contributors:

> The feedback I got when I didn't get the job said my written language skills were weak on my application form. And I had ticked the disability box and said I was dyslexic and didn't get through to the next stage. I am not doing that again!

> I always tick the box, I am so much better speaking than writing about what I can do. They never ask me about dyslexia although I often bring it up if it feels OK to do so. I try to be positive about it – it seems to work. I am better getting jobs than keeping them.

Some of the adjustments at the selection stage are extra time for any written assessment, and appropriate scribes and/or readers to support dealing with text. In the interview, taking notes to help with recall and the use of a pencil and paper to help with structuring a line of argument is also considered as reasonable. Similarly, as dyslexia awareness grow, interviewers are allowing extra time for the individual to formulate their answers and find the right words. Interviews can be anxiety-provoking events for everyone and this can affect recall of information. This can be especially important with the increasing use of online interviews. Online interviewing is another area of personal preference. Some people prefer being at home as it enables them to have all the information around them, which can relieve anxiety and lead them to perform better. Others much prefer face-to-face interviews, and actively ask for it as an adjustment:

> It is better for me, it feels more natural – I think I can present myself better – I don't have to rely on just words. If they don't like it or can't accommodate it, I don't think it is the right job for me.

## 8.16 The Workplace

Having been successful at the interview stage, conversations with human resources staff and managers can, if needed, consider other adjustments. These are most frequently the assistive technology packages outlined earlier that help with literacy and planning difficulties. However, challenges at work can present themselves at any time and for a variety of reasons. These might be changes in job routine, working from home, changes in team structures, or changes in work roles, especially those that increase administrative tasks. If this occurs, and the dyslexic person is struggling to perform, then questions such as these should be asked. What can be done to help? Can or should the job be restructured? How can others help to enable the dyslexic person to work more effectively? Solutions might be:

- additional time to complete work duties;
- additional time for administrative work;
- more feedback meetings – development chats;
- change to work hours; that is, amended start and finish times;
- someone to clarify the tasks or to bounce ideas;
- proofreaders for important long documents;
- pre-meets or meeting notes or agendas in advance.

Often some adjustment to the role may only be needed to be give the dyslexic person time to develop strategies that overcome their challenges. Some of these adjustments would also be of benefit everyone.

## Organisational Influences on Success

Similarly, when beginning a new role or in training and assessment settings, the dyslexic person may be at a disadvantage owing to unfamiliarity and the extra processing that is involved. In these circumstances, some of the suggestions listed here could be explored:

- the opportunity to shadow or observe for the first few days – to help assimilate information;
- notes in advance of any training workshops or lectures – to enable more effective processing in the meeting;
- additional training time to learn how to use equipment/techniques;
- extended time for probation or in training to develop skills and task-specific expertise;
- longer meeting times to see stakeholders, clients, or patients until expertise, knowledge, and confidence have increased.

## 8.17  The Employer's Responsibilities

This section briefly outlines the legal framework underpinning the adjustments process used in the UK at the time of writing this book. It aims to maintain fairness and equality for everyone in the workplace, and therefore is used as an example for consideration by readers.

There has long been an argument for employers to provide a work environment in which people can build their self-efficacy, as this generally increases productivity and motivation, leading people to work more effectively and so contribute to organisational success. However, employers have an additional duty of care regarding their dyslexic employees that is enshrined in UK law. Dyslexia is regarded as a disability under the Equalities Act 2010/2018. The act defines a disability 'as a physical or mental impairment that has substantial and long term effects on his or her ability to carry out normal day to day activities.' As discussed in Chapter 2, dyslexia has a genetic basis and is therefore considered a long-term condition that can impact on cognitive processes over a lifetime. This can lead to adverse effects that are can impact on day to day activities, such as persistent difficulty in reading or understanding written material. For some, there may be the inability to remember information, such as the names of people. For some, there may also be difficulties with distractibility and concentration, owing to some of the elements (feelings of worry, failure, and low self-efficacy) we have discussed in previous chapters (see Chapter 4, for example). In fact, many of the challenges that our dyslexic contributors mentioned fall into one or more of these categories.

Nevertheless, many dyslexic people feel uncomfortable about the disability label, and being seen as disabled can be a great concern for many newly diagnosed adults. While they may recognise most of the characteristics of dyslexia in themselves, they have never seen themselves as having a disability. In these cases, it can help to emphasise that dyslexia is specific in nature: it may present itself at times of transition, change of job or role, or when the demands of a job compete with other elements such as professional examinations and home life. As mentioned earlier in this chapter, an assessment is often sought when there is inconsistency in performance – for example, persistent failure in professional examinations when the individual is highly competent in other aspects of the job.

The positive side to the Equalities Act is that employers are not allowed to discriminate and are obliged to make reasonable adjustments. This has meant that there is greater awareness of dyslexia in the workplace. Organisations are required to put policies and procedures in place to comply with the law. Inclusion is the premise. They include:

## Organisational Influences on Success

- **Commitment.** This policy outlines the organisational commitment to equal opportunities, diversity, and inclusion.
- **Recruitment.** Policies around recruitment aim to ensure there is no discrimination; that is people compete for a job on equal terms. There is a question on the job application regarding any disability, and if this box is ticked, reasonable adjustments, such as extra time, are offered and are put in place if there is any assessment activity.
- **Employment.** These policies ensure induction and workplace training is accessible. Extra time should be given to re-process and learn new information. Workplace assessments can be conducted; coaching and assistive technology are offered.
- **Retention.** These policies are targeted at providing the individual with the support, including some extra time, to improve their skills to the level of competence required by the job. Probation periods can be extended; diagnostic assessments and workplace assessments can be conducted; specialised coaching and assistive technology are offered.
- **Communication.** This relates to dyslexia awareness training and the publication of policies so that managers and employers know where to go and what support is available to them. These include internal websites, in-house training, disability networks, and informal groups.
- **Promotion of diversity and inclusion.** This is not a legal requirement, but it is an example of good practice. Some employers have embraced the Act by putting policies into practice at all levels in the organisation that promote inclusion and diversity.

Despite the Equalities Act, and related positive promotion, some people who had disclosed their dyslexia in an effort to gain support found it was a very negative experience. Disclosure and fear of stigma remain an issue. For example,

Part II

> When I told my employers I had dyslexia, they did not take the issue seriously, did not find out what they needed to do in order to support me and did not want to support me in getting assessed even.

> I find people lose patience and cannot help regardless of their awareness of your dyslexia. They feel as if they are carrying you (a dyslexic person). In turn you (the dyslexic person) lose your independence, self-respect, and self-esteem due to the support required from others. It further shatters your self-confidence because you cannot be self-sufficient.

In both of these cases, the employers were not complying with the spirit of the law. It may have been a lack of awareness and knowledge about dyslexia and what could be done to help. However, there is more information available nowadays, particularly on social media, websites, and so forth, that both employers and individuals can access. As mentioned previously, there is an increasing amount of positive promotion outlining the skills and value a dyslexic employee can bring to an organisation. A large number of websites also outline the nature of dyslexia by listing the range of characteristics that dyslexic people can experience. Unfortunately, the plethora of apparently contradictory information can be confusing and unhelpful. One way to encourage understanding and to dispel the myths about dyslexia is to promote awareness training for the whole organisation. This also provides the opportunity to better inform people about the solutions, many of which are simple and cost effective, although they might require a little more time. Another example:

> Watching my children experience school as dyslexics, I realise little has changed over the past twenty-five years. However, I do feel workplaces are more accommodating in general. It still all really depends on the personalities involved and if they have an interest. Attitudes have changed for the better but I still hear people being negative about dyslexic adults and colleagues. There are still so many myths around and assumptions – I challenge these assumptions all the time.

## 8.18 Awareness, Assessment, and Implementation

Good awareness training for any of the hidden disabilities that fall under the neurodiverse umbrella is a valuable activity. It provides a platform for people to communicate, to ask and answer questions, and for people to feel better informed. This can lead to people feeling valued and better understood. It makes life easier for both the dyslexic person and their colleagues.

Awareness training should ideally be bespoke and provided by someone who has experience of the nature/culture of the organisation and an understanding of job demands. The impact of dyslexia in the emergency services is very different from those in banking or retail industries. General information on dyslexia is already on websites, hence the training may not be of great benefit unless it is personalised.

Such training is often most effective when it is presented from several perspectives. Contributions from dyslexia specialists providing the theoretical context, from human resources providing the organisational context, from managers outlining their perspectives, and from dyslexic people talking about the challenges and how they deal with them could all be considered.

Human resources is usually the department responsible for the production and implementation of adjustment policies. Large organisations usually have designated teams who look after the selection and recruitment practices outlined earlier. They also oversee any poor performance issues. If someone is struggling at work, they can seek advice from such teams/groups. In smaller organisations, there should be someone who is the human resources representative, though it can also be a manager's responsibility, and this can make it harder if there is little trust between the two parties. They will explore the reasons and discuss options, including suggesting a meeting with occupational health (OH) or an assessment to determine if there is a reason for the challenges. Initially filling in a screening questionnaire may be suggested, and depending on the results, referral for a more formal diagnostic assessment may be recommended. It must be noted that many organisations do not automatically fund these assessments. Screening questionnaires can be accessed online by anyone, and they can be a good indication – but they should be treated with caution as they can produce false positives and false negatives. However, they are a good starting point for the individual to consider reasons for their problems at work.

Occupational health procedures, which are sometimes outsourced, are often more focused on the individual's well-being. For example, if an individual experiences stress or anxiety, in addition to struggling with aspects of work, they can refer themselves or be referred to an occupational health practitioner. These usually take a more holistic approach to identifying issues. Here is an example:

> My HR rep suggested I went to OH because I did not want to disclose I was dyslexic. OH were great, they listened to me, saw the pressure I was under and made recommendations such as adjusted workload and different working hours and no hot desking – it gave me the time and space to get back on my feet.

Human resources and occupational health can refer people for diagnostic assessments, which is discussed in Chapter 2. As we discussed in Chapter 2, the aim of these diagnostic assessments is to provide a reason for the difficulties and an explanation for weak performance issues, to identify the skills and abilities of the individual (what they are good at), and to provide a range of recommendations that will mitigate the weaknesses and enable the individual to work more effectively. Assessments for dyslexia should be conducted by trained educational or occupational psychologists or teachers who have specialist training.

It is important that the assessor is used to working with adults, as the assessment process is different to that normally used with a child.

A diagnosis can be a shock, so it is worth being prepared for an assessment, such as knowing something about dyslexia. Ideally, it is best to talk to someone who can explain what is involved. In the past, diagnostic assessments have been conducted in person, so the assessor can more readily observe both verbal and non-verbal behaviour. However, the COVID-19 pandemic has led to an increasing move towards online assessment. Some of the measures of assessment have been adapted to deal with this different administration. Nevertheless, some psychologists prefer face-to-face interactions, as building of rapport is easier and observation of a person's behaviour when completing the tests is very important.

Following the diagnostic assessment, people in the UK are often referred to Access to Work for a work-based assessment. Access to Work is a UK government scheme set up to help employers make reasonable adjustments. It also makes a financial contribution to the cost of equipment. This assessment provides advice on workplace adjustments, but it is not a diagnostic assessment. It takes the information regarding the individual's skills and abilities to tailor adjustments to the job specifically for that individual. As previously mentioned, dyslexia affects everyone differently, so the interventions and solutions should be individualised. In practice, many people are offered similar technology packages, but it is the coaching that is often more personalised. There follow another two examples from one of our contributors, which sum-up many of the points in this subsection.

> Digital tools have enabled me to flourish. Especially as my dyspraxia also makes my handwriting illegible if I write too quickly. However, in spite of my comfort with using digital tools I am still grateful for the help from ATW in providing specialist software to deal with spelling and grammar issues and organise my ideas, so the IT department is my friend.

Part II

'My work-based assessment was not great, I liked the assessor and thought he listened but he just recommended a load of IT. I really struggle with technology and had only just got my head around what I needed to do at work. when boxes of stuff arrived in the office – I felt completely overwhelmed – I felt totally incompetent if I needed boxloads of help. Fortunately, my manager seem to understand and we did it bit by bit. I don't use much, just the reading and proofreading software.'

Finally, continuing the UK as an example, there are a range of independent or charitable organisations that can provide support with Access to Work and/or training and coaching. The British Dyslexia Association website (www.bdadyslexia.org.uk/) is worth looking at for information relevant to the whole of the UK; although there are other more focused organisations, such as Dyslexia Scotland (https://dyslexiascotland.org.uk/). The two authors of this book work with more regional organisations, one with Independent Dyslexia Consultants (www.dyslexia-idc.org/) which focuses on the south of England, the other with the UK Dyslexia Foundation (www.dyslexia-help.org/), which focuses on the north of England. Both support adults with dyslexia, including those in tertiary education and employment, though the Dyslexia Foundation has more of a focus on supporting adult dyslexics into work, and hence often works with adults who have more pronounced literacy difficulties. These examples emphasise the need to look around. Organisations are likely to be more experienced in different aspects of adult dyslexia and therefore one may be better placed to help than others. These are examples from the UK, but there are similar organisations elsewhere. The range of organisations is likely to be wider in the English speaking world, given the history of work on dyslexia, but they can be found all around the world.

# 9

# Personal Perspectives of Dyslexia and Career Success

## 9.1 Introduction

In this penultimate chapter, we explore the impact that dyslexia has had on people in a range of professional settings. As detailed in Chapter 1, we asked a number of adults with dyslexia to tell us about their career journeys. Those who responded to our request work in a variety of professions, including the health care service, the civil service, the police service, management consultancy, the film industry, and engineering while others are self-employed (entrepreneurs). All have achieved some degree of success in their work-life, although none have acknowledged this explicitly.

When we asked individuals to send us their stories for this book, we told them that our aim was to gain their perspectives on the impact that dyslexia had on them as individuals as well as on their careers. We asked them to consider which skills supported them in their work-life, and what challenges had influenced their job performance, as well as how they had overcome these challenges. We also asked them to talk about whether they felt that their current job was right for them. They have interpreted these points in their own ways, so there is a degree of variability in the stories. Obviously, individual differences add to this variation. This includes the fact that the contributors were diagnosed at different stages in their career, so the influence of awareness of their own dyslexia may vary across stories.

We feel that there was also a degree of consistency in the stories. Perhaps not surprisingly, most of the stories were positive. We looked for common themes emerging from them. In our view, the most striking ones were persistence, determination, and hard work: the need for hard work was mentioned many times, with determination and persistence to overcome challenges also being an often quoted personal perspective. However, people skills were also very frequently commented upon by the contributors – being able to work with others was clearly something that these dyslexic adults felt was important to them and their success in the workplace.

There was also mention of difficulties with literacy, particularly reading, with technology being one way to overcome such issues. Many referred to self-understanding and self-confidence, and the encouragement of others, including family, colleagues, and dyslexia-coaches. Again, these points are consistent with many of the themes touched on in the rest of the book.

The overriding impression given from reading the personal stories here is that most seem to feel that they are in a good job for them. Again, this fits with what we have referred to as goodness of fit in the rest of the book. This should lead to greater job satisfaction, along with higher levels of self-efficacy, which should increase further as job-specific expertise develops. Most of our contributors are in roles or jobs in which they feel they can demonstrate their skills: people skills, creative-thinking, big-picture solution finding. This, in many cases, also seems to have helped them mitigate many of their dyslexia-related challenges. They have all faced setbacks. Often, extra time in training, or to settle into a job, has helped them to develop the strategies and skills needed. However, at times, the challenges seemed to have been too great and they have had to seek further support or look for alternatives. There are examples of both of these positive and negative experiences in our contributors' stories.

Contributors' perspectives have been mentioned throughout the book, but this chapter includes a selection of fifteen longer stories, which we feel present ideas that may be useful. We have tried to select a range of views in order to show the individual differences that we see as important when dealing with dyslexia. To emphasise this, there are a couple of professions (e.g., the medical profession) where we have included multiple contributors to show how different experiences can be within similar contexts. We have avoided too much editing of stories, so as to keep to the original version sent to us as closely as possible – to show what they see as important. However, some editing has been necessary to ensure that as much as possible, identifying information was removed. We have also conducted a little bit of editing to help with ease of reading at times, so as to keep the stories to a manageable length and to keep the book within its word limit. To avoid identification of contributors in these longer stories, we have used pseudonymous initials rather than real names. Whereas in the rest of this book we have put contributions in quotation marks to distinguish contributions from our words, the stories here are contained within boxes so they appear separately.

Part II

### *SPD: Film Documentary Producer/Director – the Entertainment Profession*

One of my first memories at school was of being taken aside from the rest of the class and made to do separate lessons from everyone else. I wasn't told then that I had dyslexia but I was told that I had problems with writing and reading and speech pronunciation. This happened all the way through primary school and into secondary school. It was here that other pupils would make fun of me as I would have to go and see the special teacher and do these strange exercises in spelling that I just didn't engage with. It wasn't too long after this time that I totally checked out of school altogether. I left school with one GCSE in Science and went straight to join the infantry in the army. I felt that because I had dyslexia I was stupid and never would amount to anything so the army was my only ticket out of where I was from.

As it turned out, I am totally deaf in the right ear. This was soon found out and I was checked out of the army also. With no plan in life, I went from job to job working on farms and factories doing manual work, restaurants and kitchens, to a door-to-door salesman selling gutters. Then I found something I could do and loved. I started as a runner in the film industry. I started as a runner as in this role I could watch how things are done instead of the study classroom way.

I always thought that dyslexia was just about spelling, reading and writing, and it is only recently that I found that it is so much more. From certain behaviour traits, to low self-esteem and anxiety in certain environments or even near certain people.

Recently I have realised that dyslexia not only affects you negatively but it has also given me some gifts that have helped me live an extraordinary life. Although I might be below par for some of my reading and writing skills, I think I have over par emotional intelligence, always been highly intuitive and great at judging people and engaging with them. This has helped me while traveling the world for pleasure and with my job, as no matter where I go I can easily read the situation and mix with all kinds of people. I think I have a special skill at reading people and reading their facial expressions in a way that lets me communicate really well with them. And I am good at reading the room.

## Personal Perspectives

Also I am good with images and abstract out of the box thinking, accessing places, rooms and people, and I am very streetwise. I have a good long-term memory and can remember conversations and events. These all helped me in my work.

Although my dyslexia was diagnosed whilst I was young, I think it was dealt with in an old-fashioned academic environment that I just would never have fitted in. I think it really affected my self-esteem and I thought because of my spelling and stuff, I was stupid and below everyone else academically. Some of the behaviour issues I have had over the years left me feeling frustrated with myself and broken, and that I just didn't fit in with the rest of society in some ways. I always hid the fact that I was dyslexic from people and my employers. As my career progressed, I would hinder myself and opt to keep myself back because of the mindset mentioned above and the fact I would have to do more writing and I would be found out by my employer. But I did keep going. The amalgamation of all this has caused a few problems over the years with my confidence and self-esteem causing me much anger and anxiety.

I have recently spoken to a dyslexia consultant which helped me understand my mind and learn to love it. It showed me how dyslexia is a gift and over many sessions I have learned to overcome my fears of writing and to embrace my dyslexia. I have to say, I never picked up a pen once or typed on a keyboard in any of these sessions. It was more like therapy of understanding my mind and what dyslexia is. Doing this has helped me overcome some of my behaviour issues and I am a happier person. I feel like I believe in myself more as I have more confidence. It's hard to explain how I feel like after I got some help, but it feels like a weight has been lifted from inside me and I feel a bit more free in my life to relax. It's a little thing but it's made such a big difference for me.

I have found a few methods that have helped me. Becoming more organised in planning and helping my mind offload things. I need to do a 'to do' list that I can then organise to help me achieve them. The coaching explained why I like to plan my week so I can clear my head of all the different tasks going around my head. It helps because I suffered from office anxiety. I was working with people who had been to the best universities and felt like an imposter working with them. Someone would say, can you just send me a 'SIMPLE' email to explain something. I would instantly get massive anxiety and spend an hour or two trying to put something together, but the more I typed the worst it got. During coaching sessions, I learned to use certain software that is now part of my everyday life, such as Grammarly and Dictaphone on my laptop. And I recently used a chatbox to send a job application. It was amazing – it is so easy and quick. But I did have to tell it what to put in. I have also learned to relax when sending an email to someone and have noticed that most people make mistakes when sending them.

While I was a runner, I worked on multiple different types of films, TV, commercials, music promos and documentaries, taking everything in and working in every department. From this, I got to know lots of different people across the industry and built up my confidence. I then became an assistant director working with large film crews. Later on, I moved over into making documentaries, which is where I really excelled as I could use my people skills to my advantage and gained the trust of people who want to tell their story. Recently, I have wondered if being dyslexic helped me do this – I feel their pain. In the last five years some of the films I have worked on have been nominated for, and won, awards.

This is a really good job for me as I get to use my people skills and work with people and travel the world, which keeps the role interesting and random and creative.

### *KTS: Doctor, Training Surgeon – the Medical Profession*

Passing exams has plagued me for my entire life. It was not until during my second degree, aged 24, when I failed my first medical school exam spectacularly, that I was subsequently diagnosed with dyslexia. From early primary school age, there were clues I might be dyslexic. Aged 12, I was highlighted as under-achieving or at times 'naughty'. Due to a lack of diagnosis, and therefore appropriate support, I failed to attain the GCSE and A-level grades I was predicted.

My dyslexia is a disjuncture between my actual ability or IQ and written exam success. I am specific in stating exam success; in stark contrast to its

## Personal Perspectives

repeated exam failures. I have often scored highly on other elements of academic work, such as thesis writing and practical exams. My difficulty with exam failure is also at odds with my daily practice. I often receive very positive feedback about my abilities as a doctor or training surgeon. I have lost count of the number of times one of my senior colleagues has assured me that I will pass a written exam because of my practical competency.

It is often commented that I am very organised. This is something I have learnt to be. My true nature is slightly frazzled and quite forgetful. The more organised I am, the better I am at functioning day to day. I am also terrible at remembering names, which is particularly tricky as a doctor in training who moves departments fairly often. I tend to link people's names to certain attributes about them, like a memory game.

I have developed specific processes using colour, layout and font when making study notes or my on-call list in work (the document of patients I need to review and/or manage). Reading long and detailed written documents can be trying, I manage this by using highlighter pens, making notes along the edge of the document, using tabs and Post-it notes. I should really buy shares in a stationer!

Something I really worried about prior to graduating from medical school was prescribing the wrong medication as many of the names sound similar. To date, I have not had a problem which is likely due to implementing extra checks such as consulting my British National Formulary or checking with a colleague prior to prescribing.

I have read about the hidden gift of dyslexia. I am yet to find mine! The only benefit I can think of is that dyslexia has taken me on a rather long, meandering path with my career, but one where I have met lots of friends and had many adventures. I am also very empathetic to others with learning difficulties who have either missed out on opportunities due to lack of support or who have had to work far harder than non-dyslexic peers to progress. I am also a visual and kinaesthetic learner. Prior to commencing written work or an operation, I find visualising and drawing out the steps required helps to highlight any limiting factors and aids its completion.

Being dyslexic means that I can have difficulty retaining, processing and recalling information, particularly if it is delivered in an unhelpful format. I am far less likely to recall information during a three-hour lecture on

Part II

anatomy, compared to 'hands on' learning during a three-hour operation. Understanding the negative impact of my dyslexia has been key, but it's still a work in progress. I thought I had 'cracked' it at medical school. Following my diagnosis, the university provided specialist study skills and I passed all my written exams first time, albeit with a lot of hard work. However, my dyslexia returned to haunt me whilst sitting my written postgraduate surgical exams. Repeated exam failure was exhausting both personally and financially. Even after finally passing these exams and successfully becoming a Member of the Royal College of Surgeons, the negative impact of repeated exam failure has made me consider my career choice as I will be required to sit a final set of exams in a few years' time.

Despite knowing I had a high IQ and being told all my life that I was smart, I often felt that repeatedly not achieving what was academically expected of me was because I was stupid. I have severe imposter syndrome, feeling that my achievements are due to a lot of good luck and that one day I will be found out. This has likely been compounded by the fact that I battled through GCSEs, A-levels, a BSc Hons, Medical School entrance exams and the first Medical School written exam before being finally diagnosed with dyslexia. Only recently have I accepted that for many years my potential was not supported and that what I have achieved is due to both my intelligence and determination. There are still days when I have to remind myself of this, though!

My aim to become a consultant plastic surgeon means that I have had to, and will continue to, work incredibly hard. Revising for an exam is particularly time consuming for me. Resitting the same postgraduate surgical exam and covering the cost of that resit by working extra shifts meant that I was both exhausted and limited in the time I could spend with friends and family or on a date. Doctors often miss important life events due to work, but when you miss these events continually for an exam you repeatedly fail, it can start to chip away at happiness. I would say this is the largely uncovered aspect of a learning difference; the impact it has on one's confidence, self-worth and overall happiness.

As I was nearing the end of core surgical training, I had achieved all competencies except for two postgraduate surgical exams. Over the course of the two year surgical programme I had repeatedly asked my deanery for support with my dyslexia and repeated exam failure, but it was never provided. There had been lots of empty promises and as a result I felt quite hopeless about my surgical career. It was also starting to affect my happiness. I met with a counsellor who was wonderful and was referred to a dyslexia coach whose support resulted in me passing my exams, my core surgical training and becoming a member of the Royal College of Surgeons. I was signposted to career mentoring and trainee support, which both provided practical solutions.

I also started to make adjustments in my life to nurture confidence and positivity, such as exercising more regularly and making time to see friends and family. I truly believe that for dyslexic individuals, both the learning difference and the impact it is having upon their well-being needs to be supported in a holistic way.

### *GTR: Doctor and Training Radiologist – the Medical Profession*

I was diagnosed with dyslexia only a couple of years ago. The trigger for this assessment was repeated failure of the FRCR 2A exam. After my third attempt, my training school suggested and supported a referral for dyslexia assessment. I felt embarrassed and unsure this test was for me, but I was willing to engage in the process and was grateful for any help offered at that point. Until the day of assessment, and even after completing it, I was so sure I was not dyslexic. The diagnosis was a shock. How did I manage to go through school and so many medical exams without anyone noticing this?! I felt very upset my own brain let me down so much and it took me a long time to accept the diagnosis. I am unsure I fully understand my weaknesses, but I am now definitely more aware of them.

Somehow, discovering this big thing about my innate disability helped me love myself a bit more. Knowing I always put in extra work to reach the goals set, and despite getting frustrated when things would not go smoothly, I developed resilience and tenacity. As far as I can remember, I always felt the need to double-check with peers that my understanding on different subjects at school, or in life, was correct, but I have done this all my life, so I thought it is part of my behaviour, being communicative and interested in the world and others. Without knowing, this was most likely a coping mechanism that I

Part II

learnt very early on. Despite being a doctor, and knowing what I know about this learning disorder, I find that the diagnosis made me frustrated with myself for not being normal. Then, slowly, it opened my eyes at how I behave and actually it helped me understand myself more.

I have a very good photographic memory and always enjoyed image and chart learning, as well as group discussions and brainstorming over independent reading. Working in isolation, and making sense of the content on my own, was never something I enjoyed doing. Reading thick literature books for my school assignments was always tricky and I have never found this particularly enjoyable. However, I have always put the extra effort in to get the things done.

When I am tired, naming even the most common words is a big deal. I realised that after I found out the diagnosis I started to stutter – that I found odd as I have never done it before either in my mother tongue or in English. Things have improved over the years, but I still stutter every now and then when some particular English words (which sound right in pronunciation and intonation in my mind) are released from my mouth in such distorted ways. It almost appears ludicrous. I have learnt to disguise it at work. When things do not come to mind I try to explain them, or give the definition, or people just name that particular word for me. When situations are too embarrassing, I apologise for it and I state I am dyslexic and sometimes I find it difficult to name things or recall words. In fact, by admitting the disability, people are kinder and sympathetic rather than thinking I have poor English knowledge.

For my day-to-day work, I use a Voice Recognition system and that helps a lot. Coaching helped, but more with making peace with myself, rather than aiding with new strategies. My educational supervisor at the time, who admitted to have always thought I struggled with exams because I am a foreigner, apologised and promised me she will be more careful in the future to identify and help other trainees in difficulty. And luck, yes, that always helps. In fact I am sure that I passed all my exams having that in the bag, as well as a big brain.

Finally my parents love me the way I am. They knew me all my life with this disability, although unknown to them. In fact, my mother still believes I was misdiagnosed as she cannot imagine me being where I am today and suffering from this.

I became a doctor because I loved and I was good at anatomy and organic chemistry, two of the tested subjects to get into medical school. The decision to become a radiologist was made because I really liked the detective work and 'working a puzzle' approach employed in this sub-specialty to come up with the diagnosis and differentials. It is fun, entertaining, and very engaging. And there is loads of imaging! Lucky me. My one big goal for the future is to become an educational supervisor and mentor and help trainees who like me struggle without knowing why. Also, I would like to make more and more doctors aware of this learning disability in order to identify trainees who may be dyslexic without knowing and better support a diverse training.

I am grateful. Because of my experience and outcome I was able to identify colleagues who were dyslexic and suggested them to test. No surprise for me when they got their results. Keep open and honest. People will like you more if you state your disability rather than hiding it. Keep smiling.

## *AGP: Doctor/GP – the Medical Profession*

I have lived most of my life not knowing that I had dyslexia and blissfully unaware that all those quirky things about me were due to my dyslexic thinking abilities. I had always performed well at school and achieved excellent grades in my GCSEs and A-levels. I had worked hard but had equally enjoyed it. I went on to medical school and appreciated that I wasn't at the top of the class any more, but still managed to get through the multitude of exams and assessments along the way. After my foundation years as a junior doctor, I decided to pursue general practice speciality training. I was inspired by my uncle who was a GP and I really enjoyed my placement in general practice. I loved interacting with patients and the ability to have continuity of care.

I was diagnosed with dyslexia 3 years ago due to repeated exam failure with a multiple choice-based written exam. I was put forward for an assessment with an educational psychologist but never had it occurred to me or anyone around me that I may have had dyslexia. In truth I didn't understand what dyslexia meant for me and didn't know how to change anything.

Being diagnosed with dyslexia made me conscious, frustrated and anxious, and it really hit my self-confidence. It has taken me a while to come to terms with it. The biggest help and resource for me to understand my dyslexia and my abilities came from dyslexia coaching. I have a great relationship with my coach and she has helped me navigate this diagnosis. I now understand what it means for me and how I can improve my study skills and use particular techniques within the exam. She has helped to restore my self-confidence and belief in my special abilities.

I love working with people. I enjoy personal interactions, team work, creativity, problem-solving and thinking outside the box. These skills have helped me to be a good doctor and separate my abilities from my colleagues as I often can find a different approach. I enjoy a challenge and working in a dynamic environment. I really enjoy working as a GP registrar and I have adapted the way that I organise myself and manage my workload over many years to do what works for me. I often forget at work and at home that I have dyslexia, but the crucial challenge for me has been this particular written exam. I have passed my practical exam for GP training at the first attempt which I was very pleased about.

I can process my admin tasks (e.g., reading and acting on correspondence, processing results and prescription requests) in the same time and manner as my colleagues after some practice. But I have noticed that I less favour the electronic portfolio, writing lengthy reflections and doing the tick box exercises.

There is still a taboo associated with specific learning disabilities amongst doctors. I too have not disclosed my diagnosis to my colleagues for the fear of being treated differently. It has been important for me to network with other doctors who have dyslexia. There is great empathy amongst us for the hurdles that we have faced in training and particularly with exams, and also there is advice and support available about what others have found to be beneficial.

I have had immense support from my parents, GP supervisors and deans of medical education who have all maintained faith in my abilities to succeed and be a good doctor. I feel relieved to be able to discuss dyslexia with other friends who were diagnosed much earlier at school and university. Perhaps dyslexia was the reason that we had formed such a strong bond and understanding in our friendship. I have found it inspiring to have role models from within my profession as well as other industries.

The COVID pandemic has changed a lot for my profession, and I feel that I have had to adapt and learn a new way of working for the future. I have

Personal Perspectives

persisted with my determination and resilience, which I didn't know I had in me. Despite everything, I haven't quit my dream yet. I believe that I am a good doctor and that my dyslexic thinking abilities give me an edge over my peers to keep going whilst seeking new ways to solve problems in a holistic manner. My favourite patients are those who present with complexity.

Despite constraints, I find my job role very rewarding. I am approaching the end of my training in the next few months and the last attempt of my final exam. I feel more positive than ever before and know that all of the obstacles that I have overcome have made me stronger and a better doctor. In the future I would like to have a portfolio career as a GP and hope that I will be able to support other doctors with dyslexia. I remain inspired by all the famous people in the world who have dyslexia that have been able to make an impact in so many different industries. And just like that – doctors can have dyslexia and be brilliant too!

## HMP: Trainee GP – the Medical Profession

I was diagnosed aged 44, in my final year of graduate entry medical school. I wanted to be a GP because I enjoy building relationships with people and I have an ability to reach others through different types of communication skills. I'm gifted at building rapport with patients/colleagues and anyone really. I'm able to see situations from many points of view and I can shift perspectives quickly according to new information. I can perceive, read non-verbal cues and reassure. I can link people up and utilise team dynamics well. I see patterns clearly and am able to notice details that many others miss.

I find it difficult to process some verbal information I hear into a coherent meaningful story. I find the number of details can be overwhelming and often cannot see overviews until much later. I remember things and process according to patterns/my position in space, so whenever I rotate to a new ward I find it very confusing. All this affects me by causing me fatigue and exhaustion. I work to compensate, but I still don't have the energy to fully enjoy my own life outside of work.

My managers have not been helpful. We have an official mechanism for notifying them so that they can support us. They do not appear to have used this even after I broke down and cried due to the pressure. Of the six rotations I have worked in, only one consultant (also dyslexic) has helped me.

Friends, family and coaching have helped me to accept my difficulties in light of equal positives, but none of the tools I have tried have enabled me to actually overcome the disadvantage of dyslexia as a medical trainee in the NHS in the current climate.

I was a laboratory scientist for 15 years previously. Now as a junior doctor, I do not think I am in the right job. UK foundation training is not set up to support dyslexic doctors well enough. The system is too pressurised and therefore any help which might otherwise be available is not there at present. However, I get satisfaction from my patient interactions. This is because I can see (and receive feedback) that my ability to listen and communicate is appreciated by patients. I feel discouraged by most other aspects of my job at present as I am slow to document, clumsy to express my handovers, and worry about missing vital information as I am trying so hard to package it 'correctly'. I would really like to find an area of medicine in which my dyslexia is not such a big obstacle.

If you are a medical trainee, try to separate the medicine from the system. The system is extremely pressurised at the moment and therefore support is absent/minimal on the job from a day-to-day perspective. This does not make you a bad doctor. It makes you a person who cannot compensate for system issues quickly under pressure. They're very different things. I try to imagine my medical role away from the trials of the NHS.

I would also say that whilst some mechanisms are in place to help, you probably don't have time to access them (external providers, extra time) and they cannot help you day to day. Don't blame yourself for that, it does not mean you do not try hard enough. It means that you recognise the limitations of the resources which are available. Be kind to yourself and reach out to other dyslexic trainees. Our stories are remarkably similar. This gives me strength in an administration heavy, multiple, incompatible IT system-based organisation such as our NHS.

### DCE: Civil Engineer – Infrastructure Work Sector

I was diagnosed at 12 years old. I struggled through school and university, even with the essential help of extra time and typing in exams awarded to

## Personal Perspectives

me in my diagnosis. I had the attitude that once I leave academics behind and go to work that dyslexia will be unimportant or reduce with age. I learned the hard way that this is not true. Not only does it not go away, but I now realise that dyslexia impacts the very core of how I think. Extra time and typing were very helpful in exams (I might not be where I am now without them), but I now feel that all they did was paint over the cracks without addressing the core problem fully. In school and university, I never acknowledged just how difficult I found studying. I wish at the time that I instead understood the link with my dyslexia to my strengths and weaknesses and therefore proactively made the most of the support available to me.

I feel my dyslexia makes me stronger at communicating ideas to people. I have been told that I am very articulate and present complex concepts in a clear line of thought, which is beneficial both at work with colleagues and at home with friends/family. I am also good at making links and thinking laterally. This enables me to contribute fresh thoughts during meetings and workshops, as well as revealing issues which might otherwise go unnoticed till later along a process.

I feel my dyslexia forces me to communicate thoroughly and think strategically about everything – which if used effectively can have a positive impact on my colleagues and it helps me to work methodically. Having to think through things more carefully and slowly to understand them also has the positive effect of helping me to pick up details that others might miss. Good relationships with my colleagues are essential to pull me out of the 'rabbit hole' when I've been in there a bit too long. I therefore find it easier to work with higher-level problems than with lower-level problems.

Dyslexia is often categorised as a disability, but many also regard it as a 'difference'. Therefore, I don't think it is helpful or true to think of yourself as being a burden at work because you have dyslexia while other employees or candidates do not. It's a fact of life that every person has a unique set of strengths and a unique set of weaknesses – and if you accept this then it follows that:

- you have strengths;
- your strengths are valuable to others;
- non-dyslexic people have different weaknesses to you.

Part II

I feel that everyone whether dyslexic or not should understand this. Like anything else that may impact you negatively at work, opening-up in the right way about your dyslexia at work is essential, and if you're unsure then seek whatever help you can. Life is too short to not make the most of it.

---

### JCS: Civil Servant/Head – Civil Service Profession

When I was 17, my A Level Geography teacher suspected I had dyslexia. At 19, I had a formal assessment at university where they confirmed it. My dyslexia makes working in the workplace more challenging to read and absorb lots of complex information; to work at pace, turning round written reports or presentations for seniors; and keep myself focused and organised day to day.

Since working from home, the impact from my dyslexia has been greater, because it removed many of the tools and processes I established in the workplace to be effective. It set me back initially while I had to readjust to the new normal, and find alternative ways of adapting how I work with my dyslexia. Outside of work it doesn't affect me greatly, but when the odd dyslexic trait makes itself known, it causes a wry smile. I'm always glad I read things twice before booking the train to see friends in Stafford and I don't book it to Stratford instead!

I think being able to 'see' the bigger picture has helped me in my job. I can recognise the patterns at work – thinking in a different way. Also you are able to add to the cognitive diversity of the team, which is great – I bring skills to the team that no-one else has. I am good at working with others – building rapport and good relationships with colleagues. Seeing the bigger picture and helping colleagues to think about problems differently – provide a bit of out of the box thinking. Being an active listener. Being pragmatic and occasionally stubborn (a little bit is not a bad thing!). I ensure that I put in the hard work. I listen to the advice I receive – which can come from many places – and be realistic but positive about what it is I'm seeking to achieve. I think it is about making many small, positive, and progressive steps forward that helps me.

It was challenging when I moved between two departments. The difference in the roles between the job organisations were like chalk and cheese! I didn't have all the tools and approaches to hand to adapt as quickly as I needed to. Moving from audit work to policy work was an enormous learning curve, but one which I successfully overcame with the fantastic help of my dyslexia coach!

In the 6 years I've been in the Civil Service, it's been good to see that there's been an increase in recognition of colleagues with dyslexia (including other neurological conditions), and the civil service now has a cross-government dyslexia group which is providing a toolkit for line managers: https://civilservice.blog.gov.uk/civil-service-dyslexia-and-dyspraxia-network/

It's a small step in the right direction, and it's great that the toolkit is available for all.

## *ACS: Civil Servant/Head – Civil Service Profession*

For me, dyslexia was this strange thing that my dad used to talk about, and whenever I struggled with my reading or writing or mathematics he used to ask me if I had dyslexia, but it wasn't until I was sitting my GCSE exams at 16 that I was diagnosed. I'd just broken my wrist and was unable to write so my English teacher had sent me to what was then called our special needs department to borrow a laptop. My English teacher was surprised how much better my essay drafting was when I wasn't handwriting so put me through a number of small assessments and felt that I did have dyslexia but that it was too late to make any sort of adjustments with my exams.

When I was diagnosed with dyslexia, I was worried that my career would never really take off, but found to my great surprise and delight that the Civil Service were more than happy to adjust in terms of what was reasonable. They helped me overcome any difficulty my dyslexia presented: e.g., years of additional reading time and the flexibility to print things on different paper.

People would say that I'm verbally articulate and a great communicator, I can really engage with and hold a crowd. Looking back at my life, particularly my early years at school, I never had any issues sitting at the front of a class and sticking my hand up and asking questions to get a better understanding of what was required, and if I didn't understand I'd repeat my questions. I'm very good at seeing the big picture and helping those in my chain of command to understand risks and opportunities by contextualising operational strategy and policy in plain English, creating a common sense of purpose and single team ethos. I'm a visual thinker which helps.

My dyslexia has reduced my confidence and reliance in almost anything written because I know that I'm not as good on paper as I am in person. So much of my work is now required to be written and despite being promoted five times in my first 12 years' service, I discovered that my dyslexia was becoming a big barrier to achieving promotion at more senior grades.

I was lucky enough to have some fantastic teachers at school who inspired me to learn by breaking things into small bits and understanding them. My love of rugby was something I was just good at and helped me to learn to read a situation. My mum always encouraged and supported me to be at my best more of the time. But my (dyslexic) dad has been one of my heroes. He has no formal qualifications but is one of the most confident speakers I know – he always helps me focus on what things to say and how to say them.

At work some of the best managers and leaders I've encountered in the Civil Service have been people who simply 'got me' – people who were prepared to give me more time to read and understand written tasks so that I could complete them.

I am boy and man civil servant, having transitioned out of sixth form and university at 17 to become a civil servant. It is the right job for me because I can utilise all my strengths! Every day is slightly different, but being empowered by my director, I spend time persuading and influencing people, as part of culture transformation, to make the most of new workspaces, with new ways of working.

I get huge satisfaction out of my job, although it would be great to be promoted. I make a difference here working on national security issues, protecting people and saving lives.

Other thoughts:

1. Do not try to learn to dance 10 minutes before the ball.
2. Bring your WHOLE authentic self – dyslexic strengths.
3. Own and be proud of your BRAND – make it your unique selling point.
4. Have a huge appetite for learning.
5. Always ask for help.

Personal Perspectives

## *LCS: Civil Servant/Programme Manager – Civil Service Profession*

I was diagnosed as dyslexic when I was 18 years old. Dyslexia has impacted me in different ways in different jobs. In some roles, such as houseparent in boarding schools, I noticed that my dyslexia was barely present as the tasks I needed to complete and the information I needed at hand were all provided in a way that I could manage and re-access with ease. However, in other roles, such as in the civil service, I can see the impact of my dyslexia in almost every task. I find reading long pieces of information (often technical) difficult, keeping a neat inbox a challenge, writing briefs or submissions frankly painful. Speaking in meetings is terrible as I often forget what I'm saying and in formal presentations I regularly find I can't remember anything I need to present.

I am glad I know I am dyslexic because I find it unbearable to read instructions or guidance – and so often ask my husband to sort finances/tax/application forms. Or he reads it and then explains it to me. I know I can read it all – but I just do all I can to avoid it! Socially, I'm known as quite scatty and quirky – which I'm not, as I'd say I'm pretty conventional. But I can see that I get this reputation as I often come at things from odd angles so can appear erratic if I don't focus on my intention. Also, sometimes my brain is quite foggy so it just socially lets me down. For example, instead of saying hello, I can end up saying goodbye – adding to the quirky label. In one job, the team leader flagged this, saying that at first they wondered what on earth they had done to employ such a 'ditz' – but then she realised that this was just my 'persona' and that my actual work was very good. Since then, I've tried to keep myself 'in line' socially, but it is hard to do!

I can really see that my brain works with far more range than others. It can spot problems and predict what others may do in response better than anyone else I know – and then consider the next steps using a very big picture model. I'm more intuitive, happy to draw on non-related fields for answers, and far more open to new options and challenge than anyone else I've worked with in the civil service. In any sort of problem-solving test, where the answer is only obvious at first to a small percentage of the population, I can see the answer straightaway. It has taken me years to realise that others don't find this easy – and that it is really a gift.

Part II

Filing and inbox management at work has been key – I keep everything and like a magpie I store helpful bits of information that I can lift text from.

Working from home has been a brilliant chance to manage my difficulties with presentations. I write all I need to say visually (like a mind map) on a massive piece of A1 paper and pin it behind the laptop. It has totally changed my ability to access information and removed the need to rely on memory.

As above, if I can use someone else's written work as a starting point, then I do. It saves the agony of the blank piece of paper. Then I adapt it to my own needs.

Setting in time ahead of meetings to think through what I need to say is so important to me. For years I thought everyone else just arrived at the meeting knowing perfectly what they wanted to say – but then I realised that this wasn't the case at all. Better prep gives better outcomes and the more I practise what I need to say the more successful my meetings are.

Learning to let things slide. I think as someone who struggles with organising information that I feel out of control and anxious if everything isn't locked down and completed. With an incredibly busy job, I've had to learn that things do need to be done at speed with mistakes or just left not completed. It was hard to do this at first, but after a few test runs to see whether I would really be 'in trouble' it was fine and has changed the way I work. I RAG rate my inbox, and anything that isn't red often now just doesn't get done.

I also use two laptops. One to work from and another to read documents and for a constant RAG rated to-do list that helps me juggle lots of conflicting deadlines.

---

### *MPS: Police Officer/Self-employed Security Consultant – Security Services*

'Needs to pay more attention.' 'Scruffy work again.' 'Daydreams and needs to focus.' 'Another term where his work failed to meet his promise.' 'An articulate and promising child, if only he would focus and check his spelling.' And in the final year before leaving secondary school, my career teacher's comment: 'You will be lucky to stack shelfs in a supermarket….' So school was not the best of places.

## Personal Perspectives

Knowing that you could do better, but somehow never did, was a hard way to learn about life. So, when one day, in my early twenties, listening to the radio and hearing somebody talk about dyslexia and how it showed itself was a pivotal moment. At last I thought, I knew what was wrong and how it affected me.

Technology was an aid, I became an early adopter of Psion Personal Digital Assistants. Storing names and numbers, rudimentary spellchecking and note-taking was useful. I was, though I did not know it, an unconscious compensator for my condition, adapting to overcome the challenges that dyslexia brings.

Knowing is one thing, but it was nearly ten years later that I plucked up the courage to get help. The driver for this was the desire to get a degree. The task seemed insurmountable and as I was in full-time employment, unrealistic. I had, though, in this time joined the Police Service, gone through training school getting very good grades, but the effort to do so was exhausting. Spending the weekends re-reading course notes, which increased in volume as the eighteen weeks progressed. And, of course, having had a blinding start, seeing my results drop, with the inevitable comments about slacking off and losing focus.

It was quite an emotional occasion when, having decided and found somewhere where I could get help, I was told that yes, I was dyslexic and my condition was a combination of auditory dyslexia and a shortage of working memory: a bit like a computer which has too little working RAM, so it just dumps stuff into the long-term (hard drive) memory, but fails to effectively log where it put in. The best bit was being told that, rather than being a bit thick, I had a high IQ.

Understanding why things did not work; addressing the often-time-consuming approaches that I had unconsciously developed to overcome my condition, became the aim of the help I got. Mind maps and coloured pens were my new weapon as I moved from unconscious to conscious compensator. Also, an acceptance that being a bit of a perfectionist was not helpful. I still am, though, oddly, a bit of a pedant around grammar and spelling.

In my early thirties, practising how to plan and write essays became my mission, often doing so while working shifts. Eventually, the degree process started, and I took an Honours degree in Policing. Four and a half years later I finished, but of course, even though I was given extra time in the exam room for my dyslexia, I still missed a 2:1 by 1 per cent because of written work:

## Part II

i.e., my spelling and grammar. Still, having worked shifts, travelled at short notice, and generally written my essays on a small PDA at odd moments, I had finished, so two fingers to the career teacher's comments when I left school.

While earning a degree was something to be proud of, I also embarked on what was a long and challenging process to become a Special Branch officer in the Police Service, partly as a result of the confidence I gained from working for a degree. The assessment process involved: day-long written exams: the range of subject matter and of course having just an hour to write a report drawn from various documents would have been impossible before getting help. So being one of just 20 who were accepted, out of the 500 plus who applied, was brilliant. And of course, I was now in a world of written reports and comprehensive briefing documents, drawn from multiple sources and succinctly distilled for a wide range of readers. I managed.

I left the service over ten years ago. I became a self-employed security consultant, advising on physical security, training, and assessing security staff. It was more operations. I worked on the Olympic Park through the final year of it being built and then during the London 2012 Olympics and Para-Olympics – and now as the Deputy Head of Security for a major sporting venue, holding one of the UK's most iconic sporting events, dealing with multi-million-pound contracts and budgets to match, along with being part of the team that plans the event. But yes, more reading and a lot of writing! But more in control!

Some would say it has worked out well, and they would be right. Others may say that having been through what I did, and overcome the setbacks, made me a better person, I guess so. But then I can be a bit bloody-minded, and very much subscribe to the 'you don't have to like it, you just have to do it' approach to life.

Despite all this, I have never lost the fear (back in the classroom) when someone points out a spelling mistake. No-one is more critical of me than myself. I still triple-check my work, to the annoyance of others. My finger still hovers over the send button before I send an email. Oddly I always misspell Security, no matter how much I try not to. I am still that shy kid at heart, who was afraid to get things wrong. If you offered me the chance to correct the condition, upgrade the RAM in a way, I would bite your arm off, if only to see how much more I could achieve.

Personal Perspectives

## LPO: Police Officer – Security Services

I write this account having lived for 46 years NOT KNOWING I was dyslexic! From a really young age, I remember hearing my mum constantly say how intelligent I was! As I progressed through junior school, due to my 'intelligence', I was encouraged to sit the 11+ exam. I don't recall much of the test itself. However, thinking about it now, I do remember enjoying the non-verbal reasoning tests, shapes, puzzles and sequences. Because of this pass, I was sent to a private school! I was placed into a class and most of my peers were the year above me. One thing I do remember was I dreaded ever being asked to read allowed in class. I could read, but some words were just hard to say and I was fearful of making myself look stupid.

Moving to secondary school, I kept myself to myself for the first year or so. I was quiet, pretty and just got on with my work. I excelled at maths and sport, so I guess the teachers were happy to just let me get on with it. But I left education at 18 with an A in French and D in Spanish. Going to university was never an option.

At 18, I made my decision, I wanted to join the police, so at 22 years old I became a full-time police officer. Each day would be different and I wouldn't have to be tied to a desk writing reports, something I really disliked. I found training school quite challenging and remember being at loggerheads with so many of the training staff. I would ask 'why' many times and for more explanation to so many things. This was just me wanting to fully understand everything that was being taught, not me being intentionally disruptive; however, that's how it was portrayed/perceived.

I knew the direction I wanted to go in. I wanted to work on plain clothes proactive units catching criminals in the act! I seemed to have developed a real natural aptitude for faces, the criminal ones, and number plates of cars, and found real strength in linking crime patterns and offenders. In 2000, I achieved the highest arrest rate in my area, second highest in the entire force. I could just sense a criminal, I can't put my finger on what it was, but I had what was described as 'copper's nose'. I would put myself in crime hotspots and I could just identify stolen cars and interpret the body language of people who were committing, or about to commit, a crime.

## Part II

I started to set my sights on where I wanted to work next and focused on the National Crime Squad. I worked hard and made it to that squad. It was tough, and some people seemed to want to undermine me – I was the only female – so had to work twice as hard to prove I was good enough to be there. During this time, I remember I was asked to put an application together to get a certain tactic lawfully authorised. I had no idea where to begin. I struggled to understand exactly what information was required. I was copied in accidentally into an email chain, definitely not for my eyes, and I was mortified to see the boss saying to another boss, 'Have you seen how terrible this application is? It's as if a 5 year old has written it.' It really upset me: my bosses were laughing at my inability to write. I didn't know what to do, but I knew I was OK when it came to writing about factual experiences. So I progressed within surveillance. This was what I had always wanted to do, and as it was nearly all practically based, I did well: I could use my eyes and ears. I managed to infiltrate so many criminals as they didn't bat an eyelid at my presence. I didn't look like a police officer! But in the office, I experienced discrimination. However, that was mainly based on the fact that I was a female rather than other reasons (well, that I knew of).

In 2004, I decided to put myself forward for promotion, and the next months were just pure hard work: the day job and studying, studying, studying. I had to read everything once or twice, highlight bits as well as make my own notes for the information to have any chance of any of it registering in my brain. I worked like this and I finally became a DS. I knew the rank for Detective Inspector, which was the next step, would bring on much more written work, therefore I opted to remain as a surveillance DS for the next 15 years. It took me that long to realise I was good enough to be promoted. I decided it was time to use the DI pass I had obtained 15 years ago. I didn't have a clue what the assessment would be, so I attended a 3-day intensive course. It was HELL. Throughout the day, we had information piled onto us from PowerPoint slides. I clearly wasn't cut out for this; this is all too difficult, and I'm really stupid!! The others on the course around me seemed so much better than me. I didn't understand what I wasn't good at or exactly what it was I was finding so difficult. I became physically ill as I feared failure. I was sick every night but I would wake up and tackle it again. And I was lucky at that

## Personal Perspectives

time. I was in a role that allowed me to use some time to study. Seven months later I passed and was promoted to DI.

After 15 years, I was there, a DI, and I could apply to be a negotiator; something I always knew what I wanted – helping other people who might be in crisis. I watched several online videos about negotiation and realised it was all about listening and talking to others. This was something I could do, and hopefully would be good at. The course had a pre-questionnaire asking how I learnt. I didn't know why they were asking us that, but was fascinated to see the results I generated; none of them said I liked to read when I learn. That was so true. All my answers seemed to say watch others or get hands on and see for yourself. The course was tough, the most mentally and emotionally draining course I have ever done. History was repeating itself: it was hell. A few times I asked if I could write some notes down to enable me to jog my memory, but was told no. Then we had an exam and, surprise, I failed: I got 9. I asked to resit it on the Monday – a weekend to revise. I had spent so many hours that weekend reading, making notes, drawing pictures, using single letters to enable me to remember words. I wanted to be a negotiator so badly, of course I was going to pass. But why was nobody else needing to do this? The end of the negotiator's course came and I passed. It was a brilliant feeling.

One of the trainers had seen me cry once too many times on week one. She was the first person who said, you seem to have a processing issue! I started to look it up on the internet. Did I have Aspergers, autism or was it something else? Several pages of things I was reading were describing ME and were pointing towards dyslexia. I had heard about it, but always thought it was something the naughty kids in the class suffered from. Not clever, intelligent people like me. But I was curious now. I completed a few of the online questionnaires and got really high scores in 2 or 3 of them, which gave an indication of dyslexia. Strangely I started to feel better.

The day of the assessment, I cried the entire time. It was a really emotional day. Aged 46, yes I am dyslexic. I cried different tears that afternoon, not ones of constant sadness, ones of joy. Finally I had a WHY and some answers as to WHY I had found so many things, connected to my learning, so incredibly hard. The assessor explained working memory and the fact my brain processed in a different way. Everything started to make sense: that's why I would have to go over and over and over work to give it a chance to move through my memory. That day I instantly stopped feeling stupid: dyslexia was not in any way linked to intelligence. That word intelligence I had heard so many times as a child from my mum was clearly true. How had I gone through all of my life not knowing this was who I was?

Prior to any assessment, when the word dyslexia started to feature, my husband said you can't be dyslexic, you are far too clever. But afterwards what it did help us both realise was we both think in a polar opposite way. He reads a newspaper from front to back, I just look at the pictures and headlines. He can't put together a piece of furniture without reading the manual from front to back, whereas I can just look at the bits and work out where they go. It was great. I was no longer stupid and I understood why.

I have stayed in the same line of work for so many years because I enjoy it, because I'm good at it, but also because it's taken 23 years for that type of work and what is required to stay in my long-term memory (well, not everything). I never wanted to be put in a situation I felt out of my depth, as I didn't have enough knowledge to talk or blag my way out of it. I think I might be braver now, as I have a why and feel more comfortable to ask for help in completing tasks. Not selling myself short or focusing on my weakness, just because if somebody needs an explanation, I now know what to say. However, I have always been able to think outside the box and problem-solve whether it be in a DIY sense or how I can covertly obtain information about a criminal.

There are clearly so many different types of brains and different dyslexias. I have excellent time-keeping, am never late, can plan my day well and have a great ability to remember people's names and faces. That's not a common skill in other dyslexics. However, I lack creative thought. I can't simply imagine nor can I understand a fiction-based book unless I physically see what it is that's being spoken about.

It's been the toughest journey of my life, but it has put me into the most powerful place I can be in. I believe in my ability and finally know I'm good at what I do. I have tried to stop focusing on my negatives and sell my strengths. My goal now, if I can do one thing, is to help others identify they may be dyslexic, if they don't know, to ensure they don't spend a day longer feeling negative about themselves.

Personal Perspectives

### *SFS: Product Manager – Financial Services Industry*

I see dyslexia as challenges with cognitive processing. I was diagnosed quite young (around 7 years old) as a result of other family members previously having been diagnosed. It characterises itself differently between our family members, for example strategies and strengths. This makes me appreciate how many individual differences there are and how difficult it can be to both understand and sometimes explain to others. So I rarely actively choose to tell colleagues.

I am organised, a strong verbal communicator, and considerate of others and compassionate. I am thoughtful, precise/accurate and have good attention to detail. I find it difficult to assess which of these are influenced by dyslexia (i.e., strategies) and which are inherent or learnt from other experiences/influences.

Being dyslexic means it takes me longer to process information or make sense of new things. It slows my pace of 'doing style' work: for example where there is a tangible output. And I find ordering thoughts challenging. I plan a lot. And I overcome these challenges with hard work/persistence and willingness to put in more hours mostly. Being very organised and verbally articulate probably help too. At work, I use a lot of frameworks (e.g. SWOT, PEST, 5Ws). I focus on what do I know/can do and try not to get too overwhelmed with all the other things. I also have strong support networks, family and friends.

I joined the army. I was commissioned as an officer doing roles across HR, logistics and training. Subsequently, I joined a well-known global bank – again across various roles including fraud and risk, project management and product. At the moment I am a product manager. It is not necessarily the right job for me. It has some analytical elements which I enjoy, but lacks the sense of developing others that is important to me. I hope to find a profession I am more engaged in where I feel I can add a lot of value and that I find more personally rewarding.

I joined both the army and the bank for the same reasons. I was attracted to the learning opportunities by being in a large organisation and working with driven people from mixed backgrounds and experiences. They are both credible organisations that I'm proud to have work(ed) for and offer

Part II

good job stability. I have been able to successfully do these roles by being diligent and professional and upholding high standards alongside strong morals.

### *SDS: Data Scientist*

I was diagnosed with dyslexia in university as I was having a lot of difficulty writing my Master's thesis. I was unable to proofread my thesis. My brain would autocorrect, so I would not see the mistakes. Even though I was not diagnosed with dyslexia until I was in my early twenties, I knew from a young age that I had difficulty with reading and spelling. However, it was not until I was diagnosed that I realised that other issues I had always faced were also attributed to dyslexia, such as not being able to tell left from right, having no sense of direction, completely losing words and having sequencing issues.

I had an English teacher in secondary school who told me that it did not matter if I could not spell; to not be hung up on this, as once the person who was correcting my exams knew what I meant I would lose very few marks for not having the correct spelling. I think that gave me confidence going into exams. I think the fact that I was always good at maths also gave me confidence in school. While I may have been struggling in some areas, at least there was always something that I had confidence in. I was lucky that both my school and my family encouraged me in this area.

Overall I am glad that I got the dyslexia diagnosis. It means that I am less hard on myself and it gives me more confidence to not do something the typical way. I have always had to figure out a different way of doing things, so I am good at seeing solutions that others may not. I think having dyslexia has made me more resilient. When I am faced with a challenge I don't give up easily because I am used to overcoming challenges and figuring things out. I am a visual thinker. I can visualise what something may look like or how various scenarios may play out. This also means that I am good at connecting dots and finding new or existing patterns.

In terms of my personal life, dyslexia for the most part does not have a massive effect. That may be the way that I have structured my life. Those close to me understand that I hate messaging and that it is best to just call me. I have accepted that I will never be a bookworm, but I really enjoy listening to audiobooks. I ensure that I always have a to-do list on the go. When I am handed a form, I still panic, but then take a deep breath and realise that it may take me ages to fill out but I will get there. Both in my personal life and at work I use assistive technology, mainly text to speech. Having assistive technology has been a game changer.

In terms of work, I am still trying to figure out different ways of working. As well as using assistive technology, I try to get my colleagues to verbally explain things to me, which I find easier to understand than written stuff. When I worked in consulting, while I was given all the assistive technology I needed, I was often put in roles that were not related to data science that I found difficult because of my dyslexia: reading loads of reports, collating the information and writing it up with very tight deadlines. When I raised this, my dyslexia was acknowledged, but nobody did anything. I kept being put in roles that were hard. Ultimately I ended up leaving that job.

So far in my new job, I have not faced such issues. I am currently working as a data scientist. I chose this profession as I had an interest and an aptitude for maths and problem-solving. I think that having a different perspective and finding innovative solutions has helped me.

Is this the right job is a hard question. Yes and no. I do face difficulties with emails and paperwork overload on a daily basis that could be attributed to dyslexia, and there are loads of jobs out there that may be easier. At the same time, I have an interest in data science and I enjoy what I do even if it is at times challenging. And I enjoy creating something and problem-solving. My job allows me to do both of those things. I can come up with innovative solutions by seeing the big picture and how components all fit together. At the moment, I am trying to upskill in data visualisation.

I would say that there is always more than one way to do something. As a dyslexic, the conventional way of doing something may not work, so you have to have the confidence to do things in a way that works for you. I think my personality has helped me get to where I am today. I am naturally determined, driven and at times a bit stubborn. So when I was faced with a challenge or something I could not do when growing up, my natural response was to keep going until I overcame that challenge – and it still is!

Part II

### *CTB: Founder/CEO of a Technology Business*

Dyslexia is very personal. It's not a label I wear freely, as most people (including myself) don't fully understand what it means or how it affects someone. I've found that because there's nothing physically wrong, there's a general disbelief that you may be struggling.

I was diagnosed at 22, late in my academic life, when I was just starting university. Up till that point I felt (most of the time) I was stupid, as that's what the education system had led me to believe too. I'm not stupid, I'm smart. Academia, however, does not come easy to me – but like most dyslexics I've met I am defiant and I am a grafter!

I studied Marketing and Economics at university, so I chose to follow that as a career path. I found the corporate world a difficult one to navigate. They never understood dyslexia and how to support me. That said, where I was able to do my best work was always in smaller companies of 75–100 people. I think this is due to less bureaucracy and company politics, which meant I could just be myself at work. I'd say with work, don't go to a company just because it has a recognisable name. I've worked at one that was run by a famous dyslexic and there was no support. Corporate life always felt for me like trying to squash a round peg into a square hole. I found all the negative aspects of my dyslexia were exacerbated in larger companies, and all the positive aspects were allowed to flourish in a smaller company. It was when I was working in a small organisation that I saw a gap in the market and set up my own business, which is growing steadily.

Working for myself means I'm not managed by anyone, which makes a big difference to my day/week, as I can work in a way that best suits me. It's a luxury I know from previously working in corporates that you don't get. I think I am on the right career path because being my own boss gives me the freedom to cut out all the bureaucracy of corporate environments and focus on my strengths. I've structured my current business, and plan day-to-day work, to play to my strengths, keeping admin to a fractional part of my daily role, and (when I remember to!) I do the more detailed heavy paperwork at the beginning of the day.

I love my job! Every day I get to solve (non-client) micro-problems. By the time the day has ended there's (usually) a tangible result. As a dyslexic, I think I am best at creative problem-solving and joining the dots. I can spot things that others can't and make connections where others don't. I thrive on seeing visual

Personal Perspectives

progress. I have also surrounded myself with bright minds, which means we talk things through and solve complex problems. I can also get to an answer to solve a problem faster than most. Seeing the world differently, and not being afraid to ask 'how' or 'why', is a core skill, but this can jar with others who don't like to question the status quo and caused me problems in the corporate world. I am always thinking ahead. Professionally, I'd love to take the business international.

The single biggest factor in helping me was my diagnosis and dyslexia coaching. It enabled me to understand struggles I'd had growing up and as an adult. It has been fantastic for me. I know now that it impacts every area of my life, the good and the bad. Most obviously my time-keeping is poor; whether it's a meeting or getting the kids ready for school, I am consistently running late. I've realised I underestimate how long tasks will take so am forever rushing. In my work, I have to be a lot more organised with the structure of my day, and trying to keep a routine, while I know it's important and helpful, is also in itself a challenge.

Tips for other dyslexic people.

- Find a dyslexic coach you like – they can help you massively with tips, techniques, advice and help you build confidence.
- Setting a routine, and planning as much as possible, has been so helpful, as has having a raft of reminders on my phone.
- Seeking out the smaller companies to work in – the hidden gems that pack a punch for their size – that's where you'll find the freedom to be yourself and demonstrate your strengths. What I found is people are generally more open and inclusive in these kinds of environments.

BUT

I'm afraid to say hard work has been the only way to get to where I am currently.

## *DPS: Psychologist*

When thinking about dyslexia, the first word that came immediately to mind was 'inconvenient'. I am so worried about making a spelling or grammar error in my reports, I check, double-check, triple-check everything. I will never get

Part II

commas, and rely heavily on my proofreader/grammar guru: 'Did I switch from Sophie to Sofie halfway through the report?' 'Have I spelt Madhumetha correctly throughout?' It's very time consuming. I have always assumed that when people (possibly not in our industry) read something that has lots of spelling and grammar errors, they form a negative impression of the writer: that is that their poor literacy is a reflection of their ability.

Where does dyslexia end and personality start? If I had not been so woefully bad at literacy as a child, would I still engage in this anal-retentive, potty trained at gunpoint, neurotic triple-checking? Or am I placing too much significance on the dyslexia? Perhaps I would have been a conscientious (if I am being kind), neurotic (if I am being honest), person anyway? This reminds me of a conversation I had many years ago. If the offending collection of dyslexia-related genes could be isolated and removed, would I still be me? What would an efficient me look like?

In terms of dyslexic strengths, I have seen the commonly referred to artistic strengths at the Surrey Institute of Art and Design and the London College of Fashion. I cannot, however, even draw stick-men and feel quite hard done by.

I feel I irritate my husband when I have to ask him for help. He has just walked in the door and I am asking him something about grammar. I had a little bit of a ding-dong with the head of the JCQ some years ago. We were chatting on the phone and he said something along the lines of 'Parents commission a private assessment from someone like you, you waltz into the school, drop the report on the desk and expect everyone to jump to it and the child wears their dyslexia label as a "badge of honour"'. He really upset me. How about you walk around in my nine-year-old's shoes for a while? I remember standing outside the classroom door on days we had French, sobbing. Recently, a friend of mine did a talk on the dyslexia-friendly classroom. In order to demonstrate how hard it is to copy something you cannot read, she had us copy the Lord's Prayer in Greek. I broke into a sweat. Badge of honour my arse!

As well as my psychologist work, I have another job, which I sort of inherited. About 10 years ago, the government got busy in my industry. The annual rent review went from three lines ('Dear resident, the current rent is X, the RPI is Y, therefore next year's rent will be Z') to 9–10 pages that have to be completed individually for each tenant. If a mistake is made (including a spelling

## Personal Perspectives

or typo), the form is not valid. Best case scenario, I have to do it all again, worst case I end up in a tribunal. You can imagine the state I get in when I have to complete 96 of these each February!

But I am a big fan of tech. I particularly like 'OK Google/Alexa/Siri, how do you spell....' It makes a huge difference, but I did not realise how dependent on this I was until I was in the car with my husband-to-be trying to text a bridesmaid about my wedding dress. I did not want my husband-to-be to know the colour (yes, I know, sentimental nonsense, but at the time it seemed important). So I could not ask Google in front of him. Obergene? Oberjean? Turns out aubergine starts with an 'A'. Who knew!

## 9.2  Conclusion

We feel that these are an impressive set of stories. They are from dyslexic people and cover a range of occupational backgrounds, along with a mixture of experiences and perceptions about their dyslexia and the issues they have faced relating to their dyslexia. The individual differences in those experiences come out clearly; as do the challenges and solutions. Trying to sum them up would be impossible – and we are sure others have additional stories to tell with different experiences of success. However, we hope that the experiences presented in this chapter provide some insight and encouragement.

We are extremely grateful for these stories and all those who have shared their experiences and strategies – and have contributed so much to this book.

# 10

# Summary and Conclusions
# A Revised Framework

In this final chapter, we summarise some of the ideas presented in the rest of the book. The framework proposed argues that the cause of dyslexia is related to an inefficiency of the phonological processing system. Hence, the framework also argues that cognitive and behavioural factors associated with dyslexia lead to different consequences and outcomes. These develop based on individual differences associated with the past experiences of the dyslexic adult. The mix of underlying skills, past experiences, and current circumstances means that some dyslexic people succeed in their chosen area, whereas others are less successful. The reasons for these differences are highly complex and very individual.

One of the aims of this book is to provide ideas to help dyslexic people to become more successful. With this in mind, we have

## Summary and Conclusions: A Revised Framework

adapted the framework presented in Chapter 2 (see Table 10.1) in order to bring together theory and practice as we understand them, along with the experiences of our dyslexic contributors. We recognise that dyslexia can present huge challenges, particularly in an increasingly literacy-focused world. Therefore, Chapters 1 to 3 focus on our current understanding of dyslexia, while most of the rest of the book aims to discuss solutions, and to provide ideas and encouragement for dyslexic people who still face challenges in the modern world.

Note that the left-hand side of the framework presented in Table 10.1 is based partly on that proposed by Frith (1999). We have moved the environment column so it is between the biology/genetic and consequences columns. We have done this because it has been increasingly evident throughout the book that the environment plays an important part in our dyslexic contributors' journey. The variability in success may be related to the environment as much as their individual abilities and difficulties. This includes the environment in which they have grown up, their education, family background, and friends, as well as experiences in the workplace. How people respond to these environmental factors influences their sense of personal achievement and success. We have added two extra columns to the framework. The fourth column focuses on key ideas discussed throughout the book: self-understanding; metacognitive strategies; and self-efficacy, job satisfaction, control, and goodness of fit. The final column lists the external aids that can make a big difference to an individual's success as illustrated by our contributors.

Self-understanding is a cornerstone of many of the discussions in this book. If you know what you are good at and what you struggle with, you have a better chance of finding ways to deal with problems and emphasise the positives. This relates to the use of metacognitive strategies. Knowing how to deal with issues and when to implement

Part II

**Table 10.1 Framework for representing key elements of adult dyslexia and success**

| Bases of Dyslexia | Environment | Consequences | Fundamentals of success |
|---|---|---|---|
| **Brain/biology**<br>Genetic factors<br>Brain differences | Learning experiences<br>Workplace structure and ecosystem | **Emotional and behavioural reactions & self-concept**<br>Positive: determination and focus<br>Negative: low self-esteem/low confidence<br>Presenting self to others | **Self-understanding**<br>Understanding your challenges and your strengths |
| **Cognition**<br>Phonological processing deficit<br>Poor understanding of grapheme–phoneme correspondences | Understanding job demands<br>Developing work-specific expertise<br>Coaching/training | **Certain aspects of Language, memory, and cognition**<br>Overload of information<br>Memory weaknesses<br>Problems with novelty<br>Processing a lot of information at speed<br>**Positive skills**<br>Creative problem-solving<br>People skills<br>Bigger picture thinking | **Metacognition**<br>Identify how you learn and work best<br>Identify and use strategies that work for you |

## Summary and Conclusions: A Revised Framework

| **Behaviour** | Support from | **Work challenges** | **Self-efficacy** |
|---|---|---|---|
| Difficulty learning to read and write | managers | Promotion opportunities | Believe you can do it |
| Weaker literacy skills | Adjustments Extra time Technology | Literacy task completion Multitasking Assessments | **Job satisfaction** Motivation Goodness of fit Being in control |
| | | **Positive attributes** Determination Persistence Resilience | |

strategies in the right context should improve self-efficacy and feelings of being in control. Many successful adult dyslexics report that they generally feel in control of what they are doing. This relates to work and to education, and could generalise to most of your life. Furthermore, if you understand your strengths and weaknesses, then there is a better chance of finding a job that enables you to demonstrate those strengths; that is, of seeking a goodness of fit between you and the job you are doing. Equally, many weaknesses can be mitigated by the use of strategies, given that you know what works for you; and skills can be further supported through appropriate adjustments and positive social support systems in the workplace.

In addition to these general themes, the chapters in Part II discuss strategies, and sometimes activities, that might contribute to these elements of success. We hope that implementing them and working out what is important for you will be enjoyable. In Chapter 4, we look at strategies focusing on personal development, which should increase chances of success. The ideas again emphasise the importance of self-understanding; in terms of dyslexia and individual skills and abilities. They also focus on metacognitive and executive processing to improve performance. The strategies discussed in the chapter touch on planning, and goal-setting. We suggest some ways to overcome problems related to memory, a common cause of lack of confidence among dyslexic adults. We also cover additional aspects of confidence and self-efficacy. For example, the reflective element of metacognition can lead to increased confidence and a sense of resilient self-efficacy. These can lead to the development of task-specific expertise. Equally, we caution that overthinking and over self-analysis can sometimes be counterproductive; thinking usually needs to be replaced by action at some point. Finally, and also related to the ideas of self-awareness, we include a discussion of potential disclosure of dyslexia itself and how to promote this positively.

Chapters 5 and 6 focus on literacy, language and effective communication. Chapter 5 specifically deals with the literacy and language issues that are related to processing of words (word reading and spelling) and the processing of text (comprehension and production). Tasks and activities are included in this chapter to show some of the things that can promote basic and more advanced reading skills, and how using meaning (morphological units represent meaning) supports understanding of text. The ideas and activities suggested may not be appropriate for all, but we believe an increased linguistic understanding leads to a curiosity, respect, and appreciation of words, rather than fear. The activities can be fun, and can lead to better understanding and increase self-efficacy in dealing with text.

Chapter 6 focuses on other areas of communication, particularly those used in the workplace. It considers how listening and speaking affect participation in meetings. It also looks at attending

## Summary and Conclusions: A Revised Framework

conferences and lectures, and contributing to workshops where relatively rapid understanding of material/information may be necessary. Issues related to producing documents, reports, or minutes of meetings at speed are also discussed. This chapter also introduces another metacognitive strategy, the 4 Ms of making things manageable, meaningful, multisensory, and memorable – and shows how this may improve performance.

In Chapter 7, we look at strategies that can be targeted specifically within the workplace. The chapter focuses on a number of the challenges that our dyslexic contributors highlight, and some of the solutions that may overcome them. Such solutions include the ability to prioritise as a key skill when dealing with complex work situations. Similarly, being as organised as you can be improves your chance of success in most workplace contexts. Prioritising and organising when dealing with complex tasks (or multitasking) require an element of making things manageable, using chunks of time to achieve specific goals and avoid fatigue. We touch again on the ideas related to the 4Ms, but also consider the idea of SMART goals (making them Specific, Measured, Achievable, Relevant, and Timed). We explore ways in which to deal with potentially stressful situations, using metacognitive skills to feel more in control and be better able to deal with a rapidly changing work environment – particularly post-pandemic and when working from home. We also talk about previewing, thinking ahead, and preparing for new environments and new situations to decrease stress. We include some tips from our contributors to help with stress, including taking breaks, rewarding yourself, and making time for yourself in terms of rest and hobbies.

In Chapter 7, we also touch on change in terms of new jobs and promotion. The latter can include the need for workplace training and professional examinations or assessments. We discuss managing the competing demands of professional examinations, work, and

Part II

family life; again, flexible planning is a solution. Planning, previewing, practising, and preparing are also discussed in terms of helping to build confidence. The purpose of workplace training is to improve skills and develop task-specific expertise, which can increase resilient self-efficacy and encourages motivation and a sense of achievement. However, it can also be associated with finding your niche in work life, which brings us back to ideas of goodness of fit and job satisfaction, and being as much in control as possible – making your own decisions. We also emphasise throughout these chapters that these strategies are suggestions and are therefore most effective if they are personalised. This also means that they need not be adopted fully but might be most helpful when the underlying principles are incorporated into a personal work toolkit. As with many of the ideas presented, they need to be practised.

Chapter 8 moves on to discuss organisational factors that can lead to success. The chapter also considers the responsibilities of employers and the benefits of mentors/coaches. We discuss ideas such as a personal work passports, which allow manager and employee alike to recognise challenges and possible solutions. Ways to think about advice and feedback from others (managers, including human resources, coaches, mentors, tutors, and trainers) is also discussed in the chapter. People are often the most supportive external factors, but practical resources/tools and technology can all assist. Use of a mobile/smartphone may be the most useful tool: with day-to-day and workplace tasks, it can help to recall what has to be done. Applications on a phone or computer can also provide a range of strategies to deal with work requirements. In this chapter, we focus on a range of comments from contributors about how they use some of these tools.

In Chapter 8, we touch on the sometimes controversial issue of reasonable adjustments in workplace contexts. This leads to a

## Summary and Conclusions: A Revised Framework

discussion of legislation, as employers have to meet legal requirements to be inclusive in the workplace. Some of the key points in current legislation in the UK are presented as an example. Although these may not be applicable in other parts of the world, they provide a discussion point, both in terms of the points made in the chapter and in terms of thinking about what legislation there may be in the part of the world where you reside. Often, legislation related to disability attempts to ensure equity, though, as we discuss in the chapter, defining 'reasonable' can lead to complexity. Similarly, individual differences may make a reasonable adjustment appropriate for one person but less useful for another.

In Chapter 9, we focus on the stories of adult dyslexics themselves. Although the rest of the book is informed by the comments and views of adult dyslexics, it is in Chapter 9 where their perspectives are presented at length. These are just a sample of those we received while we were putting the book together. We thank everyone who discussed ideas with us and shared how they dealt with challenges. It is not possible to summarise all the ideas presented, but we feel that the ones we chose illustrate many that we have developed throughout the rest of the book. Many contributors suggested that being nice to yourself is important. We would agree. It is also particularly evident that working hard and being determined are overriding themes in their stories. We hope that some of their experiences will resonate with the dyslexic reader and provide a basis on which to further develop skills and strategy frameworks in the future. We also hope that those who work or live with dyslexic people will gain insight into the issues they face.

In conclusion, we explore in this book what dyslexia in adulthood can mean, and what might be done to deal with the challenges: there is no single, correct answer for all, so taking an individual differences approach, looking at your individual abilities, skills, and experience, and knowing how it affects you, is important. With this in mind, we present a large number of ideas and strategies in the hope that there is something in this book for most readers. We hope you explore those that you feel might help and build your own professional toolkit or framework for success. The most effective strategies are likely to be those that have been personalised and refined. Self-understanding should be constructive and personally motivating, and it should lead to good strategy selection, good communication, and, therefore, individual success.

Thank you again to all our contributors, and to the many people we have worked with who have been the inspiration for this book.

# References

Aarts, H., Dijksterhuis, A., & Midden, C. (1999). To plan or not to plan? Goal achievement or interrupting the performance of mundane behaviors. *European Journal of Social Psychology*, 29, 971–979.

Abele, A. E. & Spurk, D. (2009). The longitudinal impact of self-efficacy and career goals on objective and subjective career success. *Journal of Vocational Behavior*, 74, 53–62.

Bailey, C. E. (2007). Cognitive accuracy and intelligent executive function in the brain and in business. *Annals of the New York Academy of Sciences*, 1118, 122–141.

Bandura, A. (1986). *Social foundations of thought and action: A social cognitive theory*. Englewood Cliffs, NJ: Prentice-Hall.

Bandura, A. (1997). *Self-efficacy: The exercise of control*. New York: Freeman.

Bandura, A. & Locke, E. A. (2003). Negative self-efficacy and goal effects revisited. *Journal of Applied Psychology*, 88, 187–199.

Banich, M. T. (2009). Executive function: The search for an integrated account. *Current Directions in Psychological Science*, 18, 89–94.

Baum, J. R. & Bird, B. J. (2010). The successful intelligence of high-growth entrepreneurs: Links to new venture growth. *Organization Science*, 21(2), 397–412.

Billett, S., Harteis, C., & Gruber, H. (2018). Developing occupational expertise through everyday work activities and interactions. In K. A. Ericsson, R. R. Hoffman, A. Kozbelt, & A. M. Williams (Eds.), *The Cambridge handbook of expertise and expert performance*, 2nd ed. (pp. 105–126). Cambridge: Cambridge University Press.

Birney, D. P., Beckman, J. F., & Wood, R. E. (2012). Precursors to the development of flexible expertise: Metacognitive self-evaluations as antecedences and consequences in adult learning. *Learning and Individual Differences*, 22, 563–574.

## References

Borokowski, J. G. & Burke, J. E. (1996). Theories, models and measurements of executive functioning. In G. Reid Lyon & N. A. Krasnegor (Eds.), *Attention, memory and executive function* (pp. 235–261). Baltimore, MD: Paul H. Brookes.

Bowling, N. A. & Hammond, G. D. (2008). A meta-analytic examination of the construct validity of the Michigan organizational assessment questionnaire job satisfaction subscale. *Journal of Vocational Behaviour*, 73, 63–77.

Brooks, P., Everatt, J., & Fidler, R. (2016). *Adult reading test 2 (ART2)*, 2nd ed. Hayling Island: ART.

Butler, D. L. (1998). Metacognition and learning disabilities. In B. Y. L. Wong (Ed.), *Learning about learning disabilities*, 2nd ed. (pp. 277–307). San Diego, CA: Elsevier Academic Press.

Butler, D. L. & Schnellert, L. (2015). Success for students with learning disabilities: What does self-regulation have to do with it? In T. Cleary (Ed.), *Self-regulated learning interventions with at-risk youth: Enhancing adaptability, performance and well-being* (pp. 89–112). Washington, DC: APA Press.

Cain, K. (2010). *Reading development and difficulties*. Chichester: BPS Blackwell.

Chen, G., Gully, S. M., & Eden, D. (2004). General self-efficacy and self-esteem: Toward theoretical and empirical distinction between correlated self-evaluations. *Journal of Organizational Behavior*, 25(3), 375–395.

Chevalier, T. M., Parrila, R., Ritchie, K. C., & Deacon, S. H. (2017). The role of metacognitive reading strategies, metacognitive study and learning strategies, and behavioral study and learning strategies in predicting academic success in students with and without a history of reading difficulties. *Journal of Learning Disabilities*, 50(1), 34–48.

Chinn, S. J. & Ashcroft, J. R. (2017). *Mathematics for dyslexics and dyscalculics*, 4th ed. Chichester: Wiley.

Cianciolo, A. T. & Sternberg, R. J. (2018). Practical intelligence and tacit knowledge: An ecological view of expertise. In K. A. Ericsson, R. R. Hoffman, A. Kozbelt, & A. M. Williams (Eds.), *Cambridge handbook on expertise and expert performance*, 2nd ed. (pp. 770–792). Cambridge: Cambridge University Press.

Clarke, P. J., Truelove, E., Hulme, C., & Snowling, M. J. (2014). *Developing reading comprehension*. Chichester: Wiley.

## References

Cornoldi, C. & Oakhill, J. (Eds.). (1996). *Reading comprehension difficulties: Processes and intervention*. Mahwah, NJ: LEA.

Cousins, K. (2020). *Dyslexia and Success: The winning formula*. Dyslexia and Success Publishing.

Covey, S. R. (1991). *The seven habits of highly effective people*. Provo, UT: Covey Leadership Center.

Daloiso, M. (2017). *Supporting learners with dyslexia in the ELT classroom*. Oxford: Oxford University Press.

Davis, R. D. (1997). *The gift of dyslexia*. New York: Perigee Books.

de Beer, J., Heerkens, Y., Engels, J., & van der Klink, J. (2022). Factors relevant to work participation from the perspective of adults with developmental dyslexia: A systematic review of qualitative studies. *BMC Public Health*, 22(1), 1–20. https://doi.org/10.1186/s12889-022-13436-x

Diamond, A. (2013). Executive functions. *Annual Review of Psychology*, 64, 135–168.

Doyle, N. & McDowall, A. (2015). Is coaching an effective adjustment for dyslexic adults? *Coaching: An International Journal of Theory, Research and Practice*, 8, 154–168.

Du Pre, L., Gilroy, D., & Miles, T. (2007). *Dyslexia at college*, 3rd ed. Abingdon: Routledge.

Dweck, C. (2017). *Mindset: Changing the way you think to fulfil your potential*, 6th ed. Boston, MA: Robinson.

Dwyer, C., Hogan, M., & Stewart, I. (2014). An integrated critical thinking framework for the 21st century. *Thinking Skills & Creativity*, 12, 43–52.

Dwyer, P. (2022). The neurodiversity approach(es): What are they and what do they mean for researchers? *Human Development*, 66(2), 73–92.

Edwards, J. (1994). *The scars of dyslexia*. London: Cassell.

Efklides, A. (2008). Metacognition: Defining its facets and levels of functioning in relation to self-regulation and co-regulation. *European Psychologist*, 13(4), 277–287.

Elbeheri, G. & Everatt, J. (2016). Principles and guidelines in test construction for multilingual children. In L. Peer & G. Reid (Eds.), *Multilingualism, literacy and dyslexia*, 2nd ed. (pp. 49–60). Abingdon: Routledge.

Elbeheri, G. & Siang, L. (Eds.). (2022). *The Routledge international handbook of dyslexia in education*. Abingdon: Routledge.

## References

Ericsson, K. A. (2018). The differential influence of experience, practice, and deliberate practice on the development of superior individual performance of experts. In K. A. Ericsson, R. R. Hoffman, A. Kozbelt, & A. M. Williams (Eds.), *The Cambridge handbook of expertise and expert performance*, 2nd ed. (pp. 745–769). Cambridge: Cambridge University Press.

Everatt, J. (Ed.). (1999). *Reading and dyslexia: Visual and attentional processes*. London: Routledge.

Everatt, J. (2011). Dyslexia in adult students with English as an additional language. *Journal of Inclusive Practice in Further and Higher Education*, 3(1), 5–17.

Everatt, J. & Denston, A. (2020). *Dyslexia: Theories, assessment and support*. Abingdon: Routledge.

Everatt, J., Steffert, B., & Smythe, I. (1999). An eye for the unusual: Creative thinking in dyslexia. *Dyslexia*, 5, 28–46.

Fawcett, A. & Nicolson, R. (1994). *Dyslexia in children*. New York: Harvester-Wheatsheaf.

Feltovich, P. J., Prietula, M. J., & Ericsson, K. A. (2018). Studies of expertise from psychological perspectives: Historical foundations and recurrent themes. In K. A. Ericsson, R. R. Hoffman, A. Kozbelt, & A. M. Williams (Eds.), *The Cambridge handbook of expertise and expert performance*, 2nd ed. (pp. 59–83). Cambridge: Cambridge University Press.

Fernandez-Duque, D., Baird, J. A., & Posner, M. I. (2000). Executive attention and metacognitive regulation. *Consciousness and Cognition*, 9, 288–307.

Ferrer, E., Shaywitz, B. A., Holahan, J. M., Marchione, K., & Shaywitz, S. E. (2010). Uncoupling of reading and IQ over time: Empirical evidence for a definition of dyslexia. *Psychological Science*, 21(1), 93–101.

Fidler, R. & Everatt, J. (2012). Reading comprehension in adult students with dyslexia: Areas of weakness and strategies for support. In N. Brunswick (Ed.), *Supporting dyslexic adults in higher education and the workplace* (pp. 91–100). Chichester: Wiley-Blackwell.

Fink, R. P. (1998). Literacy development in successful men and women with dyslexia. *Annals of Dyslexia*, 48, 311–343.

Flavell, J. H. (1979). Metacognition and cognitive monitoring. *American Psychologist*, 34, 906–911.

Frith, U. (1999). Paradoxes in the definition of dyslexia. *Dyslexia*, 5, 192–214.

## References

Garner, J. K. (2009). Conceptualizing the relations between executive functions and self-regulated learning. *The Journal of Psychology*, 143, 405–426.

Gerber, P. J. (2012). The impact of learning disabilities on adulthood: A review of the evidenced-based literature for research and practice in adult education. *Journal of Learning Disabilities*, 45, 31–46.

Gerber, P. J. & Raskind, M. H. (2013). *Leaders, visionaries and dreamers extraordinary people with dyslexia and other learning disabilities.* Hauppauge, NY: Nova Science Publishers.

Gerber, P. J., Ginsberg, R., & Reiff, H. B. (1992). Identifying alterable patterns in employment success for highly successful adults with learning disabilities. *Journal of Learning Disabilities*, 25, 475–487.

Gillon, G. T. (2018). *Phonological awareness: From research to practice*, 2nd ed. New York: Guilford Press.

Glover, J. A., Ronning, R. R., & Bruning, R. H. (1990). *Cognitive psychology for teachers.* London: Macmillan.

Gollwitzer, P. M. & Oettinger, G. (2011). Planning promotes goal striving. In K. D. Vohs & R. F. Baumeister (Eds.), *Handbook of self-regulation: Research, theory and applications*, 2nd ed. New York: Guildford Press.

Hall, D. T. (2002). *Careers in and out of organisations.* Thousand Oaks, CA: Sage.

Hall, D. T. & Chandler, D. (2005). Psychological success: When the career is calling. *Journal of Organisational Behaviour*, 26, 155–176.

Heslin, P. A. (2005). Conceptualising and evaluating career success. *Journal of Organisational Behaviour*, 26, 113–136.

Heslin, P. A., Keating, L. A., & Ashford, S. J. (2020). How being in learning mode may enable a sustainable career across the lifespan. *Journal of Vocational Behavior*, 117, 103324.

Hock, M. (2012). Effective literacy instruction for adults with specific learning disabilities: Implications for adult educators. *Journal of Learning Disabilities*, 45, 64–78.

Hogan, R., Chamorro-Premuzic, T., & Kaiser, R. B. (2013). Employability and career success: Bridging the gap between theory and reality. *Industrial and Organizational Psychology*, 6, 3–16.

Horn, J. L. & Blankson, N. (2005). Foundations for a better understanding of cognitive abilities. In D. P. Flanagan & P. L. Harrison (Eds.), *Contemporary intellectual assessment.* New York: The Guilford Press.

# References

Hughes, E. C. (1958). *Men and their work*. Glencoe: Free Press.

Hulme, C. & Snowling, M. (Eds.). (1997). *Dyslexia: Biology, cognition and intervention*. London: Whurr.

Irlen, H. (1991). *Reading by the colors*. Garden City Park, NY: Avery Publishing Group.

Jackson, H., 2005. *Good grammar for students*. London: SAGE Publications.

Jackson, N. E. & Doelinger, H. L. (2002). Resilient readers? University students who are poor recoders but sometimes good text comprehenders. *Journal of Educational Psychology*, 94, 64–78.

Judge, T. A., Cable, D. M., Boudreau, J. W., & Bretz, R. D. (1995). An empirical investigation of the predictors of executive career success. *Personnel Psychology*, 48, 485–519.

Kail, R. & Salthouse, T. A. (1994). Processing speed as a mental capacity. *Acta Psychologica*, 86, 199–225.

Kanfer, R. & Ackerman. P. L. (2005). Work Competence: A person orientated approach. In A. J. Elliot & C. S. Dweck (Eds.), *Handbook of competence and motivation*. New York: The Guildford Press.

Kaufman, J. C. (Ed.). (2009). *Intelligent testing: Integrating psychological theory and clinical practice*. Cambridge: Cambridge University Press.

Kelemen, W. L., Frost, P. J., & Weaver, C. A. (2000). Individual differences in metacognition: Evidence against a general metacognitive ability. *Memory and Cognition*, 28(1), 92–107.

Kim, A.-H., Vaughn, S., Wanzek, J., & Wei, S. (2004). Graphic organizers and their effects on the reading comprehension of students with LD: A synthesis of research. *Journal of Learning Disabilities*, 37, 105–118.

Kintsch, W., Patel, V. L., & Ericsson, K. A. (1999). The role of long-term working memory in text comprehension. *Psychologia*, 42(4), 186–198.

Kirby, P. & Snowling, M. J. (2022). *Dyslexia: A history*. Montreal: McGill-Queens University Press.

Knoop-van Campen, C. A. N., Segers, E., & Verhoeven, L. (2018). How phonological awareness mediates the relation between working memory and word reading efficiency in children with dyslexia. *Dyslexia*, 24, 156–169.

Košak-Babuder, M., Kormos, J., Ratajczak, M., & Pižorn, K. (2019). The effect of read-aloud assistance on the text comprehension of dyslexic and non-dyslexic English language learners. *Language Testing*, 36(1), 51–75.

## References

Leather, C. (2018). *Explaining the relationship between aspects of metacognitive and cognitive function and the workplace success of dyslexic people.* PhD Thesis, University of Surrey, UK.

Leather, C., Hogh, H., Seiss, E., & Everatt, J. (2011). Cognitive function and work success in adults with dyslexia. *Dyslexia*, 17(4), 327–338.

Lesaux, N., Pearson, M., & Siegel, L. (2006). The effects of timed and untimed testing conditions on the reading comprehension performance of adults with reading disabilities. *Reading and Writing*, 19, 21–48.

Lezak, M. D., Howieson, D. B., Loring, D. W., Hannay, H. J., & Fischer, J. S. (2004). *Neuropsychological assessment*, 4th ed. New York: Oxford University Press.

Locke, E. A. & Latham, G. P. (2002). Building a practically useful theory of goal setting and task motivation. *American Psychologist*, 57, 705–717.

Logan, J. (2009). Dyslexic entrepreneurs: The incidence, their coping strategies and their business skills. *Dyslexia*, 15, 328–346.

Lunenburg, F. C. (2011). Self-efficacy in the workplace: Implications for motivation and performance. *International Journal of Management and Business Administration*, 14(1), 1–6.

Madaus, J., Zhao J., & Ruban, L. (2008). Employment satisfaction of university graduates with learning disabilities. *Remedial and Special Education*, 29, 323.

Magno, C. (2010). The role of metacognitive skills in developing critical thinking. *Metacognition and Learning*, 5(2), 137–156.

Mather, N. & Wendling, B. J. (2012). *Essentials of dyslexia assessment and intervention*. Chichester: Wiley.

McLoughlin, D. (2012). Dyslexia in employment: The impact of affective factors. In N. Alexander-Passe (Ed.), *Dyslexia and mental health: An investigation from differing perspectives* (pp. 165–178). New York: Nova Science Publishers.

McLoughlin, D. & Leather, C. A. (2013). *The adult dyslexic: Interventions and outcomes – an evidence based approach*, 2nd ed. Chichester: Wiley.

McLoughlin, D., Leather, C. A., & Stringer, P. E. (2002). *The adult dyslexic: Interventions and outcomes*. London: Whurr.

Miles, T. R. (1993). *Dyslexia: The pattern of difficulties*, 2nd ed. London: Whurr.

Miyake, A. & Friedman, N. P. (2012). The nature and organization of individual differences in executive functions: Four general conclusions. *Current Directions in Psychological Science*, 21(8), 8–14.

## References

Miyake, A., Emerson, M. J., & Friedman, N. P. (2000). Assessment of executive functions in clinical settings: Problems and recommendations. *Seminars in Speed and Language*, 21, 169–183.

Moats, L. C. (2010). *Speech to print: Language essentials for teachers*, 2nd ed. Baltimore, MD: Paul H. Brookes Publishers.

Moran, S. & Gardner, H. (2007). 'Hill, skill and will': Executive function from a multiple-intelligences perspective. In L. Meltzer (Ed.), *Executive functions in education: From theory to practice* (pp. 19–38). New York: The Guilford Press.

Nicolson, R. I. & Fawcett, A. J. (2019). Development of dyslexia: The delayed neural commitment framework. *Frontiers in Behavioral Neuroscience*, 13, 112. https://doi.10.3389/fnbeh.2019.00112

Norman, G. (2005). From theory to application and back again: Implications of research on medical expertise for psychological theory. *Canadian Journal of Experimental Psychology*, 59(1), 35–40.

Peng, P., Barnes, M., Wang, C., Wang, W., Li, S., Swanson, H. L., Dardick, W., & Tao, S. (2018). A meta-analysis on the relation between reading and working memory. *Psychological Bulletin*, 144(1), 48–76.

Rack, J. P., Snowling, M. J., & Olson, R. K. (1992). The nonword reading deficit in developmental dyslexia: A review. *Reading Research Quarterly*, 27, 29–53.

Raskind, M. H., Goldberg, R. J., Higgins, E. L., & Herman, K. L. (1999). Patterns of change and patterns of success in individuals with learning disabilities: Results from a twenty-year longitudinal study. *Journal of Learning Disabilities Research and Practice*, 14, 35–49.

Reid, G. & Clark, J. (2021). *Dyslexia tools: Workbook for teens*. Emeryville, CA: Rockridge Press.

Reid Lyon, G. & Krasnegor N. A. (1996). *Attention, memory, and executive function*. Baltimore, MD: Paul H. Brookes Publishing.

Reiff, H. B., Gerber, P. J., & Ginsberg, R. (1997). *Exceeding expectations: Successful adults with learning disabilities*. Austin, TX: Pro-Ed.

Ruban, L. M., McCoach, D. B., McGuire, J. M., & Reis, S. M. (2003). The differential impact of academic self-regulatory methods on academic achievement among university students with and without learning disabilities. *Journal of Learning Disabilities*, 36, 270–286.

## References

Salthouse, T. (2012). Consequences of age-related cognitive declines. *Annual Review of Psychology*, 63, 201–226.

Schnieders, C. A., Gerber, P. J., & Goldberg, R. J. (2016). Integrating findings of studies of successful adult with learning disabilities: A new comprehensive model for researchers and practitioners. *Career Planning and Adult Development Journal*, 31(4), 90–110.

Schraw, G. & Dennison, R. (1994). Assessing metacognitive awareness. *Contemporary Educational Psychology*, 19, 460–475.

Schraw, G. & Moshman, D. (1995). Metacognitive Theories. *Educational Psychology Review*, 7(4), 351–371.

Shaywitz, S. E. & Shaywitz, J. (2020). *Overcoming dyslexia*, 2nd ed. New York: Random House.

Shimamura, A. P. (2000). Toward a cognitive neuroscience of metacognition. *Consciousness and Cognition*, 9, 313–323.

Shin, J. (2020). A meta-analysis of the relationship between working memory and second language reading comprehension: Does task type matter? *Applied Psycholinguistics*, 41(4), 873–900.

Siegel, L. S. (1988). Evidence that IQ scores are irrelevant to the definition and analysis of reading disability. *Canadian Journal of Psychology*, 42, 201–215.

Simmons, F. & Singleton, C. (2000). The reading comprehension abilities of dyslexic students in higher education. *Dyslexia*, 6, 178–192.

Sleeman, M., Everatt, J., Arrow, A., & Denston, A. (2022). The identification and classification of struggling readers based of the Simple View of Reading. *Dyslexia*, 28(3), 256–275.

Smith-Spark, J. H., Henry, L. A., Messer, D., & Ziecik, A, (2016). Executive functions in adults with developmental dyslexia. *Research in Learning Disabilities*, 53–54. 323–341.

Smith-Spark, J. H., Henry, L. A., Messer, D. J., & Ziecik, A. P. (2017). Verbal and non-verbal fluency in adults with developmental dyslexia: Phonological processing or executive control problems? *Dyslexia*, 23, 234–250.

Smythe, I. & Everatt, J. (2009). Checklist for adults with dyslexia. In I. Smythe (Ed.), *Employment and dyslexia handbook 2009* (pp. 15–17). Bracknell: British Dyslexia Association.

Snowling, M. J. (2000). *Dyslexia*, 2nd ed. Oxford: Blackwell.

## References

Snowling, M. J., Dawes, P., Nash, H., & Hulme, C. (2012). Validity of a protocol for adult self-report of dyslexia and related difficulties. *Dyslexia*, 18(1), 1–15.

Stein, J. (2019). The current status of the magnocellular theory of developmental dyslexia. *Neuropsychologia*, 130, 66–77.

Sternberg, R. J. (1999). The theory of successful intelligence. *Review of General Psychology*, 3(4), 292–316.

Sternberg, R. J. (2005). Intelligence, competence and expertise. In A. J. Elliot & C. S. Dweck (Eds.), *Handbook of competence and motivation* (pp. 15–30). New York: The Guilford Press.

Stipanovich, N. (2015). Metacognitive strategies in the career development of individuals with learning disabilities. *Career Planning and Adult Development Journal*, 31(4), 120–130.

Stordy, B. J. & Nicholl, M. J. (2000). *The LCP solution: The remarkable nutritional treatment for ADHD, dyslexia and dyspraxia*. New York: Ballantine Books.

Suttle, C. M., Lawrenson, J. G., & Conway, M. L. (2018). Efficacy of coloured overlays and lenses for treating reading difficulty: An overview of systematic reviews. *Clinical and Experimental Optometry*, 101, 514–520.

Swanson, H. L. (1990). Influence of metacognitive knowledge and aptitude on problem solving. *Journal of Educational Psychology*, 82, 306–314.

Swanson, H. L. (2012). Adults with reading disabilities: Converting a meta-analysis to practice. *Journal of Learning Disabilities*, 45, 17–30.

Swanson, H. L. (2015). Intelligence, working memory, and learning disabilities. In T. C. Papadopoulous, R. K. Parrila, & J. R. Kirby (Eds.), *Cognition, intelligence and achievement* (pp. 175–196). Boston, MA: Elsevier.

Swanson, H. L. & Zheng, X. (2013). Memory difficulties in children and adults with learning difficulties. In H. L. Swanson, K. R. Harris, & S. Graham (Eds.), *Handbook of learning disabilities* (pp. 214–238). New York: The Guildford Press.

Tallal, P., Miller, S. L., Jenkins, W. M., & Merzenich, M. M. (1997). The role of temporal processing in developmental language-based learning disorders: Research and clinical implications. In B. A. Blachman (Ed.), *Foundations of reading acquisition and dyslexia: Implications for early intervention* (pp. 49–66). Mahwah, NJ: LEA.

Thiede, K. W., Anderson, M. C. M., & Therriault, D. (2003). Accuracy of metacognitive monitoring affects learning of texts. *Journal of Educational Psychology*, 95, 66–73.

## References

Thompson, P. A., Hulme, C., Nash, H. M., Gooch, D., Hayiou-Thomas, E., & Snowling, M. J. (2015). Developmental dyslexia: Predicting individual risk. *Journal of Child Psychology and Psychiatry*, 56, 976–987.

Thomson, M. (2009). *The psychology of dyslexia*, 2nd ed. Chichester: Wiley/Blackwell.

Torgesen, J. K. (1996). A model of memory from and information processing perspective: The special case of phonological memory. In G. Reid Lyon & N. A. Krasnegor (Eds.), *Attention, memory, and executive function* (pp. 157–184). Baltimore, MD: Paul H. Brookes Publishing.

Trainin, G. & Swanson, H. L. (2005). Cognition, metacognition and achievement of college students with learning disabilities. *Learning Disabilities Quarterly*, 28, 261–272.

Tunmer, W. E. & Chapman, J. W. (1996). A developmental model of dyslexia: Can the construct be saved? *Dyslexia*, 2, 179–189.

Van Bergen, E., de Jong, P. F., Maassen, B., & van der Leij, A. (2014). The effect of parents' literacy skills and children's preliteracy skills on the risk of dyslexia. *Journal of Abnormal Child Psychology*, 42(7), 1187–1200.

Vancouver, J. B. & Kendall, L. N. (2006). When self-efficacy negatively relates to motivation and performance in a learning context. *Journal of Applied Psychology*, 91(5), 1146–1153.

Veenman, M. V. J. & Spaans, M. A. (2005). Relation between intellectual and metacognitive skills: Age and task differences. *Learning and Individual Differences*, 15(2), 159–176.

Vinegrad, M. (1994). A revised adult dyslexia checklist. *Educare*, 48, 21–23.

Warmington, M., Stothard, S. E., & Snowling, M. J. (2013). Assessing dyslexia in higher education: The York adult assessment battery-revised. *Journal of Research in Special Educational Needs*, 13(1), 48–56.

West, T. G. (1991). *In the mind's eye*. Buffalo, NY: Prometheus.

Whitmore, J. (1992). *Coaching for performance: A practical guide to growing your own skills*. Boston, MA: Nicholas Brealey Publishing.

Wilkins, A. (2005). *Reading through colour*. Chichester: Wiley

Winner, E., von Karolyi, C., Malinsky, D., French, L., Seliger, C., Ross, E., & Weber, C. (2001). Dyslexia and visual-spatial talents: Compensation vs deficit model. *Brain and Language*, 76, 81–110.

## References

Wissell, S., Karimi, L., Serry, T., Furlong, L., & Hudson, J. (2022). 'You Don't Look Dyslexic': Using the job demands-resource model of burnout to explore employment experiences of Australian adults with dyslexia. *International Journal of Environmental Research and Public Health*, 19(17), 10719. https://doi.org/10.3390/ijerph191710719

Wong, B. (1996). Metacognition and learning disabilities. In B. Y. L. Wong (Ed.), *ABCs of learning disabilities* (pp. 120–139). San Diego, CA: Academic Press.

Yost, E. B. & Corbishley, M. A. (1987). *Career counseling: A psychological approach*. San Francisco, CA: Jossey-Bass.

Zimmerman, B. J. (2006). Development and adaptation of expertise: The Role of Self-Regulatory Processes and Beliefs. In K. A. Ericson, N. Charness, R. J. Feltovich, & R. R. Hoffman (Eds.), *The Cambridge handbook of expertise and expert performance*. Cambridge: Cambridge University Press.

Zimmerman, B. J., Bandura, A., & Martinez-Pons, M. (1992). Self-motivation for academic attainment: The role of self-efficacy beliefs and personal goal setting. *American Educational Research Journal*, 29, 663–676.

# Index

'4 M's', 22, 168, 170, 172, 181, 189, 190, 193, 194, 197, 202, 204, 217, 305
5-w rule, 121

Access to Work, 253, 265, 266
accessible, 109, 179, 181, 187, 212, 215, 217, 248, 261
accommodations, 9, 33, 41
achievement, 18
adjustments, 61, 111, 134, 224, 225, 228, 245, 252, 253, 255, 257–261, 265, 275, 283, 303, 306
advocate, 93, 96, 100, 137, 232
anxiety, worry, 17, 26, 49, 50, 56, 65, 69, 96, 97, 128, 139, 203, 205, 217, 227, 243, 254, 257, 264, 270–272
applications, 165, 166, 225, 248, 257
apprenticeship, 213
assessors, 4, 35, 36, 38, 46, 47, 57, 156, 223, 234, 240, 253
assistive technology, 86, 99, 172, 179, 225, 240, 258, 261, 295
attention, 4, 9, 13, 69, 71, 78, 119, 121, 124, 185, 196, 211, 235, 247, 286, 293
attribution, 22, 111, 115, 116
audience, 178, 244
automatic, 77, 106, 107, 109, 142, 144, 170, 197, 221
automaticity, 12, 78, 106–108, 125, 197

Bandura, A., 61, 65–68, 75, 128
behaviour, 17, 19, 69, 71, 74, 98, 99, 103, 112, 123, 265, 270, 271, 275

big picture, 269
biological, 13, 28, 32, 57
bullet points, 181, 186

career success, 4, 22, 61–64, 68, 85, 267
chairing, 187
charitable organisations, 266
childhood, 5, 7, 30, 39, 56, 57, 75, 80, 91, 93, 96, 134, 142
chunking, 31, 104, 119, 120
civil service, 221, 267, 282–285
coaching, 8, 92, 93, 116, 179, 180, 225, 228, 229, 240–244, 253, 261, 265, 266, 271, 278, 280, 297
communication, 18, 22, 100, 134, 139, 146, 168, 169, 177, 188, 210, 230, 233, 252, 279, 304, 308
comorbidity, 8–10
compensatory, 9, 25, 34, 39, 43, 46, 56, 76, 108, 164
control, 19, 22, 48, 49, 71, 73, 81, 82, 111, 124, 125, 128, 132, 189, 193, 196, 199, 204, 217, 247, 286, 288, 303, 305, 306
counsellors, 239
Covey, S.R., 194, 195
Covid-19, 86, 191, 197, 210, 234, 239, 265
creative, 26, 43, 47, 49, 91, 98, 118, 147, 148, 181, 217, 226, 247, 269, 272, 292, 296
creativity, 26, 46, 57, 81, 205, 221, 278
criticism, 126, 177

321

# Index

decoding, 6–8, 15, 17, 29, 30, 39, 40, 42, 44, 46, 55, 108, 142, 143, 145, 148, 150, 156–159, 164, 167
definition of dyslexia, 6
definitions of success, 21, 60
diagnosis, 45, 97, 138, 174, 178, 240, 265, 272, 274–278, 294, 297
dictionaries, 152, 155
disclosure, 134, 136, 137, 224, 232, 234, 245, 304
distraction, 31, 97, 181
Dweck, C., 67, 128
dyspraxia, 4, 9, 13, 265, 283

effort, 17, 39, 60, 65, 68, 92, 96, 101, 107, 108, 115, 122, 123, 125, 130, 170, 177, 199, 203, 222, 237, 261, 276, 287
emails, 121, 169, 172, 175, 177, 178, 192, 196, 197, 221, 224, 244, 295
emotional, 17, 25, 32, 34, 56, 67, 82, 130, 226, 227, 243, 270, 287, 291
employment, 3, 5, 13, 18, 20, 26, 32, 37, 57, 62, 63, 72, 246, 266, 287
engagement, 161, 163, 165, 171
engineering, 47, 267
entrepreneurs, 79
equity, 252, 307
errors, 21, 79, 100, 103, 108, 148, 150, 176, 178, 179, 233
Everatt, J., 6, 9, 12, 16, 18, 40, 42, 45, 47, 49, 57, 68, 78, 155, 156
exaggeration, 202, 216
examinations, 33, 35, 40, 60, 66, 92, 128, 134, 190, 200, 210, 215, 219, 253, 254, 260, 305
executive functioning, 12, 48, 49, 57, 71–74, 81, 105, 170
expectations, 67, 69, 96, 193, 194, 235, 238, 249
extra time, 33, 40, 134, 135, 137, 192, 207, 224, 225, 232, 234, 252–254, 257, 261, 269, 280, 287

familiarity, 81, 107, 125, 174, 197
family, 4, 42, 60, 64, 90–92, 99, 121, 126, 131, 135, 136, 160, 204, 235, 239, 268, 274, 275, 280, 281, 293, 294, 301, 306
feedback, 67, 78, 97, 126, 128, 135, 173, 180, 230, 237, 238, 240, 257, 258, 273, 280, 306
film industry, 267, 270
flexibility, 64, 71, 75, 77, 86, 147, 252, 283
Frith, U., 27–29, 301
frustration, 49, 95, 138, 139, 144, 153, 169, 176, 179

Gerber, P.J., 19, 21, 49, 81, 82, 84, 90, 100, 125, 131, 221
gist, 40, 46, 104, 143, 173
goal-setting, 22, 67, 69, 70, 82, 84, 90, 109, 129, 194, 243, 304
goodness of fit, 22, 82, 84, 191, 220, 221, 226, 228, 229, 256, 268, 303, 306
grammar checkers, 176
Grammarly, 244, 272
graphemes, 15, 30
GROW model, 240

hard work, 60, 84, 213, 215, 268, 274, 282, 290, 293, 297
health care service, 267
highlighting, 99, 162, 202
human resources, 4, 204, 239, 245, 258

inclusion, 260
individual differences, 9, 17, 22, 46, 49, 52, 57, 112, 123, 136, 140, 268, 269, 293, 299, 300, 307
inferences, 31, 40, 162
information processing, 82, 101, 102, 103, 106, 107, 110, 141, 215
instructions, 75, 133, 172, 192, 200, 202, 285

**322**

## Index

intelligence, 37, 47
International Dyslexia Association, 6
interventions, 4, 7-9, 16, 18, 20, 30, 42, 240, 265
interviews, 42, 257

job demands, 23, 84, 85, 190, 207, 263
job satisfaction, 64, 65, 86, 191, 207, 222, 226, 229, 268, 306
job specific expertise, 190, 191, 213, 220, 269

key words, 150, 159, 160, 181, 182, 187

learning difficulties, 9, 16, 27, 46, 49, 273
learning disabilities, 278
learnt helplessness, 110
Leather, C., 12, 46, 57, 64, 72, 241
lecture, 181, 273
legislation, 229, 252, 253, 307
listening, 78, 103, 132, 155, 161, 164, 165, 182, 183, 185, 186, 188, 189, 211, 212, 287, 291, 295, 304
lists, 118, 123, 171, 172, 200, 231, 240, 246, 247
Logan, J., 79, 82

manageable, 120, 124, 127, 128, 130, 158, 170, 172, 174, 182, 187, 197, 198, 202, 269, 305
managers, 4, 23, 126, 133, 135, 169, 180, 199, 207, 221, 223, 227, 229-235, 237, 239, 242, 245, 258, 261, 263, 279, 283, 284, 306
maps, 118, 163, 165, 212, 246, 287
mastery, 66, 80, 126, 127, 128
McLoughlin, D., 66, 80, 128-130
meaningful, 31, 69, 79, 170, 171, 202, 217, 279, 305
meetings, 23, 121, 137, 168, 169, 181, 183-186, 192, 193, 196, 197, 201, 203, 210, 232, 235, 243, 248, 258, 281, 285, 286, 304
memory aids, 170, 217
memory span, 45, 49, 72, 98, 104
metacognitive, 19, 22, 32, 48, 49, 57, 73-75, 78, 84, 89, 90, 109-112, 116, 128, 159, 161, 168, 170, 174, 194, 217, 301, 304, 305
Miles, T., 39, 46
mindset, 67, 100, 128
misinterpretation, 104, 218
Moats, L.C., 146, 156, 157
monitoring, 22, 73, 74, 111, 128, 162, 220
morphology, 22, 73, 74, 113, 130, 162, 220
motivation, 59-61, 65, 68, 78, 82, 90, 119, 125-127, 129-131, 157, 166, 194, 203, 221, 226, 242, 259, 306
multisensory, 118, 171, 202, 217, 305
multitasking, 169, 172, 173, 192, 195-197, 220, 235, 305

neurodiversity, 8, 13, 14, 244
non-verbal ability, 38, 53
non-word reading, 55
novelty, novel, 190, 191, 205, 206, 208, 211, 225

occupational health, 264
organisation, 18, 22, 59, 63, 109, 120, 123-125, 131, 192, 199, 208, 229, 243-245, 249, 253, 256, 261-263, 266, 280, 293, 296
orthography, 150, 151
overload, 103, 192, 197, 198, 203, 243, 295

people skills, 100
persistence, 8, 68, 69, 81, 84, 125, 237, 268, 293
phonemes, 15, 30, 37

**323**

## Index

phonological processing deficit, 9, 27
phonology, 10, 45, 141, 145
phrases, 144, 184–187, 189
planning, 18, 22, 70, 73, 74, 81, 84, 90, 100, 104, 107, 109–111, 115, 116, 121–123, 125, 143, 167, 170, 173, 176, 177, 181, 182, 188, 189, 193–195, 199, 206, 209, 210, 216, 220, 222, 232, 242–244, 249, 258, 271, 297, 304, 306
police service, 267
practice, 9, 15, 16, 20, 24, 29, 30, 32, 35, 39, 40, 42, 43, 47, 54, 56, 75, 77, 78, 80–82, 90, 99, 106, 107, 116, 119, 130, 139, 141, 143–146, 148, 150, 153, 156–158, 176, 179, 182, 188, 210, 213, 219, 221, 235, 261, 265, 273, 277, 278, 286, 301
practitioners, 5, 13, 19, 27, 35, 77, 155, 245
predicting, 104, 182
prepare, 185, 187, 188, 208
pre-reading, 159, 161
presentations, 23, 61, 127, 168, 169, 183, 187, 214, 243, 282, 285, 286
preview, 211, 214, 217
prioritisation, 125, 211, 214, 217
problem-solving, 71, 74
profile, 48, 50, 53, 98, 99, 240
promotion, 23, 26, 50, 63, 64, 66, 95, 96, 169, 207–209, 225, 229, 239, 244, 261, 262, 284, 290, 305
pronunciation, 151, 157, 160, 188, 270, 276
proof-reading, 144, 173, 179, 180

qualifications, 16, 32, 35–37, 60, 63, 99, 191, 214, 284
questioning, 19, 165, 171, 204
questionnaires, 42, 112, 264, 291

rapid naming, 45, 55
reading comprehension, 8, 15, 34, 40, 43, 56, 98, 99, 145, 244

reading speed, 35, 98, 99, 143, 173, 175
Reading Test, 35, 56
reasonable adjustments, 252
recruitment, 254, 256, 261, 263
reflection, 110–112, 115, 116, 254, 256, 261, 263
remembering, 31, 117, 118, 132, 144, 146, 188, 189, 200, 201, 233, 273
reports, 26, 61, 97, 121, 122, 144, 160, 169, 172, 174, 175, 177, 178, 224, 240, 244, 282, 288, 289, 295, 305
re-reading, 40, 74, 109, 110, 143, 165, 287
resilience, 67, 128, 131, 132, 275, 279
revising, 194, 215, 256

second language, 154
self-awareness, 23, 26, 33, 82, 84, 109, 110, 221, 243, 304
self-belief, 59, 61, 67–69, 117, 127–129, 204, 219, 227, 237, 254
self-efficacy, 32, 64–69, 73, 78, 82, 86, 90, 111, 116, 127–129, 131, 133, 137, 153, 191, 197, 207, 221, 225, 226, 228, 229, 237, 242, 259, 268, 303, 304, 306
self-employed, 267, 286, 288
self-esteem, 16, 17, 26, 32, 49, 56, 61, 65, 66, 96, 99, 133, 139, 234, 262, 270, 271
self-regulation, 82, 112
self-understanding, 19, 22, 26, 32, 47, 73, 84, 89, 93, 94, 112, 137, 156, 232, 243, 268, 304
Shaywitz, B.A., 28, 29
SMART, 198, 243, 305
Smith-Spark, J.H., 48
Snowling, M.J., 6, 27, 42, 45
social ecologies, 82, 90, 133, 226, 229
societal success, 32, 63
spell checkers, 166, 225, 248

Index

spelling, 6–8, 18, 33, 35, 39, 40, 55, 93, 98, 103, 107, 108, 128, 136, 141–145, 147–151, 165, 170, 175, 179, 181, 188, 192, 221, 248, 265, 270, 271, 286–288, 294, 304
Stanford-Binet, 38
Sternberg, R.J., 73, 75, 78, 79, 101
strengths and weaknesses, 22, 24, 84, 97, 281, 303
stress, 10, 23, 50, 64, 66, 192, 203–205, 219, 238, 249, 264, 305
study skills, 37, 140, 162, 177, 274, 278
summarising, 162
Swanson, H.L., 20, 72, 74, 76

task analysis, 22, 111, 170, 194, 197
temporal processing, 11
text-to-speech, 33, 159, 161, 162
time management, 23, 90, 120, 123–125, 192, 194, 195, 199, 200, 219, 243
time pressure, 18
tiredness, 203, 205, 225, 253
tongue-tied, 183
trainers, 4, 214, 291, 306
typing, 176

university, 4, 91, 95, 172, 173, 215, 278, 280, 282, 284, 289, 294, 296

verbal reasoning, 37, 38, 46, 48, 52, 53, 54, 97
verbal skills, 16, 52, 54, 155
vicarious, 66, 226, 229
visual, 10, 11, 35, 46, 48, 53, 107, 163, 212, 273, 283, 294, 296
vocabulary, 15, 31, 32, 37, 38, 43, 46, 48, 54, 99, 106, 115, 145, 146, 153–155, 157–161
voice-activated, 165, 248

Wechsler, 37, 53, 54, 56
Woodcock-Johnson, 38, 53, 54, 56
word origins, 151
word parts, 150, 157
word reading, 7, 8, 39, 42, 140, 159, 164, 304
work passport, 234, 235, 306
working from home, 124, 169, 191, 192, 197, 199–202, 210, 239, 248, 258, 282, 305
working memory, 12, 30–32, 37, 38, 41, 45, 48, 49, 55, 71, 72, 102–105, 107, 109, 117, 206, 254, 287, 291
writer's block, 176
writing style, 174

Printed in the United States
by Baker & Taylor Publisher Services